O wh_____
wa_____

Never Ask "Why"

ED GARVEY

Edited by CHUCK CASCIO

———

With a foreword by JUDGE ALAN PAGE
and a historical introduction by DR. SARAH K. FIELDS

Never Ask "Why"

Football Players' Fight for
Freedom in the NFL

TEMPLE UNIVERSITY PRESS T *Philadelphia* • *Rome* • *Tokyo*

TEMPLE UNIVERSITY PRESS
Philadelphia, Pennsylvania 19122
tupress.temple.edu

Library of Congress Cataloging-in-Publication Data

Names: Garvey, Ed, 1940–2017, author. | Cascio, Chuck, editor. | Page,
  Alan, 1945– writer of foreword. | Fields, Sarah K., 1968– writer of
  introduction.
Title: Never ask "why" : football players' fight for freedom in the NFL /
  by Ed Garvey ; edited by Chuck Cascio ; with a foreword by Judge Alan
  Page and a historical introduction by Dr. Sarah K. Fields.
Description: Philadelphia : Temple University Press, 2023. | Includes
  index. | Summary: "In this autobiography, the founder and first
  executive director of the NFL Players Association recalls the early
  years of the union's establishment, empowerment, and negotiations with
  the league and commissioner"—Provided by publisher.
Identifiers: LCCN 2022012186 (print) | LCCN 2022012187 (ebook) | ISBN
  9781439923153 (cloth) | ISBN 9781439923177 (pdf)
Subjects: LCSH: Garvey, Ed, 1940-2017. | National Football League. Players
  Association—History. | National Football League—Management. | Labor
  unions—United States—Officials and employees—Biography. | Collective
  bargaining—Football—United States. | Collective labor
  agreements—Football players—United States.
Classification: LCC GV954.3 .G37 2023 (print) | LCC GV954.3 (ebook) | DDC
  796.332/6406—dc23/eng/20220630
LC record available at https://lccn.loc.gov/2022012186
LC ebook record available at https://lccn.loc.gov/2022012187

Printed in the United States of America

9 8 7 6 5 4 3 2 1

This book is dedicated to the three hundred courageous football players who agreed to take on the National Football League to establish a union. Many of these players risked their careers by challenging the league and the National Labor Relations Board at federal district court to advance all players through collective bargaining.

The union leadership of John Mackey, Kermit Alexander, Brig Owens, Alan Page, and Randy Vataha were committed to racial integration and to every player's economic advancement within the NFL.

When we began this process, Black players were barred from the National Football League Hall of Fame and from meaningful player or front-office leadership positions. The combined efforts of the player representatives, each of whom is elected by his respective team, had a major impact on athletes in all professional sports.

Ed Garvey

Contents

Photos follow page 114

Foreword

JUDGE ALAN PAGE

Ed Garvey's posthumous book, *Never Ask "Why,"* is essential reading for anyone who wants to understand the journey and sacrifices pro football players made in order to establish their rights as professionals. This book, in Ed's own words, provides a clear-eyed view of the long and difficult road players and the National Football League Players Association (NFLPA) had to navigate against America's most powerful sports business—the National Football League (NFL). In these pages, Ed sheds light on the struggles of the players and the union and on what it took for football to achieve the status it holds today.

Players used to believe they should never ask why the status quo existed. They were expected to accept their roles, their pay, and a system that denied them the individual rights today's players take for granted. As head of the NFLPA, Ed Garvey relentlessly asked, "Why?"

Some say Ed was a bomb thrower, a revolutionary bent on destroying the NFL. That assertion is belied by the success of the game today. In reality, Ed's efforts created the foundation for labor peace, which has allowed today's game to thrive.

These pages show Ed's passion and commitment to the belief that players were workers whose performance was integral to the success of the business of football and who were due appropriate compensation, health protection, a pension, and other benefits. The goal he pursued was for players to receive a fair share of the wealth they were an integral part of creating. In pursuit of that goal, Ed's voice resonated with conviction and integrity, as it does here. He believed that by sharing the wealth in an equitable manner, players would become true professionals and the game itself would become better. Ed was correct.

Ed Garvey: Bomb thrower? Occasionally. Revolutionary? Certainly. Game changer? Most definitely.

Alan Page is a National Football League Hall of Fame player whose career as a defensive tackle spanned fifteen seasons with the Minnesota Vikings and Chicago Bears before he retired in 1981. Page was a National Football League Players Association player representative from 1970 to 1974 and again from 1976 to 1977 and a member of the NFLPA Executive Committee from 1972 to 1975. In 1992 he won election in Minnesota and became the first African American to hold a seat on that state's supreme court, a position he was reelected to four times until he faced mandatory retirement in 2015.

Historical Introduction

Dr. Sarah K. Fields

Luck can be a key element in understanding and interpreting history. One historian attributed the production of good histories to "accident, luck, and serendipity," by which he meant the fortuitous constellation of things such as asking or being asked the right questions and finding a source.[1] The publication of Ed Garvey's autobiography about the early years of the National Football League Players' Association (NFLPA) some five years after his death in 2017 is a found document for historians— its posthumous appearance at a moment when the NFL, America's clear national pastime, continues to be controversial is a matter of accident, luck, or serendipity.

But who was Ed Garvey, and why does this manuscript matter? As a young lawyer, recently graduated from the University of Wisconsin School of Law, Garvey worked in labor law. In 1971 he became involved with the fledgling NFLPA before the National Labor Relations Board (NLRB) recognized it as a union. He advised NFLPA president John Mackey, a future Hall of Fame tight end, as the young union tried to negotiate its first collective bargaining agreement (CBA) with the NFL owners. Garvey became the NFLPA's executive director soon thereafter and would remain in that role until 1983. During his tenure, he oversaw and helped navigate players' strikes in 1974 and 1982 as well as several significant lawsuits, including

---

1. James E. McClellan III, "Accident, Luck, and Serendipity in Historical Research," *Proceedings of the American Philosophical Society* 149, no.1 (2005), pp. 1–21.

Mackey v. NFL. In *Mackey*, first the district court in 1975 and then the Eighth Circuit Court of Appeals in 1976 concluded that the NFL was subject to federal antitrust law and that the Rozelle Rule (a rule that allowed Commissioner Pete Rozelle to award compensation from the team signing the free agent to the team losing the free agent) was subject to collective bargaining.[2] The Rozelle Rule restricted free agency signings to such an extent that free agency almost didn't exist because the price of compensation, often draft picks or cash, on top of paying the player was usually high. This meant that ownership and the league held significant power over the players, who had little hope of ever playing for a team or in a location of their choice. Garvey, whose mission was in part to end the Rozelle Rule, was not a popular figure: NFL owners and many in the media were not fans. Neither were some of the football players. After the 1974 strike, he survived a vote of no confidence from the players as well as continued attacks from the league's owners, but the strike helped build a more cohesive union. Much has been written about the NFL and the NFLPA's battles during Garvey's tenure, and he himself gave many interviews. This document, though, is truly his perspective on what happened while he was with the NFLPA, particularly his first five years.

To recount the stories of the past and to explain how the past relates to the present, historians rely on shards of evidence gleaned from a variety of sources, but these sources are limited to those that have been discovered and identified. In fact, history buffs often fantasize about finding new, unknown artifacts. For example, in 2009 a preservation society found a box in the attic of a house they were restoring, and, curious, the discoverers found important letters and postcards from World War I. Similarly, in 2018 a judge discovered, just outside of his courtroom, a locked vault previously hidden by bookcases, which contained documents from 1831.[3] Although the Garvey family knew about his manuscript, historians did not, and thus, this is a found document from a voice thought to have been silenced.

Garvey's autobiography gives historians new evidence to examine and ponder, allowing new interpretations of the past. Douglas Booth theorized that history has moved away from the "craft of recovering facts towards his-

---

2. Mackey v. NFL, 407 F. Supp. 1000 (D. Minn. 1975), *aff'd in part and rev'd in part*, 453 F.2d 606 (8th Cir. 1976).

3. Frank MacEachern, "Historic Documents Found in Home," *Greenwich (CT) Time*, November 27, 2009, p. A1; Sophia Veneziano, "Judge Warren Edwards Working to Breathe New Life into Marion County Courthouse," *Marion (OH) Star*, October 31, 2021, https://www.marionstar.com/story/news/local/2021/10/31/judge-warren-edwards-working-restore-marion-county-courthouse/8539347002/.

tory as the practice of interpreting remnants from the past." He argued that historians should recognize that although we can learn from each piece of evidence, no evidence gives us the truth of the past.[4] Garvey's autobiography allows us another tool to examine his own story in conjunction with the other historical documents about this era.

Because the rise of the NFLPA was in the recent past and because of the present power of the NFL, much has been written about the league, the union, and their early battles. Garvey has been maligned in some of these accounts. The media documented the events contemporaneously, sometimes blaming Garvey for strikes and contract agreement limitations, but their perspective, like all, is biased. Garvey is adamant in his autobiography that sports journalists were in the owners' pockets and did their bidding both intentionally and inadvertently. Former players such as Bernie Parrish and Jim Brown have written about their experiences in the league in this era, and scholars and journalists have drafted many biographies of players, coaches, owners, teams, the games themselves, and Garvey's chief nemesis, NFL commissioner Pete Rozelle. David Harris, journalist and author, wrote an extensive exposé on the business side of the NFL in 1986, in which he asserted that the "mention of Ed Garvey's name alone was enough to turn most NFL conversations unanimously ugly."[5] Scholar Michael Oriard wrote about this time period from a unique perspective: He was an NFL player from 1970 until 1974 and was on the strike lines during the 1974 players' strike, only to be cut by his team when the strike resolved. After that he went to graduate school.[6] Historian Richard C. Crepeau offered a more recent interpretation of the early labor battles between the players and the league, in which he noted Garvey's challenging relationship with the owners and his reliance on the courts to give him what the owners would not.[7] Now in this autobiography, Ed Garvey tells his own stories.

By itself, Garvey's account is an important evidentiary document. One can read his autobiography as a piece of the puzzle already being assembled by other contemporary accounts and scholars, or one can read it as an entry

---

4. Douglas Booth, "Evidence Revisited: Interpreting Historical Materials in Sport History," *Rethinking History* 9, no. 4 (2005), pp. 459–483.

5. David Harris, *The League: The Rise and Decline of the NFL* (New York: Bantam Books, 1986), 80.

6. Michael Oriard, *Brand NFL: Making & Selling America's Favorite Sport* (Chapel Hill: University of North Carolina, 2007).

7. Richard C. Crepeau, *NFL Football: A History of America's New National Pastime* (Urbana: University of Illinois Press, 2014).

point and a chance to learn more. Frankly, the document is a good and exciting read. Garvey's commitment to the players, particularly the mid- and lower-tier players who didn't get star treatment, and his passion for getting them a fair deal are palpable. He fought hard for what he thought the players as a whole deserved, and he was unafraid of the owners' power and privilege; indeed, he seemed unafraid of much beyond failing the union. He knew the owners and the media often hated him, and at times—perhaps all the time—he hated them right back because they got in the way of his achieving that fair labor deal. In some ways the book is frenetic and chaotic, which likely reflects how Garvey himself felt, and it contains amazing, provocative stories that, while set in the past, have ties to the present. For example, Garvey's tales of racist, elitist NFL leaders may surprise some and yet remind them of more recent stories of NFL leaders' racist and elitist comments. Garvey almost offhandedly introduces critical labor law decisions such as *Mackey, Kapp v. NFL*, and *Radovich v. NFL*,[8] and those unfamiliar with the cases should be inspired to learn more. Although the last collective bargaining agreement in 2020 was reached with relatively little turmoil and no work stoppage, its very existence is due to Ed Garvey and those early battles with NFL owners and Pete Rozelle, as well as the lawsuits Garvey waged. Simply put, today's NFLPA exists in part because of Ed Garvey, and this is, finally, Ed Garvey's version of what happened.

Sarah K. Fields is a Professor of Communication at the University of Colorado, Denver. She is the author of Game Faces: Sport Celebrity and the Laws of Reputation *and* Female Gladiators: Gender, Law, and Contact Sport in America *as well as the coeditor of* Sport and the Law: Historical and Cultural Intersections. *She is the president-elect of the North American Society for Sport History.*

---

8. Kapp v. National Football League, 390 F. Supp. 73 (N.D. Calif. 1974), *aff'd*, 586 F.2d 644 (9th Cir. 1978) and Radovich v. NFL, 352 U.S. 445 (1957).

In Appreciation

Betty Garvey

In memory of my husband, Ed Garvey, and on behalf of our daughters, Pamela Garvey, Kathleen McNeil, and Lizzie Garvey, I would like to thank Brig Owens, Judith Blank, David Sheridan, editor/adviser Chuck Cascio, agent Joseph Perry, and the Temple University Press and its editor, Ryan Mulligan, for their help in turning this dream of Ed's into a reality.

As anyone who knew Ed will confirm, Ed was not one to give up on *any* project. In late 2016 and early 2017, his complications from Parkinson's disease increased, but nonetheless he maintained his commitment to complete this manuscript. At the same time, I made a commitment to him to do everything possible to get his writing published. With the help of all these people, that has now happened.

Ed died on February 22, 2017. Through this book, which captures his intense efforts to help professionalize football for the thousands of athletes who commit themselves to this career, his brave legacy lives on.

Note on Language

In 2020, the NFL team based in Washington, DC, ended its use of a team name considered a slur against Native Americans. This change came after Ed Garvey wrote this manuscript and after his death in 2017, and the manuscript used the team's name of the time. Temple University Press has chosen to redact instances of the slur in accordance with our policy on the treatment of derogatory language.

Never Ask "Why"

Introduction

I decided to write this book sometime during the National Football League (NFL) players' strike in 1974. There have been books by former players on the inhumanity in team sports, but nothing fully explained how sports owners manipulated the players, courts, Congress, sportswriters, and media to maintain monopoly status and protect the reserve system . . . and the inhumanity resulting from that system. Few people understand the role of the commissioner in professional sports, and even fewer understand how Congress made it extremely difficult for players and their unions to gain concessions from management, let alone a fair share of the enormous revenues generated by pro sports in the United States.

If we, the union and its representatives, wanted the public to understand the reserve system, the power of the owners, the suppression of dissent within the NFL, or the manipulation of the government by the owners, we could not leave it to the sports press. Much of the sports press was heavily influenced by the commissioner and club owners. I felt compelled to demystify that system or else the public and future professional athletes might never understand the constant battle waged to secure dignity for the professional athlete—in short, the struggle to have athletes treated as people instead of property.

The athlete-as-property concept began in the 1870s. Baseball owners decided they could make larger profits if they stopped competing with one another for players, so they agreed to divide the most talented players among themselves. They then agreed that because each player was "reserved" to a team, the other teams would refuse to offer that player employment. Because the player would be given only one club to play for, he would be forced to accept the salary offered and that club's working conditions. It worked so well that the reserve system became a fixture in sports.

The NFL's system controlled entry into the league by use of the draft; by teams' retention of veteran players through the use of option and compensation clauses; by the elimination of discussions between players and potential employers through antitampering rules; and by team control of players through the Standard Player Contract and the commissioner as the arbitrator of last resort.

The NFL's eventual tremendous box office and television success convinced owners and their commissioner that their genius and restrictive systems were largely responsible for football claiming to be *the* national sport starting in the 1960s. They had a heavy stake in maintaining the system that was in place. So, in the 1970s, the NFL dug in its heels and told players and their new union that they were in for the fight of their lives if they tried to change the system. Anyone who challenged the league by asking *why* the system worked the way it did would be labeled a subversive. Anyone— whether a player or union official—threatening any part of the reserve system was an enemy to be banished from the game. NFL management fought to keep players in that subservient role, desperately trying to break the union and making our people do as we were told.

As with any totalitarian regime, the NFL used the media as an important weapon against those who opposed them. Super Bowl week became a major scheme, with hundreds of sportswriters, TV announcers, color commentators, radio announcers, producers, and directors gathered in the best hotels in the Super Bowl city to be wined, dined, propagandized, and corrupted by the league office and its highly skilled public relations department.

In the absence of objective or investigative reporting, the public had little or no opportunity to understand the reserve system, eventual legal cases like the *Mackey* case or the *Kapp* case, the discrimination in hiring, the fifty-two-day strike for player freedom in 1974, or the New England Patriots' strike in 1975. It is my goal to provide here a better understanding of those events and that system—events that changed professional sports for all time and a system that robbed athletes of their freedom and dignity.

I discuss the crucial role John Mackey in particular played in helping to achieve players' goals in more detail later, but knowing his background is important for perspective.

In 1970, Mackey, a tight end for the Baltimore Colts, became the first president of the National Football League Players Association (NFLPA), holding that position until September 1973. In his first year as president, Mackey organized a players' strike, which resulted in millions of dollars in increased fringe benefits from the league. However, it also resulted in John being temporarily blackballed from any NFL team until the San Diego Chargers signed him just as the 1972 season started. He retired as an active player at the end of that season, concluding a ten-year career as tight end that eventually led to his Hall of Fame induction. His contributions to the NFLPA continued in his role as president through 1973 and well beyond when John and several other players brought an antitrust lawsuit against the NFL, the landmark *Mackey* case.

This book is about NFL myths and realities. It is about management's control of the media and the athletes. It is about a young union struggling to achieve dignity for the athletes . . . and about union busting, NFL style.

This book is written in the hope that professional football players' struggles to change the system within which they must work can serve as an example to those exploited workers in our society who must struggle outside the limelight for a more just society, for decent wages, and, yes, for freedom and dignity.

1

All about Control

When I became executive director of the National Football League Players Association (NFLPA) in 1971, team control of any NFL player began and, in a sense, ended with the NFL Standard Player Contract, a device like those used in the entertainment industry or anywhere employers would insist that *their* form be used. It was not a contract from the player's standpoint because he gained little, if anything, under the terms, while it allowed the club owner to gain almost total control over the player both on and off the field. It was a one-way street. The club could insist that the player perform only for the club, fire the player at any time with no obligation to pay him for the balance of the contract, keep him from playing other sports in the off-season, refuse to allow the player to endorse a product and receive compensation from that endorsement, fine him any amount for any reason, suspend him from a game or for life without so much as a glance at his constitutional protections, trade him, or sell him. As for the player, he was paid for every game he performed in. If he played the entire season, he earned the salary agreed to when he signed the "contract" for that year. When he was cut, he stopped getting paid.

The NFL lawyers drafted the "contract" and included a clause in which the player agreed to incorporate into it all current and future bylaws of the NFL, which were unavailable to the player or his lawyer at the time of signing. For example, while a player may have reached an agreement on bonuses for outstanding performance, he could learn that the owners, through an amendment to the Constitution and Bylaws, had outlawed performance

.ɹuses and thus that that clause in his contract was null and void because he agreed to be bound by future bylaws.

The owners came up with another clause to make certain that no "soft-on-players" owner gave anything away. They decided that no contract was valid until the commissioner approved it. The NFL Constitution and Bylaws established no standards for disapproving a contract; therefore, Commissioner Pete Rozelle's judgment alone became the standard, adding to his power. The commissioner could protect all league rules and practices, written and unwritten, by refusing to approve any contract that would violate whatever he claimed at the moment to be his standard.

In addition to giving Rozelle complete control, this power gave general managers tremendous leverage in negotiating with players and their lawyers or agents. If an owner wanted to avoid a proposed concession, he would say, "The commissioner will never approve that." Players were told everything from "It is a violation of league rules to eliminate the option clause" to "It is a league rule that you must sign three one-year contracts."

Now that is power, that is player control, and it was all located at the league office.

Most players came into the league through the draft. Once selected and told by the commissioner where they *must* perform, the players were forced to sign a commissioner-drafted, one-way form contract before they would be allowed to step onto the practice field. The commissioner had to approve every comma and every clause in that contract. Prior to 1977, even if fired by their respective clubs, players were not free to select their next employer because they were placed on waivers. In truth, the waiver system was another draft, and those players had been "awarded" by Rozelle to their new teams.

The *Kapp* Case: How It Started

The owners had gotten the best of us when the NFLPA tried to negotiate a fair collective bargaining agreement with the league in 1970 because of their power and, in part, because they hired lawyers who argued for hundreds of hours over the most insignificant points. For example, a mutually agreed upon point said that when a player was waived or traded, he had to report to his new team ASAP. We agreed to that, but no one said whether he would fly tourist or first class. Some players are huge; most are bigger than the normal passenger. To fly cross-country, tourist class for a 265-pound tackle is uncomfortable, to say the least. I argued for first-class fare; the owners insisted on coach. Guess who won? Players fly coach.

The owners had made their point: Never give in! Never compromise! Never let the union take credit!

I should have learned from that experience, but I didn't. Most of us assume that other people see things as we do. Ever notice how a person arguing a point gets annoyed that you won't agree? The reason many people nod and say, "Yes, I agree" is to avoid conflict, not because they agree. Because we wanted a new relationship with the NFL after we signed the collective bargaining agreement, I assumed they felt the same way. Boy, was I wrong.

That was Rozelle. Never talk settlement. Stick to your position at all costs. Say stuff like, "Our lawyers have never lost, and they say . . ." Never express uncertainty. Compromise is for losers, for the weak, not for the NFL.

I believe Rozelle was reasonably bright though quite insecure and had never been in a position to make decisions before he became the league's commissioner. A tendency among insecure people is to mask it with stubbornness. Once their advisers tell them what to do, they do it. They fear that if they compromise, their opponents—or even their allies—will sense weakness and indecisiveness; worse, they may have to defend a new position. Quarterback Joe Kapp played out his option with the Minnesota Vikings in 1969 and became a free agent on May 1, 1970. However, no team signed Kapp to a contract, despite the fact that he had led the Vikings to the Super Bowl in 1969, had enormous charisma, and was named First Team All-Pro that year. Kapp waited. Training camp passed. The preseason went by, as did the first few regular-season games. Would he ever play again?

The answer came from New England Patriots president Billy Sullivan. The Patriots, a hapless lot for years, had a new stadium under construction in Foxborough, twenty miles outside of Boston. To sell tickets, they needed a star, and Kapp was the answer. Kapp agreed to a four-year guaranteed contract with the Patriots, but that contract was drafted by the Patriots' lawyer and reviewed by Kapp's lawyer, John Elliott Cook. It protected Joe Kapp, not the NFL. It was not, to say the least, the NFL's Standard Player Contract. Kapp flew to Boston, signed the contract at a press conference, bought a home in Boston, and looked forward to the challenge of helping turn the Patriots into a winner.

On July 13, 1971, less than a year after Kapp signed with New England and only a month after the owners had signed a collective bargaining agreement with the NFLPA, I received a call from Cook, Kapp's lawyer, who said, "I have just been informed by Commissioner Rozelle that Joe, in order to play in 1971, must sign the Standard Player Contract because the *union* insists that players sign it. Is that true?"

due process?

"Mr. Cook, you must have misunderstood," I said. I explained that Commissioner Rozelle must have said that it was the NFL Constitution and Bylaws making that requirement, *not* the collective bargaining agreement.

"No, I believe I understood him correctly," replied Cook.

I said, "Let me call Rozelle and get back to you. Maybe *he* is confused."

I reviewed the events in my mind: After more than twelve months of negotiations, unfair labor practice charges against the owners, and constant turmoil, we had finally executed a collective bargaining agreement on June 17, 1971. I had been elected executive director of the NFLPA in mid-May that year, and I hoped to carry on a decent relationship with Rozelle and the league while the contract was in force. Rather than jump to conclusions on the Kapp matter, I figured I should listen to Rozelle's side of it before making a decision.

I called Rozelle, repeated my conversation with Cook, and said, "Pete, I'm sure you mean the Constitution and Bylaws of the NFL require Joe to sign your contract."

"No," he said. "Ham Carothers [Covington and Burling lawyer for the NFL] says it's the collective bargaining agreement in article III, section 1."

I quickly grabbed my printer's proof of the recently signed agreement. It read, "All players shall sign the Standard Player Contract." I was shocked that Rozelle would use it as a union endorsement. Looking back, I shouldn't have been shocked. In effect, the league had put one over on us. In the past, every player had been forced to sign the Standard Player Contract pursuant to league rules. In negotiations for the collective bargaining agreement, we revised the contract substantially, and we said so in that same article III. No one had said we would force people to sign it.

I said, "Pete, listen, claim the Constitution and Bylaws if you like, but we will never support the view that the collective bargaining agreement *forces* players to sign the Standard Player Contract until it has been revised. Read the next section. It says we will 'revise the Standard Player Contract'!"

"Talk to Ham. I believe that's his position," came Rozelle's curt reply.

"I don't give a damn what Ham says. I'm telling you that you can't use *us* to force Joe Kapp to sign the Standard Player Contract. He signed a year before we even reached agreement on article III."

"Talk to Ham" was his response.

"Okay. But our position won't change."

Hamilton "Ham" Carothers worked for perhaps the most powerful of the "super law" firms in Washington, DC. He treated the union and players with disdain. I always felt that I might receive a bill after having the privilege of talking to him. We referred to Carothers as the de facto commissioner of the NFL because of Rozelle's total reliance on his judgment.

I called Carothers, and, sure enough, he argued that it was the collective bargaining agreement that required Joe to sign the form contract. It was another NFL trick. Carothers was the NFL's antitrust expert, not their labor expert. He had not been involved in a negotiating session, yet he was basing his argument on the collective bargaining agreement, an agreement reached many months *after* Joe Kapp had signed his Patriots contract.

So began yet another disruptive, expensive, time-consuming, unnecessary battle with the NFL. Ultimately, arrogance alone stood between settlement and lawsuit. The Rozelle-Carothers bond was keeping Joe out of football.

My goal was compromise. At that moment, I wasn't trying to challenge the legality of the Standard Player Contract, though that was within the power of the union. I only wanted to allow Kapp's contract to continue to exist alongside it. I knew Joe Kapp wanted to play, and I believed that Sullivan wanted him to play for the Patriots. At the outset, it was really Kapp and Sullivan against Rozelle and Carothers. The latter duo had never forgiven John Elliott Cook, Kapp's lawyer, for getting an $800,000 contract for quarterback John Brodie in 1966 from the San Francisco 49ers. Now they wanted revenge.

There was talk by some in the NFL-controlled press that Cook had duped Kapp into signing a contract that gave Cook general power of attorney over all of Kapp's affairs. In fact, Kapp and Cook did not have any agreement beyond a handshake, but they were both honest men who believed people should live up to their word.

Carothers was particularly vehement in conversation with me, saying, in reference to Cook, that there was "no point in talking to the old man."

So I found myself in the role of mediator, although obviously trying to help Joe. Rozelle finally ordered Kapp to leave the Patriots' training camp unless he would sign the Standard Player Contract. Joe insisted that he already had a contract and saw no need for another one. Rozelle told him, in effect, to sign it or he would be out of football. Joe refused and was ordered to leave the day after camp opened.

Some sports pages read, "Kapp Quits Pats!" but Joe Kapp never "quit" anything. If we had a warrior class in America, Kapp would be at the front of it.

During the next six weeks, I spent so much time on the Kapp problem that I began to wonder if I had become executive director for the Patriots and Kapp rather than for all of the league's 1,300 players.

What was bothering Rozelle? That question plagued me throughout the six weeks. After all, the league could have made an exception for Kapp, warned owners that Rozelle would never make the same mistake of allowing a player to perform unless he signed the Standard Form Contract, and fined Sullivan, and the problem would have disappeared. Instead, they fought Kapp tooth and nail. Was it their hatred of Cook? Were they getting back at the union? At the time, I did not understand the tremendous importance of the Standard Player Contract as the center of the reserve system. But even if I had, the NFL's intransigence would still have mystified me.

I thought of a possible reason and asked one of our attorneys, Leonard Lindquist, and his associates to research the transferability of personal service contracts in Massachusetts. Their conclusion: The contract was not transferable. I thought perhaps this might be the NFL's problem with Kapp's nonstandard contract. Maybe Sullivan wanted to trade Kapp because the Patriots had acquired highly regarded quarterback Jim Plunkett.

I called Cook. "Would you agree to an addendum to make the contract assignable?"

"No," he responded.

"Why not?" I asked.

Cook said, "Because Joe should have some say on which team he plays for."

I agreed and asked permission to talk with Kapp. Cook had Kapp call me for what was my first conversation with this incredible person after hours and hours of wrangling over his contract. He said he just wanted to play football and urged me to do everything I could to get him back to the Patriots.

I asked, "Is there any team you wouldn't play for?"

A pause and then, "No! Any team that wants me, I'll play for!"

With Joe Kapp, there were no mealymouthed responses.

I said fine and added, "Please ask Mr. Cook to give me permission to make the contract assignable."

"Okay. Just get me back playing football under my existing contract."

"I'll do my best."

The next morning, with considerable excitement, thinking that the problem had ended, I called Carothers with the offer: "We agree to make the contract assignable."

Carothers responded, "I'll get back to you." Later, he called and said, "You are missing the point. He must sign the Standard Player Contract."

"He won't," I said.

"Well, that's your problem."

Now what the hell was bugging them, if not allowing Kapp to be traded? Goddammit, we had spent hundreds of hours trying to find the solution.

Rozelle started the public relations machine. The line was unmistakably anti-Cook. Never attack the player—always the adviser. He told William Wallace of the *New York Times*, "Cook was good for Joe twice. I hope it's not two out of three. If so, Joe's career is over."

The writers had a field day at Cook's expense. The public was beginning to think Kapp was crazy, and they were saying things like, "Everyone else signs the standard contract, why not Kapp?" as if everyone else had had a choice and decided to sign.

My last inspiration was that maybe Rozelle was concerned that without the standard contract he might be unable to expel Kapp from football if he were caught gambling (not that Kapp was a gambler). I called Cook. "Would you agree to an addition to the contract that would allow Rozelle to expel Joe for gambling?"

"I guess so."

"How about conduct detrimental to football?"

Long, long discussion. Finally, and to my surprise, Cook agreed!

The next day, back to drafting.

I was excited. I hadn't had such a feeling since June 17, 1971, when we finally mutually approved the collective bargaining agreement. That duel was fun for a while, but it brought a great sense of relief when we reached agreement. Now surely we were about to settle the Kapp dispute. Joe would play; he could and probably would be traded; the commissioner would emerge with the Standard Player Contract intact; and everyone would be reasonably happy. Then we would get on with revisions of the standard contract. We thought we had satisfied all of the real or imagined concerns that Rozelle and Carothers might have about the Kapp agreement:

1. Kapp could now be traded.
2. The commissioner's power to discipline Kapp had been established.
3. The NFL could still appear powerful because Cook and Kapp had been forced to compromise.

We also agreed not to use the Kapp agreement as a precedent for future players during the term of the collective bargaining agreement. Our naive hope was to change the Standard Player Contract to make it fair to the players.

It was close to Labor Day, and time was running out. Rozelle seemed ready to make a deal. To be on the safe side, I called Billy Sullivan again and suggested an off-the-record meeting with him, Rozelle, Kapp, and me. Sullivan insisted the problem was Cook. I said it was Rozelle but suggested that if he could control Rozelle, I could influence Cook. When I pushed for a weekend meeting, Sullivan demurred: "Can't do it."

"Why not? We are almost out of time."

"I have to flush the toilets," responded Sullivan.

"You what?"

"The Sanitary Commission says we can't open the Foxboro Stadium this weekend unless the sewage system can handle all toilets being flushed at the same time, so we have to flush all of them at the same time."

"Great! But why do you, the president of the club, have to be there? Isn't Kapp a little more important?"

"I have to be there for the morale of my employees."

My weekend suggestion got flushed down the Foxborough sewage system. My next thought was to have my friend and fellow attorney Leonard Lindquist meet with Rozelle to close the deal. Rozelle would be reluctant to give me credit for solving the dispute. He would feel better having the older Lindquist there. Lindquist agreed, called Rozelle for an appointment, and left for New York.

When he arrived, Leonard headed immediately for the NFL office. Rozelle's secretary asked him to wait for a few moments. Lindquist called me and told me that after waiting for nearly three hours outside Rozelle's office, he was finally called in, only to learn that Rozelle wasn't ready to sign. Rozelle suggested Lindquist go to Washington to await word from Carothers, the de facto commissioner. Rozelle had conned us again. He wanted to help, but someone else had said no.

The next day Carothers, the hatchet man, called Lindquist, who had returned to DC: "Mr. Lindquist, there will be no compromise. I suggest you tell Mr. Kapp to sign the Standard Player Contract if he wants to play football, and I suggest you tell Mr. Garvey to live up to his responsibilities under the collective bargaining agreement."

Leonard responded briefly. Ham Carothers had prevailed again. The NFL never compromises. They assumed the player would give in; after all, he wants the money, so he wants to play football.

Well, Hamilton Carothers didn't understand Joe Kapp.

League attorneys took a new approach. They filed a grievance against Kapp and the union for not living up to the collective bargaining agreement.

My initial reaction was to think they must be joking. How in the world could they expect Kapp or the NFLPA to participate in such a grievance?

Who, after all, would be the arbitrator of the complaints of the player, his union, and the commissioner of the NFL? You guessed it: Pete Rozelle! The question before "Arbitrator" Rozelle would be simply this: "Was 'Commissioner' Rozelle right in kicking Joe Kapp out of football?"

I called the NFL's labor attorney, Ted Kheel, and told him that we would not participate in a farce. We also informed Rozelle and the Patriots that we would not participate, which prompted a call from Billy Sullivan.

"Why won't you participate?" he asked.

"Obviously, Mr. Sullivan," I said, "it is absurd to ask Rozelle to be a judge of his own conduct. We aren't crazy."

"Listen, Ed. That statement proves to me that you haven't been around the NFL long enough. If you had been, you would understand that when Rozelle puts on the arbitrator's hat, he is completely objective about his own conduct as commissioner."

I couldn't believe what I was hearing. My response: "You are correct. I haven't been around football long enough to believe that! If I ever do believe it, I'll know it's time to get out!"

Cook and Kapp joined me in refusing participation in this most outrageous affront. Nevertheless, the NFL went forward. Rozelle broke all records for promptness and held a hearing almost immediately. The transcript of the hearing reveals that, on September 1, 1971, at 11:10 A.M., Pete Rozelle and his attorney, Paul Tagliabue, Carothers's understudy at Covington and Burling, called the Kapp hearing to order. Kheel and another attorney from his firm, Ray Gregory, were present for the Management Council.

Kheel began: "To me, it is sad that the union is abdicating in the face of the claims of a lawyer [John E. Cook] or so it appears to me. . . . I would hardly think that this is the way for the union to build up its status and position as the collective bargaining agent . . . but it's not for me to tell them what to do."

On the question of the commissioner's role, Kheel said, "At various times in its many letters and telegrams the union said that the commissioner, in view of a prior decision with regard to Mr. Kapp, is not qualified to make a decision based on this record. I would submit that this reveals a total lack of understanding of the functions of the office of the commissioner and the intent of the collective bargaining agreement . . . the powers of the commissioner were created before there even was a union."

Billy Sullivan was their only witness. Their contention was that the collective bargaining agreement required Kapp to sign. Unhappily for them, Kapp had signed his Patriots contract on October 22, 1970, and there was no collective bargaining agreement until June 1971, eight months later. That didn't bother Sullivan that September morning in 1971:

> Q: "Did you ever indicate that a contract could be entered into with Joe Kapp without his signing the Standard Player Contract?" (Note that the question was not whether he affirmatively told him he must.)
> A: "At no time."
> Q: "And you understood that that was a requirement of the collective bargaining agreement?"
> A: "Absolutely."

Apparently, Billy Sullivan could read the future, for at the time there was no collective bargaining agreement. How could he have possibly known it would be a requirement of the collective bargaining agreement in October 1970 when the agreement wasn't signed until June 19, 1971?

The "hearing" came to a close at 2:30 P.M., and Kheel, despite the fact that there was no formal opposition, asked for two weeks to file a brief.

The NFLPA reported in the *Audible*, our monthly newsletter, that players should "sit on the edge of their chairs" awaiting a decision from "Arbitrator" Rozelle on "Commissioner" Rozelle's decision to kick Kapp out of football.

I later described Rozelle's decision to the National Academy of Arbitrators by borrowing from Mark Twain: "With the calm confidence of a Christian holding four aces," "Arbitrator" Rozelle found that "Commissioner" Rozelle had been correct. Comedy, farce, or tragedy, the NFL once again shunned compromise, turned its back on common sense, and followed Carothers and Rozelle into federal court. Joe Kapp filed suit against the NFL.

Three years later, on December 19, 1974, U.S. District Court Judge William Sweigert returned his judgment on Kapp's case against the NFL, invalidating his contract with the Patriots. Kapp's case depended on an argument that the NFL had acted as a monopoly to induce the Patriots to breach their contract with Kapp and then subsequently keep him out of professional football. That day, our staff gathered for a small Christmas party. There wasn't much joy at that party until suddenly I received a call from Leonard Koppett of the *New York Times*.

"Ed, I have some news for you. The judge ruled for Kapp."

"He what?" I was almost shouting.

"He held the Standard Player Contract, the draft, and the Rozelle Rule illegal!"

"Holy mackerel . . . can you hold a second?"

I shouted to everyone that Kapp had won! With the Rozelle Rule declared illegal, any team that lost a free agent to another team would no longer be entitled to compensation by the team signing the free agent. The party started. The union was saved. Although it was a victory, it should be noted that while Kapp had won a judgment, the jury incredibly said he wasn't injured—which is to say the NFL's violation did not directly cause the harm Kapp experienced—so whether doing so was considered legal or not, the NFL continued to insist that players sign the contract.

At the time of the Sweigert decision, only 350 NFL players had paid dues to the union. We were in financial trouble, and, more important, we were arguably not a majority union. Forces among the players were gathering to fire me and the so-called radicals who were challenging the league. It might have worked had it not been for the decisions by Rozelle and Carothers in July and August 1971 to kick Joe Kapp out of the NFL and their subsequent refusal to compromise. Carothers's arrogance and Rozelle's fear of losing face probably saved the union because it allowed us to punish their over-reach and show their vulnerability for the first time. And the guts of Joe Kapp had led the way.

A strong military strain existed in the NFL. Coach Hank Stram played martial music over a loudspeaker at his practices as the cherry picker lifted him above his "troops" to get a better view. Sportswriters described games as great battles, and many owners seemed to believe they had the same control over their men as a marine drill sergeant would. The NFL draft and the Standard Player Contract were elements of control that permitted other, more specific measures of control to exist.

In the NFL, discipline of the player was another important element of control. Without limitations on an employer's ability to discipline, the employee would have no rights, allowing management to dominate employees' lives. The NFL hierarchy always argued that discipline was absolutely essential to the success of a team. There is some truth to that. When you have a team sport, you have to make sure people work together. But discipline in the NFL was not limited to on-the-field conduct. It was also used to control the lifestyles of the players off the field to impress upon them the fact that the NFL controls them at all times. Due process in the imposition of discipline was not an important concept to the NFL moguls.

The Standard Player Contract and the NFL Constitution and Bylaws gave the clubs and the commissioner unlimited power to discipline players both on and off the field for almost anything that offended the commissioner, coach, owner, or general manager. Prior to the dramatic changes made in the 1977 collective bargaining agreement, managerial authority went unchecked because the only appeal was to Rozelle himself. The case of wide receiver Lance Rentzel best illustrated the inherent problems.

Discipline as Control: Lance Rentzel

Our antitrust counsel, Ed Glennon, who was handling the *Mackey* case for us, met me in Los Angeles to take Don Klosterman's deposition on July 23, 1973. Klosterman was the Rams' general manager. The deposition was to be held in the Rams' offices, and I felt it would be courteous to call Rams owner Carroll Rosenbloom to suggest an informal meeting. Over dinner, Rosenbloom asked, "You don't think Rozelle will do anything about Rentzel, do you?"

I was surprised by the question. Lance Rentzel had been arrested for possession of marijuana, but other players had been accused of worse crimes with no action taken by Rozelle. Rentzel's previous run-in with the law for indecent exposure was far from my mind; he had come through an extremely difficult and embarrassing situation, and everyone who knew him was proud of him. I responded that I couldn't imagine Rozelle doing anything about Rentzel's marijuana charge.

During the deposition, Klosterman seemed nervous. Ham Carouthers was there too, but he wasn't nervous—only impressed that the previous night he had been at Rosenbloom's for dinner and Jimmy Stewart had stopped in.

The deposition ended around 3:30 P.M., and that evening I met Glennon back at the hotel, got ready for dinner, and headed for the Rosenbloom's Bel Air estate. We arrived and were given a tour of the palace by Rosenbloom's son. Soon Carroll Rosenbloom's wife, Georgia, appeared, introduced us to the other guests, and fixed drinks. Just before Carroll himself arrived, another dinner guest, actor Ross Martin, turned to Georgia and said, "Isn't it terrible about what they have done to our Lance?"

Georgia seemed disturbed by the question and quickly said, "Not now."

Her reaction increased my curiosity. I asked Martin what "they" have done to "our" Lance, and he responded, over Mrs. Rosenbloom's protestations, that Rozelle had suspended him for at least a year. I couldn't believe it. "For what?" I asked.

"For this drug charge," came the reply.

Just then Carroll came in and I exploded. "He did what?"

"Calm down, Ed, we'll talk later," said Rosenbloom, moving around the room greeting guests.

"No, let's talk now. This is outrageous."

Within minutes, Rosenbloom drew me and Glennon aside to discuss Rozelle's action. He began by telling us that he thought of Rentzel as his "own son," but he calmly explained that he had no choice but to accept the commissioner's decision.

Glennon was incensed. "Do you know what I would do if it were my son? I'd fight like hell!"

I told Rosenbloom that the union would take immediate action in court to enjoin this arbitrary and capricious action by Rozelle. I insisted that players, like other workers, have a right to due process. I was confident we would succeed in having Lance reinstated. Although an ordinary employer can fire an employee for smoking marijuana, the head of an unregulated monopoly should not be allowed to fire the player and make it impossible for him to perform with anyone else, including the Canadian Football League (CFL). (Even when a player is suspended, his contract remains intact, and the CFL honors NFL contracts even when the player is not being paid.)

I had no doubt that we would prevail in court. Had the Rams waived him and then allowed him to sign with another team, I would have said okay, but who gave Rozelle the power to end Rentzel's career? Carroll privately offered to give us legal assistance and, at one point, offered to pay legal fees for Rentzel. We declined but did promise to stay in touch with him and his lawyer.

Glennon and I went back to the hotel to find two messages—one from John Mackey and one from the Rams' player rep, Tom Mack. I assumed both messages related to Rentzel, so I called Mack first in order to give Mackey all of the details.

Mack was extremely disturbed about Rozelle's decision on Rentzel. I informed him about our dinner meeting, and he agreed that we should pursue court action immediately. I called Mackey next. Before anything was said about Rentzel, John told me that he had officially retired. The guy who held the association together, who had made the fundamental decisions for years, was now leaving. We agreed to meet for breakfast. He said Rentzel would join us.

Mackey arrived the next morning and seemed relieved, relaxed, and cocky as ever. He was glad to be out of football. First, the rumors were that he had lost a step following the 1970 negotiations. Some in the media called him militant, accusing him of leading the players astray and saying he was under my control. When Mackey was waived by Baltimore after a short dispute with management in August 1972 and he became a free agent, not one NFL team claimed him for $100. Voted the greatest tight end to ever play in the NFL, he was not worth $100? They never broke John Mackey. He and Joe Kapp would show that a few people can change a system.

At breakfast the next morning, Mackey was clearly more concerned about Rentzel than himself. Rentzel was understandably nervous: If he fought the suspension, would he cause more embarrassment to himself, friends, and family? Would the league blackball him? What would Rosenbloom's reaction be? (Rosenbloom had earlier advised the "boy" to take his "medicine like a man." So much for his offer of help for his "son's" defense.)

We told Lance that we would sponsor his case, in part because Rozelle had wronged him, but also to establish a precedent to protect players in the future. Mackey urged him to take a stand. Rentzel decided: "Let's go with it."

Ed Glennon worked with his partner, Bob Atmore, to prepare papers for a temporary restraining order. If granted, the order would prevent Rozelle from interfering with Rentzel's employment contract with the Rams.

On August 1, I flew to Los Angeles to meet Atmore, Glennon, and our local counsel. We worked until 3:00 A.M. finishing the affidavits and the memorandum of law in support of our request for a restraining order. Because of the potential national impact, disputes involving the NFL and a player were considered more appropriately brought to federal court, but we wound up preparing for state *and* federal courts because our case would be heard by Los Angeles Judge Charles Carr, and our local counsel warned that we could not win with this judge.

The irony was incredible—to avoid Rozelle and his arbitrary and unfair system, we had to prepare to get beaten in federal court and then walk across the street to the state court, where we hoped for a fair hearing.

We arrived at the federal building at 10:00 A.M. The clerk treated us like enemies. After an hour's wait, we were told to proceed to the judge's chambers. Before we were allowed to enter, we were interrogated by a court official. He asked each person to identify himself. "Are any of you reporters?" he asked.

By then we were concerned because Bob Atmore hadn't arrived yet. He stayed behind while the typing of the law memo was being finished. I volunteered to wait in Judge Carr's outer office for Atmore as Ed Glennon and our local counsel entered his chambers with the local counsel for the NFL. When Atmore arrived, the judge's secretary allowed him to enter chambers but refused to let me through the door.

Turned out that she was Florence Nightingale compared to the judge.

Glennon had seen and dealt with many judges over his thirty-year trial practice, but he had never come across anything like this. The judge virtually shouted at them: "Who do you think you are? I'm a busy man! I've practiced at the top of the federal bar for forty years and you have no right to be here! You are not important!"

My mind raced back to the dinner at Rosenbloom's where I had assured him that "no federal judge in his right mind would allow Rentzel's suspension." Guess I was overconfident.

We then dismissed the federal case, grabbed some lunch, and went over to state court to file.

———————

As soon as we decided to represent Rentzel, the NFL, through its pipelines in the sports press, started raising questions about our decision. The undertone was clear as they revived Rentzel's previous arrest and asked why NFL players would come to the aid of one who had been arrested for a perverted act, despite the fact that the point at issue, and precedent being set, was the league arbitrarily policing possession of marijuana. The unspoken question: "Is Garvey really representing the best interests and the true feeling of his constituents?"

We knew criticism would come hot and heavy, but as usual, the Executive Committee and the Rams players supported the idea of instigating a suit—not because it would be popular but because it was our duty to help one of our members. You can't pick your plaintiff. I assumed the public would oppose our action, in part because the sports columnists would support the commissioner and exploit Rentzel's past. We were pleasantly surprised when the *New York Times* did a telephone survey in the Los Angeles and New York areas and determined that more fans supported our position than the NFL's. Apparently, most people believed strongly in fair play between employers and employees, despite the sports press.

The attitude expressed in the poll didn't affect the writing in other newspapers, whose writers would never ask Rozelle the pertinent questions:

"What is the NFL drug code, and where is it written?"

"What type of 'probation' was Rentzel on?"

"How is the 'integrity of the game' at stake in this case?"

"What type of hearing did you give Rentzel before suspending him?"

DP

✱ DP

"Did you notify Rentzel's union that you were holding such a hearing?" The answers to these questions made Rozelle's action difficult to support.

The "hearing" conducted by Rozelle had been a trap. Rozelle told Lance that he wanted to talk to him about his latest episode with the law and informed him that he could bring counsel if he so desired. <u>Had Rozelle warned Rentzel that their talk might lead to indefinite suspension</u>, Lance might have contacted the union to represent him. Instead, thinking that he would only get his knuckles rapped, he took two lawyers with him for a "chat." Because his lawyers had never dealt with the NFL before, they were somewhat awed by the procedure and unprepared for what Rozelle had planned. They were surprised to find a court reporter present to take down every word. They were unfamiliar with the sections of the NFL Constitution and Bylaws provisions read to them by Rozelle's lawyer. They should have left, but they stayed, in part because they believed that Rozelle would be fair and that it was a paternalistic scolding. They believed the commissioner would protect the player.

notice

The result was disastrous. Rozelle suddenly notified Rentzel that he was <u>suspended indefinitely</u> and that he would remain suspended until he was "rehabilitated" in the judgment of the commissioner. Rozelle even suggested that Lance do some community work to demonstrate that he was rehabilitating.

The Texas judge who had put Rentzel on probation did not think that possession of marijuana warranted revocation of probation, but Rozelle decided that his *unwritten* probation had been violated. Who appointed this man, a football commissioner, as the one who should determine standards of a citizen's probation? Given his power, he could enforce his decision. The so-called hearing was also our undoing before the California state court judge, who ruled that the league had not violated due process because Rozelle had afforded him a "hearing" and given Rentzel a chance. Rozelle and his new in-house counsel reveled in the state court's decision. Their sham hearing was enough to convince the judge that <u>procedural due process had not been violated</u>; the union had been defeated; Rozelle's authority as disciplinarian had been upheld by a California court; the NFL could continue to say, "We have never lost."

But there was something Rozelle did not count on: The decision made us even more determined to curb his powers as commissioner and to replace him with an impartial arbitrator. Yes, Rentzel was a defeat for the union in the short run, but in the long run it helped to convince the membership that we could never accept Rozelle's arbitrary powers in a collective bargaining agreement. No matter the court, the players understood that Rentzel had received NFL "justice" from Rozelle. The kangaroo court was plus one: The owners plus their "impartial" arbitrator.

If the Rentzel case demonstrated Rozelle's power to discipline, the San Diego 8 incident upheld his power to intimidate.

To understand the San Diego 8, some background on misuse of drugs in the NFL is essential. For many years, NFL teams bought and distributed amphetamines to the athletes, apparently thinking that if someone needed a lift at halftime or before the game and it would help the team win, it was justified. The attitude for years was "The other team is doing it, why shouldn't we?" Like a lot of other problems, Rozelle ignored this one until it became public because when it did, the commissioner had no choice but to act. Naturally, he found it easier to crack down on the athlete than on his masters, the club owners.

Houston Ridge, a player for the San Diego Chargers, brought a lawsuit against the team and its doctor because they had given him drugs. He claimed that the drugs allowed him to play injured and thereby exacerbated his injury, which left him partially crippled for life. The team settled out of court in 1979 for close to a quarter of a million dollars.

When the press got ahold of the story, all hell broke loose. The NFL's potential loss could be in the millions if other players brought similar suits. Players began to relate stories about teams passing out amphetamines like candy. Washington R°°°°°°s offensive lineman George Burman told a reporter that one out of three R°°°°°°s used pep pills, and Congressman Harley Staggers of West Virginia decided to hold a congressional hearing on the "drug problem in sports." The heat was now on the commissioner's office to do something about the "drug scandal" in the NFL, a scandal brought about by management, not the players. The commissioner discussed with Congressman Staggers and some writers the possibility of urinalysis for players.

Rozelle was invited to attend our Board of Representatives meeting at the NFLPA in June 1973, one year before negotiations would begin. This would be Rozelle's first meeting with player reps in over a decade. John Mackey was still president of the NFLPA, and he welcomed Rozelle to the meeting. We had decided as a group not to discuss in advance the questions put to Rozelle, believing that spontaneity would be more effective.

Most often if Rozelle met with players, it was at a social gathering. Players in these settings were somewhat in awe of the commissioner because of his powers, his position, and the pedestal the press had placed him on for years. Those of us who knew him from 1970 negotiations and beyond knew that he would destroy himself in a question-and-answer session in front of the reps. Rozelle could not have been more nervous. Reps peppered him with questions for over two hours, and, as he did so well with the press, he ducked each one. The reps, however, would not let him get away without answering.

Steve Tannen of the New York Jets asked what he thought of the NFL Standard Player Contract, and Rozelle responded that it was "somewhat unclear" and that he had never read it all the way through. He had never read it—and he is the man who had forced Joe Kapp out of football because he had not signed a Standard Player Contract and who, under the league rules, must approve every Standard Player Contract signed.

Tannen almost screamed at him: "*What the hell have you been doing for the past thirteen years?*" Rozelle had no answer. He wasn't used to such a direct challenge.

Then Mike Stratton, twelve-year veteran, raised his hand. Rozelle called on him, and Mike summed up Pete's answers over the past two hours. It went something like this: "Mr. Rozelle, you have refused to answer any of the questions put to you . . . you haven't read the contract . . . you can't comment on Joe Kapp . . . you have no opinion or explanation on why it takes so long to rule on obvious grievances . . . you have no position on artificial turf . . . frankly, you are wasting our time." Well, that was about all Rozelle could take, but, of course, he still didn't answer questions.

As the meeting was about to end, I asked Rozelle if the NFL had any plans to force the players to submit to urinalysis to test for drugs. He ducked, but I asked again, and he ducked again, so I asked again. Finally, as he looked more and more ridiculous before the players, I said, "Pete, I want to assure you that if you institute urinalysis, we will go on strike. Is that clear?" He said, "Yes," it was, but he would not give us any commitment one way or the other. He almost bolted for the door.

When he left, all of the reps knew what a few of us had known for a long time about the "iron commissioner." In my judgment, that meeting convinced Rozelle that he had to do something dramatic about amphetamines in order to win back the respect and fear that had allowed so little resistance to that point. Something short of urinalysis, because he now understood he couldn't get away with urinalysis. Eight players in San Diego would eventually pay the price of his decision.

The San Diego 8

Miami had beaten Minnesota in Super Bowl VIII at Rice Stadium in January 1974, and as a warm-up to upcoming collective bargaining negotiations, we met with a group of owners in Houston the following day to get a feel for their mood. Cleveland Browns owner Art Modell, New York Giants owner Wellington Mara, and their handpicked negotiator John Thompson were there. Modell was the primary spokesman. Almost all of the NFLPA representatives, including Bill Curry, Kermit Alexander, and Tom Keating, went to the owners' palatial hotel for the meeting. The session was short and electric.

Modell had wanted to get something off his chest for a long time. He asked me, "Why didn't you support the league on the blackout issue?" in reference to Congress's vote that owners had to televise home games that were sold out, which the NFL predicted would destroy the game.

I explained our position as we had explained it to Rozelle some months before the anti-blackout bill swept through Congress like a brush fire. We had urged a compromise—lift the blackout for playoff games but keep it for regular-season games. We told Modell that Rozelle vehemently rejected any compromise even though we had found some receptivity to it on Capitol Hill. I told him that we had asked Rozelle what his fallback position was, and his response had been, "After football is destroyed, we will go back to Congress and say, 'See what you have done!'" I had laughed, and when Rozelle rejected the compromise, we withdrew.

"Why?" demanded Modell.

I said, "Because it was going to lose, and lose bad. Why should we give our support to a totally futile effort when Rozelle rejected, out of hand, our compromise?"

Modell seemed surprised by the Rozelle story but ended by saying that there "is value in support even if you know it's for a losing effort." He is right, of course, and that was my point too: Had the NFL tried to deal with the union, support might have been possible.

The meeting ended shortly thereafter on a discussion of the league's expansion plans. We wanted to know if the league planned an expansion of two or four teams and how those teams would acquire veteran players. Modell asked why we were concerned. We responded that Kermit Alexander would like to know before waking up in the morning to hear that he has been drafted and sent to Seattle.

Modell, in one of the more insensitive moments in NFL-NFLPA relations, looked at Alexander and said, "I don't see why a boy would care whether he was drafted, sold, or traded!" In fairness, Modell did not intend to make a racial slur by use of the term "boy." He didn't understand its significance. To Modell, all players, white or Black, were "boys." And that fact made his insensitivity to the humanity of all players all the more apparent to the assembled.

The owners were eager to break up the meeting, and after a few more comments, the meeting ended.

We left Houston feeling a little uptight. The meeting had been extremely hostile—unnecessarily so in our view. It should have been a signal to us that they were out to punish us for questioning the league's plans. We left for Las Vegas for a golf outing that would raise some money for the association and provide a few days off, which we needed before going into the long struggle for a contract.

Before we could unpack, a San Diego Chargers player told me he had to discuss something with me immediately. We went to my room. He told me a bizarre story about a local narcotics officer coming to his home to warn him to be careful of his associations because several of his teammates were under investigation. The officer then named several San Diego players suspected of using marijuana and other drugs. I was curious: "Why would he give you the names?"

"That's what bothers me," the player said. "I don't know whether he is legit or whether he works for Rozelle and was simply pumping me." He was scared.

I promised to look into it and urged him to stay in touch. We talked to various people in San Diego but couldn't really nail down the story. We knew that Chargers officials had warned the players that they were under police surveillance. Everyone on the team was uptight. Five years earlier, San Diego had been the site of an NFL drug scandal, the *Houston Ridge* lawsuit and subsequent out-of-court settlement. Ridge, a defensive lineman of four seasons, filed and won a class action suit against the Chargers for giving him amphetamines and steroids, which he believed led to his career-ending injuries in 1969. Evidence revealed that the Chargers' management bought pep pills and handed them out as if they were harmless. Because of the adverse publicity over the use of amphetamines and the *Ridge* lawsuit, the league was cracking down and looking to shift blame from the team to the players.

Two writers in San Diego were zeroing in on the use of drugs by players. Both were normally so pro–NFL establishment that we assumed they were setting the stage for action that would get the league off the hook. Soon the drug problem would be center stage.

League security was run by former FBI agent Jack Danahy for nearly eighteen years. Danahy traveled around the league every year to talk to the players about gambling, women, and drugs. He never mentioned alcohol.

He had an assistant for several years named Bernie Jackson. Jackson, who was Black, was the type of person the NFL hierarchy used in order to present a friendly face in otherwise dramatic moments, and he always told us to call "if there is anything I can ever do for you." When we would call, there was nothing he could do, so he wasn't really any different from the other league people.

Many players complained of phone taps and of being followed. Were their fears well founded? We used to laugh at some of our friends on the left who "exaggerated" when they recounted FBI excesses. We thought they were paranoid—the FBI may be bad but not that bad. With the revelations about J. Edgar Hoover's attempts to ruin Jean Seberg's and Martin Luther King's reputations, not to mention the wiretaps, the infiltration, the break-ins, and the efforts to undermine organizations, we now realize the "exaggerations" were pretty accurate. We will never know about the NFL's excesses. Who knew what was in NFL files about players or union officials? One thing we did know was that the NFL guarded those files and would not open them to players or the union.

In any event, Jackson and Danahy went to San Diego on a mission to investigate "drug users." A grand jury could warn people of their rights, possibly grant immunity; the FBI would give a Miranda warning; local investigators would be concerned about due process—the right to face your accusers, the right to counsel. NFL security, by contrast, was worried about one thing: The image of the commissioner of the NFL.

———

Almost every paternalistic despot in American industry tried to keep union organizers out of their industry by talking to workers about "family." Football team owners did the same, working the term "NFL family" to death. When collective bargaining negotiations began in 1970, Rozelle urged Mackey to keep the dispute "in the family." In other words: Don't talk to the press.

To some extent, the family talk worked. People generally like to feel that their boss will be as kindly as a father. Players felt the same way. When Danahy and Jackson came to San Diego and settled into their comfortable hotel suite, they knew how to get information. They had softened up the players by warning that everyone was under surveillance, and they had local narcs talk to players about those who were under investigation.

The press was alarmed by the investigation, but not by its tactics. An unnamed "NFL official" publicly called San Diego the "drug cesspool of the NFL." The impression was created that some players were using drugs stronger than marijuana. Jackson and Danahy "invited" players to come to their hotel suite individually and asked if they had any objection to the discussions being taped. They told the players that their goal was to keep it within the *family*. They explained their mission: To find out if there was a problem with serious drugs—"not marijuana."

The National Organization for Reform of Marijuana Laws (NORML) estimated that 80 percent of college students had at least tried marijuana, the third most popular drug in the United States after alcohol and tobacco. The surgeon general said it was not dangerous. President Gerald Ford's Panel on Drugs urged decriminalization of marijuana in 1974. The American Bar Association did the same a year later. NFL players were only a few years out of college, so when their employer sent security people to investigate "drugs," the players assumed they were concerned about hard stuff, not grass. When players were told that investigators were not concerned about pot, they felt free to confess to smoking it.

Friendly Bernie Jackson and Happy Jack Danahy put the players at ease: "Tell us so we can keep the authorities out; tell us or face the bright lights of a congressional hearing." Thus, they had all the forces at work, and the easy answer was "Tell us everything and nothing will happen. We will keep it within the family." Father Rozelle will protect you.

Some players fell for it. They not only confessed their own use of marijuana but told on teammates. After all, they wouldn't get into trouble: This wasn't like a "real" investigation, this was Rozelledom. This was the family.

A month after the NFL investigation, ten Chargers players received a letter from the mount: "You have been found *guilty* of violating the NFL drug code . . . you may demand a hearing but if in the best interests of the league, the club and yourself, you decide to *waive* a hearing, you will not be suspended." There was another choice: "You may retire and not pay the fine."

What were they guilty of? Who said so? Was there a jury? Is this how the "family" works? What in hell is the NFL drug code? The league said it didn't care about pot. These questions and comments flowed through my telephone shortly after the letters arrived.

Kermit Alexander and I headed for San Diego to meet with the accused, or the "guilty," and decide on a course of action. An attorney came with us to handle legal representation for the eight players.

We gathered in a crowded room at the Towne and Country on San Diego's hotel circle. Everyone was upset. Careers were on the line. Those who told on their teammates and those who had refused to even talk to Danahy all stood "guilty" according to Rozelle. All felt helpless. The only hope rested with the NFLPA. They were there to hear what we could do.

First, we ascertained what had been told to NFL security. Then, we talked about a common defense, but everyone had his own lawyer, and most thought they could help themselves better by working individually, under the assumption that the NFLPA had no power. Nevertheless, all agreed to let us handle negotiations with the league, and all agreed to keep us advised.

We left San Diego for Washington. We knew that our only chance rested with pressure on Rozelle. Given Rozelle's intense dislike for me in particular following our interactions so far, I suggested that the entire Executive Committee confront Rozelle on the issue, on the methods employed by Danahy and Jackson, and demand that "charges" be dropped.

A week later, on April 4, the Executive Committee was in New York for a bargaining session. After lunch we headed for Rozelle's office at 410 Park Avenue. Rozelle wasn't there, and no one there knew why we wanted to see him, but everyone there was clearly nervous. We were told he would gladly see us later in the day.

We returned to Rozelle's office about 3:30 P.M. He was nervous, as always, around players. In a conference room around a huge table, we began: "It's unfair to pick out a few people. . . . They were tricked. . . . There is no drug code. . . . They did not have a hearing. . . . You can't be prosecutor and judge and jury."

Rozelle bristled. He had no place to hide. We didn't buy the lines that he had to do *something*, lines later gobbled up by sportswriters. Rozelle couldn't believe how angry the players were. Player reps Tom Keating, Bill Curry, and Kermit Alexander all took turns telling him that it would be crazy if he named these people. We accused him and Danahy of "gestapo" tactics. The meeting ended forty-five minutes later. It was an eye-opener for the new NFLPA president, Bill Curry, who had never seen Rozelle under pressure and was not impressed with what he saw. We left with no indication of Rozelle's plans, but he walked away aware of the line he'd be crossing by releasing names.

A few weeks passed. All of the attorneys representing the Chargers players were told by Rozelle's house counsel, Jay Moyer, that if they demanded a hearing, "Suspensions were possible," but if they "waived" a hearing, "a fine would be the maximum penalty." Given those "choices," nearly all of them waived the hearing. Why take a chance on losing a career on a meaningless hearing before Rozelle? They remembered Rentzel from the year before, and Kapp in 1971. Two of the ten Chargers players chose retirement.

To review, Rozelle "investigated" the charges of drug abuse; only he knew the offense because it was the UNWRITTEN *Rozelle drug code*;

Bruh this guy

Rozelle as prosecutor examined the evidence and decided to prosecute; Rozelle as judge and jury decided they were guilty, and now Rozelle as appellate court would review the circumstances. "Why bother?" said the attorney of one of the players. "It's a complete farce."

Still, Rozelle had not yet released the names of those accused. Maybe there was some hope.

————

I gave it one more chance. I called Bill Curry and Kermit Alexander to tell them that I planned to see Rozelle alone to discuss the Chargers problem. With their approval, I went to New York to urge Rozelle privately to keep the names quiet.

Our discussion lasted about an hour. I said the players would pay the fine, but I almost begged him not to release names. I related the story about a young man I had represented who was sentenced to jail and how the trauma and embarrassment could have ruined his life. No one can judge the ultimate impact of this type of public humiliation on a person. I told him about the post-football career plans of the players involved and talked about the tremendous contributions those players had made to the game and to the NFL over the years. I thought I was getting to him, but then he looked at me and said, "Ed, I hope you don't think that anything you have said has had an effect on me."

My mind flashed back to the fall of 1969, to President Nixon's dismissal of the National Day of Protest against the Vietnam War: "Under no circumstances will I be affected whatsoever by it." Rozelle and Nixon would not yield to the rabble.

We shook hands, and I left. Even then I couldn't say anything to Rozelle for fear that it would hurt the players. When I walked onto Park Avenue, I had a strong urge to throw up. I felt dirty. I had exposed my concern to the point where Rozelle could laugh and say, "We got him." I had accomplished nothing.

————

My last shot to save the situation was a call to Edward Bennett Williams, the NFL's "liberal" owner of the Washington R******s. I met with him at his office on Connecticut Avenue in DC. If any owner would be concerned about the players' civil liberties, I thought it would be Williams, an attorney with an outstanding reputation who had defended many unpopular clients, from Jimmy Hoffa to John Connolly.

Williams did seem shocked. There was an owners' meeting scheduled for that weekend. He agreed to discuss the issue with Rozelle and the other owners. He would stay in touch with me, and he even called me at home later to tell me how to reach him over the weekend in New York.

I anxiously awaited word from him. He never called. Finally, I called him to find out what had happened. He said, "I never raised it because there was no support, not even from Klein" (Gene Klein, Chargers owner).

I couldn't believe it. He never even raised it, weighing the regard of his owner peers against this outrageous disregard of civil liberties.

A few days later, while returning to Washington, I called my office and found out that Rozelle indeed had released the names to the media. One player's wife had called hysterically because her husband had been named publicly but had received no advance notice. Incredible, even for those of us hardened to the NFL's tactics. Rozelle was issuing a press release: "The amount of the fine indicates the severity of the offense." Process of law, past contributions, and future careers be damned. The commissioner's image must be protected at any cost, and the family was kicked to the side without a second thought. The heat was relieved from the owners (Gene Klein was fined and the doctor hired by Klein to give out the pills was "barred for life" from the NFL) and moved onto the players.

Another sad day in the NFL. Another reason players hardened their position. Was this the NFL's strategy for bargaining? Would they intimidate others who had tried grass or used amphetamines? Was this Rozelle's Hoover-like move to warn us to take it easy on him? Or was it more simple: Was it so he could now wash his hands of the "drug problem" his owners had created?

Who knows? All we do know is that the totalitarian regime of Rozelle won again. Once again, the NFLPA lost and couldn't protect the players. Supposedly, according to how Rozelle always described his position, "The commissioner represents the owners, fans, and players." Eight players, their wives, and their families found out that was a lie. No one at 410 Park Avenue gave a damn about the potential impact on those players' lives. Intimidation was just another part of the NFL's program.

From Joe Kapp to the San Diego 8, the NFL's control over the individual was clear. Due process was irrelevant; the rules were unwritten; an appeal to the commissioner was a joke. Not only was the player controlled by the draft and the reserve system; he was controlled and intimidated by the arbitrary disciplinary system headed by the commissioner. How could he obey the rules when the rules were only published in the commissioner's head? How could he have respect for the NFL when investigators used tactics that had been ruled illegal for law enforcement officials years ago?

As we prepared our bargaining position in the late winter and early spring of 1974, we were angry. Kapp, Rentzel, the San Diego 8, the arrogance of the commissioner and his attorneys—these were the underlying problems. Latter-day analysts would claim that I had decided to make the commissioner into a convenient figurehead for the larger hated system of the NFL, which was the target of our wrath. They suggested that his was a calculated decision to spur the troops. They could not be more wrong. We tried at every juncture to give Rozelle a way to be decent, to compromise, to show compassion. He refused every gesture, laughed at our weaknesses, rejected every compromise. It is easy to say we "made" Rozelle the enemy, but if you had talked to the wives of the San Diego players, or to Lance Rentzel, or if you had been the one talking with Joe Kapp, you would know that Rozelle made himself the scapegoat, the enemy. Fair play, compassion, impartiality were meaningless words in this totalitarian system.

"No Freedom, No Football" became the battle cry in 1974. It might well have been "No Fairness, No Football" or "No Dignity, No Football," but "Freedom" seemed to sum it all up.

2

Accumulation of Power

need check & B's

How did it happen that a public relations man called "commissioner" could dominate the lives of 1,300 professional football players? Who gave him that power? The easy answer is: The owners. But where did they get the power?

It helps to be a monopoly, but monopolies don't just happen.

The NFL rarely faced outside competition for player services and fan support over its first seven decades of existence. Competing leagues existed for only ten of those years. The NFL destroyed all pretenders to the crown and, like some mythical monster, grew in strength as it devoured each of the bodies. Then, in 1960, along came the American Football League (AFL).

Had the NFL been willing to meet the wealthy oilmen who created the AFL halfway or even 20 percent of the way, there never would have been an NFL-AFL "war" or an AFL, or the eventual American Football Conference (AFC). One or two expansion teams would have avoided the emergence of the AFL. But once again, the arrogance of the NFL hierarchy forced the issue.

There were plenty of large metropolitan areas eager to receive pro football: Houston, Kansas City, Boston, Denver, Oakland, San Diego, New York, Buffalo, Cincinnati, Miami. But the NFL was paralyzed by success. In 1960, NFL teams were making lots of money, and, with huge TV revenue coming in, the twelve owners looked forward to millions more. Why share TV money twenty ways instead of twelve? They dismissed the idea of a new league; they ignored the warning signals. They failed to expand sensibly. Basically, the league fell victim to its own propaganda: "We can't dilute the quality of football. There aren't enough good players!"

On top of their self-imposed problems, Commissioner Bert Bell had died in October 1959, leaving the NFL leaderless during a critical period.

While Lamar Hunt, Billy Sullivan, Bud Adams, and other AFL owners were plotting their invasion of the NFL, the NFL moguls stumbled around seeking a new leader. Most NFL owners were prepared to accept longtime league counsel Marshall Leahy as commissioner when the owners met to select Bert Bell's successor in January 1960.

Leahy, a warm and decent man, represented the best in the NFL. He respected the law, and he respected his adversaries. While he fought hard for his clients, his adversaries respected Leahy as a man of integrity.

Leahy could have had the job, but he insisted that the NFL office move to San Francisco, his home. The request was too much for the Eastern-dominated league. When it became obvious that Leahy was out, having achieved a majority but not the 75 percent required by the NFL Constitution and Bylaws, the owners looked for an interim commissioner while they searched for the right man. Paul Brown and Wellington Mara approached Pete Rozelle, who was then the Rams general manager, and asked if they could submit his name. They felt, according to Rozelle, that a new name might break the impasse and end the bitter meeting. Rozelle agreed to have his name submitted.

Rozelle was informed of his election on the twenty-third ballot by Carroll Rosenbloom. His term was for three years beginning January 26, 1960. The three-year term became five, ten, fifteen, twenty.

Leahy had been the NFL's lawyer and general counsel to the 49ers. He understood the league and its problems. On the surface, he appeared to have all of the credentials to become an excellent commissioner. Interestingly, Rozelle and the owners were highly critical of my ability to lead the NFL players who hired me as executive director because "Garvey never played pro football." Their inconsistency never bothered them. Rozelle acknowledged he did not play football in high school or college, although he did play a "flag game once."

At the time of his election, Rozelle was thirty-three years old with a BA in English from the University of San Francisco. He worked as publicity director and assistant athletic director at the university and then handled public relations (PR) for the Los Angeles Rams before moving to a small PR company in San Francisco that worked for the Australian government during the 1956 Olympic Games. He went on to become general manager of the Rams for three years before being named NFL commissioner. Would this background prepare him for the tough decisions in 1960–1963?

Rozelle's primary concern was to consolidate his position as commissioner by doing his job while gaining control of the mechanisms of power. One way to consolidate his position was to destroy the rival AFL. Pete would encourage the NFL owners to focus on the AFL as an enemy. During this critical period, Rozelle learned the value of a hated enemy. If the enemy is bad enough, he can be blamed for anything and can be used as a diversion from one's own performance. From 1960 to 1966 it was the AFL, and from 1967 to 1968 it was the Teamsters, who threatened to organize the players. From 1970 on, Black players, the union, and I were all trying to break down the city walls and take over the NFL "civilization." Rozelle, without a common enemy, might be forced to answer a tough question: "What do you do all day, Pete, at $1,000 per day?"

He was not prepared for tough decisions. He had never been asked to put his beliefs on the line. He was a PR man, trained to make excuses in defeat and take credit for success. After all, a PR man doesn't make mistakes; he just comments on them and puts the best face forward. He was never in the ring, only in the stands.

The AFL was a strange group to start with. Owners had little in common other than oil and money, and few would have predicted ultimate success and even domination of the combined NFL once the merger occurred. But one thing the AFL had at the beginning was the ability to have fun, to be innovative, to laugh at themselves. They also had enough money to succeed and people smart enough to outthink Rozelle and his coterie.

The AFL didn't go crazy trying to get the big names. They sensibly went out to establish a league primarily in non-NFL cities and gradually went after big-name college players. Lamar Hunt and Al Davis recognized that there were plenty of good players available for twelve NFL and ten AFL teams. After all, the pro "minor leagues" (colleges) turned out hundreds of excellent players every year. They didn't need training, for they had trained since junior high school. All they needed was a job, and the NFL often made mistakes in cutting players. Pittsburgh once cut Johnny Unitas! Len Dawson, Daryle Lamonica, and others never made it in the NFL, but they had a chance in the AFL. *doesn't do shit how he such trouble* ○ ✳

Rozelle moved in to destroy the AFL through ridicule, with Vince Lombardi as the primary advocate of the NFL's stubborn strategy. Saint Lombardi had already turned the Packers around and was rapidly becoming the George Patton of football. Americans needed a hero, and Lombardi fit the mold. Tough, hard-nosed, violent-tempered, religious, Vince was to change pro football. He would chuckle at the AFL brand of football, and Americans would laugh. He would make fun of the fledgling league, and the AFL was supposed to go away.

The Lombardi Era coincided with the NFL-AFL war. Was it coincidence? Was the Lombardi mystique, self-serious and self-assured, responsible for Rozelle's refusal to recognize and deal with the AFL? Was it the Lombardi's unflinching commitment to total victory following the examples of military generals like LeMay and Patton that forced the NFL to try every means to destroy the AFL? No one knows, but it's a safe bet that thirty-five-year-old, insecure PR man Rozelle was more inclined to follow a Patton than a Henry Clay. Compromise requires confidence.

It is no accident that Lombardi never lost a draft choice he wanted to the AFL. It is no accident that Lombardi led the fight against agents and lawyers representing players. A lawyer for perennial all-pro center Jim Ringo entered Lombardi's office to announce that he was there to negotiate for Ringo. He was told to wait a minute. When Lombardi returned, the lawyer was informed that Ringo was no longer with Green Bay because Lombardi had just traded him to Philadelphia. After that, how much guts would it take for a lesser-known player to confront Lombardi with a lawyer?

When Lombardi said the AFL would be destroyed, he meant it. It was the enemy. Lombardi, who praised players who played with injuries and looked down on those who would not, was the NFL symbol of the 1960s. "Winning is not everything—it's the only thing" and other such nonsense attributed to Lombardi became part of American life. Who knows how many young football players ruined potential pro careers as a result of would-be Vince Lombardi's running around screaming, hitting, shouting, and cursing at players to allow themselves to be exploited for the programs that used them?

The Lombardi spirit forced the NFL establishment and its titular head, Rozelle, to fight the AFL until it was too late. It became too late in 1964 when NBC agreed to televise AFL games. Finally, in 1965 or 1966, a merger was proposed. After all, it was foolish to go on squandering thousands of dollars bidding on rookies to get them into the NFL when a common draft—the old way—would work again to keep the cost of rookies down. And the AFL decision in 1965 to go after veteran NFL quarterbacks such as John Brodie really forced the issue. True, in a merger, the TV money would be split up twenty-four ways, but so what? The amounts saved on rookies through a common draft, not to mention veterans like Brodie, would more than compensate for the TV money lost. Wellington Mara, owner of the Giants, was given credit by many for forcing the decision to merge.

Mara was never one to rock the boat. He believed in the NFL Constitution and Bylaws. He loved tradition. He never went out of bounds. Yet Mara signed placekicker Pete Gogolak to a contract in 1966 after Pete had become an AFL free agent having played out his Buffalo option. Even though they were at war, the two leagues respected each other's contracts. An owner told me and John Mackey in 1972 that Mara's action forced the merger.

Following these signings, the AFL would now be free to raid the NFL of its stars and vice versa. No longer would the battlefield remain in the parking lots outside college bowl games. Now everyone was fair game, including veterans. Prior to the Gogolak signing, there had been a quiet (and illegal) agreement among owners in each league to stay away from veterans from the other league. But then negotiations began with Brodie, Jim Ninowski, Alex Karras, Joe Kapp and other veterans. Rozelle still fought the merger, fearing he would lose his job if one occurred. Then, according to Carroll Rosenbloom, after the Gogolak signing and a few others, Lombardi went to Rozelle and said a merger was inevitable. The owners assured Rozelle he would remain as commissioner. Hearing his job was secure, Rozelle dropped his opposition to the merger.

An AFL-NFL merger signaled doom to the competition for football players between pro football leagues in the United States. With the top twenty-five TV markets taken up, it would be nearly impossible for another league to compete successfully for fans, and gradual expansion would use up other markets. The immediate question became how the NFL would keep its awesome power by getting the merger through Congress.

———

Congress had always been a happy hunting ground for sports owners. The last thing a congressperson wants is blame for hurting sports or causing a franchise to move out of his or her district. When it came time for the merger, league attorney Hamilton Carothers was confident of quick action. The league assumed that everyone in Congress would be happy to bring an end to wild bidding for athletes. There would be few obstacles to passage of yet another exemption from federal antitrust laws for millionaire owners of football teams.

Senator Philip Hart (D-MI), a liberal on nearly all issues, had a peculiar blind spot when it came to sports. Hart married the daughter of Walter Briggs, owner of Briggs Stadium and the Detroit Tigers, and Hart was once general counsel to the Tigers. Because of his unblemished record in the Senate, I personally did not believe that Hart supported pro sports' monopolistic practices for any personal or family gain. But his views on this subject were formed by the sports establishment, and he never took the time to search out the players' perspective. Also, at the time, a union to represent players was just beginning, so players had no real voice yet to speak for them. Had there been an established and organized players' union at the time of the merger, I believe Phil Hart would have been on our side.

In any case, Senate Bill 3817, the AFL-NFL merger bill, was reported out of Hart's Antitrust Subcommittee without hearings and sent to the House in 1966.

The Senate Monopolies Committee set forth numerous conclusions with no supporting data: the league would keep its "twenty-four teams in the same locations," large rookie "bonus money could now go to raise veteran salaries," and broad statements were issued that the merger would be "beneficial for all concerned." Carothers had earned half of this money. He got the bill through the Senate without having one witness appear, without answering a single question.

Congressman Emanuel Celler (D-NY) was chairman of the House Antitrust Subcommittee and chairman of the full Judiciary Committee. Celler devoted his life to the rule of the law, believing passionately in fairness and due process. He gaveled the football merger hearings to order at 10:50 A.M. on October 6, 1966. After reviewing Senate Bill 3817 and various amendments, Celler read an opening statement saying the subcommittee would "explore thoroughly the extent of the immunity requested, and the results that would flow from any such grant of immunity." Celler quoted from an Attorney General Committee's report on antitrust protections published in 1955:

Antitrust is a distinctive American means for assuring the competitive economy on which our political and social freedom under representative government in part depend. . . . They reinforce our ideal of careers open to superior skills and talent, a crucial index of a free society.

It would be difficult to state the issue better. Then he stated his own philosophy:

The antitrust laws have been a valuable protection to individuals possessing the superior skills and talents that are required to participate in professional football. . . .

The policies embodied in the antitrust laws generally have been considered to be of such great importance in the American business world that exemptions have been granted only after the most thorough-going examination. And when the Congress has seen fit to exempt industries from the antitrust laws, the normal procedure is for Congress to erect a mechanism or procedure which would serve to perform the same function that competition is expected to perform. . . .

The Antitrust Subcommittee, if an antitrust exemption is to be granted, must consider carefully what is to take the place of the antitrust laws as a safeguard to the interests of the general public as well as the participants in professional football. Should a government regulatory body be established? Is the office of the commissioner of professional football adequate to protect the interests of the players and the general public if an antitrust exemption is granted?

Celler made all of the important points. The primary question that emerged was how the participants and the public could be protected absent competition. Regulatory control is one answer; the commissioner as "protector" is not.

––––––––

On Tuesday, October 13, 1966, Rozelle, Lamar Hunt, Tex Schramm, and Hamilton Carothers appeared before the subcommittee and the circus began. On October 11, I was one month into law school at the University of Wisconsin and could not have cared less about merger hearings in football. The war in Vietnam, President Lyndon Johnson's credibility gap, and other issues were more pressing. But football owners would get their merger.

Rozelle read his opening statement. This "bill of very limited scope . . . will be beneficial to the colleges and high schools and millions of sports fans. Football operations will be preserved in the 23 cities and 25 stadiums where such operations are presently being conducted. That alone is a matter of considerable public interest to the local economies, stadium authorities and consumers."

How could you go wrong by voting for a bill that will help local economies, high schools and colleges across the land, and millions of fans, the NFL asked. Not only that, "A drafted player will receive a minimum of $12,000, and pension plan benefits to all AFL players will increase substantially." Thus, the workers would also be helped. A perfect law that helped everyone! Would Congress be swayed by this PR campaign?

For support, the chief PR man of organized sports naturally turned to the sportswriters of America. Lloyd Larson of the *Milwaukee Sentinel*, Bob Maisel of the *Baltimore Sun*, and Bob Burnes of the *St. Louis Globe Democrat* were all quoted to the effect that the merger was in the best interests of the fans. Players who favored merger were widely quoted by Rozelle's friends in the sports press, while those who opposed the merger were ignored.

Celler continued the hearings, but long before they concluded, the bill approving the merger was introduced on the floor of the House and passed, despite objections from Chairman Celler and Judiciary Committee members on the last night before Congress adjourned for the 1966 congressional election. It was then tacked onto a conference committee compromise bill on investment tax credits and adopted by both houses. President Johnson signed the bill without hesitation. The deed was done. Competition killed. The NFL would gather enormous strength, and pro football players would lose an unprecedented opportunity to see the leagues compete for their services.

Looking back, it's difficult to believe that Congress would approve creation of a monopoly with no hearings in the Senate and incomplete hearings in the House. The Senate never took a vote on the merger. What was the hurry? The 1966 season was almost over, the 1967 season months away. But hurry they did, before opposition could crystallize.

Hale Boggs of Louisiana, House Democratic Whip, was the key to quick passage in the House. He was aided by Speaker John McCormick and Congressman Tip O'Neill, friends of the Boston-born Billy Sullivan, who owned the New England Patriots. Senator Russell Long of Louisiana made certain the Senate approved. How would Boggs and Long of Louisiana benefit from passage? Within months it was announced that New Orleans would get an NFL franchise immediately, despite being just one of seven applicants. Boggs and Long were pleased, and the NFL was pleased. Years later (January 9, 1977) reporter Daniel Rapoport of the *Washington Star* quoted Long as saying, "Rozelle said that if the merger went through, New Orleans would likely get the next franchise."

A merger occurred, though not, as Celler had hoped, with a thorough examination or with a regulatory agency to protect players and fans. The merger went through, as Senator Sam Ervin said, as a result of "legislative chicanery" at best. Some would call it bribery, but other would call it smart politics.

The NFL would brag about its achievement. They had pulled off an end run around Celler and the Antitrust Subcommittee. They were home free.

But in their haste to avoid questioning, they may have committed some strategic errors. If they had sought exemption for the draft or Rozelle Rule, they might have been successful. There was no real opposition, so why didn't they try?

Still, as Rozelle observed his kingdom in December 1966, things couldn't have been more in control. NFL clubs could bargain collectively with broadcast networks without fear of antitrust attack. Because of the 1961 antitrust exemption, the NFL would dominate the networks. No one could oppose Rozelle on the air because Pete could have them fired. There was no competition for the NFL now. A common draft, the unwritten Rozelle Rule, and other restrictive practices would hold salaries down and keep profits up. There was a weak, disorganized union and a kept sports press that was thirsty and hungry. Fans flocked to the new national pastime. Money rolled in. The NFL had beaten the odds and stood as the shining example of success in professional sports. Its power would not be successfully challenged for almost a decade, and one reason for Rozelle's success was the NFL's control of the media.

The NFLPA, such as it was in the early years, tried to get labor writers to cover what was a labor problem, but with few exceptions the story ended up on the sports page, even though we may have been making labor history. Generally, labor writers shied away from what was considered sports and sportswriters avoided business. Nightly news programs had three distinct segments: News, weather, and sports. "Sports" can't be "news" and vice versa. Similarly, newspapers confined all news related to sports to the non-serious sports section. Labor disputes generally appeared in the general news section, reported by writers with some understanding of the labor movement, the National Labor Relations Board (NLRB), strikes, and lockouts. But in the 1970s, the football strike was covered as sports by reporters who knew nothing about labor disputes.

Editors did not generally hold sportswriters to the same standard as other reporters. (George Solomon, sports editor of the *Washington Post* from 1975 to 2003, said in May 1981 to the American Society of Newspaper Editors, "It's time sportswriters were looked at as reporters.") Newspaper publishers at the time believed that the sports page was designed only to sell newspapers and that the page had no other intrinsic value. Because publishers considered sports pages as part of their entertainment coverage, they were less concerned about bias, accuracy, and fairness than with their "news" coverage. So what if a sports columnist was "controversial"? Why should the paper be concerned if he or she was unfair, wrote that unions were bad for sports, that unions would kill the game, that players were greedy? It helped sell papers, and besides, sports were only a diversion from "important" things. If play is the work of children, we must be amused when adults work at children's games.

The NFL played on the media companies' anti-union sentiment while pouring drinks down open throats. Spokesmen for management have been quoted about the sports unions:

"Unions are ruining America and now they are going to ruin sports."

"Players don't want a 'union,' they want an 'association.'"

"Players aren't like truck drivers or other laborers that need unions, they are 'professionals.'"

Many writers felt the same way.

The league constantly talked of "professionals," as if the players were doctors or lawyers in a position to negotiate between many competing offers. In their view, "professionals" were not supposed to be unionized. In the stadium clubs and the touchdown clubs of America, the talk was that unions "drag people down . . . they reward incompetence, not talent." And many of the sportswriters enjoyed being around wealthy owners. Some were delighted to have dinner at an expensive restaurant or attend a league extravaganza in the Astrodome or Rivergate or the *Queen Mary*. Conflicts could be put aside because writers shared many of the basic attitudes held by owners, and sports sections were not held to the same standards as news sections.

When the AFL-NFL merger was consummated in 1966, the commissioner announced that a championship game to be called the Super Bowl would follow that season. Rozelle, ever the public relations man, seized upon the Super Bowl as an opportunity to buy and ensure the loyalty of the nation's sports press. All the league had to do was provide journalists covering the event with first-class facilities; a tremendous party; constant entertainment; remembrances in the form of suit bags, briefcases, jewelry, and watches; and limited access to the coaches, owners, and athletes. Journalists soon understood that failure to participate in these events and accept these gifts might limit their coverage. The NFL would put on a show to end all shows, making baseball, basketball, and hockey appear amateurish in their PR efforts

While writers would drive to the race track in NFL-furnished cars or play in an NFL-sponsored golf tournament for NFL-purchased prizes, Don Weiss, the league's PR director, and his staff would videotape and mimeograph all of the daily interviews. The writers would return from the track or golf course, pick up three or four previously recorded interviews, file the stories, and convince their bosses back home that they were busting their humps. The league would furnish a twenty-four-hour bar and lavish parties in private clubs.

The NFL used to spend about $200,000 on the press during Super Bowl week. That's right: *Two hundred thousand dollars* on 1,500 writers, announcers, and hangers-on! By 1979, at his Super Bowl XIII press conference, Rozelle admitted that the league would spend close to $1 million during Super Bowl week! The press party cost was estimated by the Associated Press at $600,000.

In Los Angeles, NFL employees served writers lobster Newburg on the NFL bus. When it came to writing an appraisal of Rozelle's performance as commissioner, who could forget the lobster Newburg? When sportswriters decided who was right and who was wrong in the players' strike, would that wonderful week in New Orleans, Miami, Houston, or Los Angeles be remembered? The answer is that I know a few, but only a few, reporters who supported the players during the strike.

Paul Hendrickson wrote about the "press pack" at Super Bowl X in the now-defunct *National Observer*. The pack consisted of 1,700 media people from some 850 news organizations. He described their accommodations at the Konover Hotel, which was once the Playboy Club in Miami Beach: The press room established by the NFL had a Western Union setup, a bank of dictation phones, eight long rows of tables with 125 typewriters, and a "free bar that is open from 12 to 12." Hendrickson described free luncheons for hundreds of writers, and endless prepared press releases, and he discussed the "pack" mentality. He described the Super Bowl press as "The Boys in the Box," quoting from Timothy Crouse's *The Boys on the Bus*, a book about writers who cover political matters: "It was just these womblike conditions that gave rise to the notorious phenomenon called 'pack journalism.'"

Crouse was describing the 1972 presidential campaign press corps, but Hendrickson successfully drew a parallel with the NFL press corps. Crouse discussed why few writers stray from the pack by quoting a former *Newsweek* correspondent: "You delude yourself into thinking, 'Hell, if I get on the bad side of these guys, then I'm not gonna get all that good stuff.' But pretty soon the realization hits that there isn't any good stuff, and there isn't gonna be any good stuff. Nobody's getting anything that you're not getting, and if they are, it's just more of the same bullshit."

Therein lies the story. At first, I thought sportswriters feared not receiving an invitation back to Super Bowl IX or X or XI, but the stakes were higher for them than just the party and party favors. The paper paid for the writer to attend, and the NFL couldn't openly discriminate against a writer once he or she arrived on scene. Friend and foe alike gained access to the press room, free bar, and interviews. Sycophants and independents got their watches, press kits, and jewelry. The real reason they don't "stray from the pack" is fear—a groundless fear, but a real one to them, that they wouldn't get the "good stuff" if they got on the bad side of Weiss or the high commissioner. They were afraid Rozelle wouldn't call on them by name at the press conference or that little favors and access would no longer be there during the long off-season.

bought the press

Ah yes, the "no such thing as a free lunch" quote roared through my mind as I thought of the sports press at the Super Bowl.

———

Super Bowl money, booze, and trinkets set the mood for writers, but the story didn't end there. Writers needed access to the locker room, to the coaches, to the "inside story" because they believed their job would end without a postgame interview. In this respect, the sportswriter was no different from the political columnist who needed White House access.

Tom Dowling, an excellent writer and former sportswriter for the *Washington Star*, was once forced out of a Washington R******s locker room after a game by a R******s official who accused him of "not being on our team." Presumably, the other writers were.

Similarly, when a Pittsburgh reporter caught Steelers coach Chuck Noll violating the collective bargaining agreement by having veterans in pads in an off-season camp in the spring of 1978, Noll accused the reporter of sabotage. He even suggested the reporter was a spy and questioned his "loyalty to the Steelers." The teams behaved as if media were dependent on their favor, and the NFL sought to keep it that way.

Another reason a sportswriter would be inclined to support management is linked to familiarity. The writer got to know management. Players would come and go, but management stayed the same. Like most people, sportswriters were more comfortable with management "friends" than with the younger athlete "strangers" who would come and go. Reporters would talk about players associations and labor issues with management staff but rarely, if ever, with the athletes.

Sportswriter Leonard Koppett explained to me that baseball writers were different from football writers because they get to know the athletes over the longer, more relaxed season—and career. A writer covering a baseball team would see the players in 162 games, whereas in football, there was an annual 25 percent player turnover, the season was short, and playe... access was limited. But football management was always available.

Finally, the NFL had the greatest job corps going. Rozelle used the Associated Press (AP) as his minor league. Nearly all NFL staff people came from AP. Most club PR men were sportswriters at one time.

Any underpaid sportswriter who dreamed of moving up outside the newspaper world would consider the NFL teams or the NFL office. Jobs at the club level paid well by newspaper standards. It did not require a genius to recognize that one would not be selected for a club PR position or a job at NFL headquarters if one supported the players' right to strike, or reported Chuck Noll for violating the collective bargaining agreement, or suggested that Rozelle was doing a lousy job.

Because the league could usually count on sportswriters, fans almost always received a distorted view of players' salary negotiations, owners' profits, and labor-management disputes. It was no accident that Rozelle testified that "sportswriters across the nation" supported the NFL's opposition to Congress's anti-blackout legislation blocking league owners from taking games off TV until stadium tickets sold out, saying, "We maintain an excellent national press clipping service. A review of the commentary offered by sportswriters generally throughout the country indicates that the League's position is supported by somewhere between 80 percent and 90 percent of American sportswriters for the simple reason that they have a greater understanding of professional sports than is common within Congress or among the public generally."

He added, "We also have the support of the only two members of Congress who have had any personal connection with professional football, Senator (Philip) Hart, who at one time had an interest in an NFL team, and Congressman (Jack) Kemp, who actually played professional football."

Senator Torbert MacDonald, who had played on Harvard's football team, responded, "I would not say that you are paranoiac, but you indicated Congress is picking on you. That the Administration is picking on you. That the Justice Department thinks this is a good bill. The fans think it is a good bill, and everyone, except you and an anonymous 80 percent of the sportswriters, thinks in a way which is contrary to what you think."

Rozelle, Kemp, and 80 percent of the sportswriters were the only ones opposed to the legislation, which passed by an overwhelming majority. Maybe no one in Congress believed sportswriters were infallible.

Despite overwhelming press opposition to the players' strike in 1974, and despite vicious attacks against the union and its leadership by columnists, pollster Louis Harris reported that fans supported the players by

ne. Few papers carried that story because it showed up the
otball News claimed that its own survey showed 80 percent
.e owners, but didn't even mention the Harris survey.
? Not so strange. See you at the Super Bowl cocktail party. After
vs, weather, *and* sports.

3

The Opposition Emerges

N FL owners had always dealt decisively with opposition. Through nearly all of its history, it eliminated player dissent by getting rid of individuals who spoke out. Despite strenuous efforts, however, owners could not eliminate the threat from players as a collective force.

At first, players were no obstacle. Individual dissenters who talked of organizing were eliminated with little fanfare. Fear of owner retaliation kept players from joining together in an association until the mid-1950s. Various old-timers told me that anyone who opposed the NFL establishment in the 1930s, 1940s, and early 1950s was cut and banned. The NFL's power to do so and get away with it had a chilling effect on those who would attempt to organize a union.

For example, in the early 1950s Washington R******s players met and decided to ask owner George Preston Marshall for fifty dollars in compensation per preseason game. Star quarterback Sammy Baugh led what was, according to a former member of the team, a short meeting. Marshall said, "We will never pay you for preseason games. This meeting is over." Marshall added that any player who wasn't satisfied with the decision would be fired. He then turned to Baugh and said, "And that includes you, Mr. Baugh!" It was a while before the players stepped forward again.

The NFLPA was formally organized on December 28, 1956. The NFL had twelve teams at the time. At the organizational meeting, ten of eleven elected player representatives attended. One rep missed the meeting because of illness, and one team, the Chicago Bears, voted not to join the organization after George Halas, one of the few owners who paid players for exhibition games, threatened to cut off his players' preseason pay if they voted to join. Halas also promised a pension fund for Bears players if they would stay outside the fledgling NFLPA.

At the first meeting, the reps decided on some proposals that they ultimately submitted to Commissioner Bert Bell in January 1957. Bell immediately refused recognition of the organization and denied all of their proposals. Coincidentally, one month later, the Supreme Court decided *Radovich v. NFL*, finding that football, unlike baseball, was subject to the antitrust laws. Panic broke out among owners as they learned of the decision. Living within the law was too much to bear. They gathered their forces and headed for Congress to seek a reversal, asking Congress to pass a law exempting the NFL from federal antitrust laws, which would put them on the same footing as baseball.

When Bert Bell appeared before the Monopolies Subcommittee of the House in support of the exemption, he was asked whether an antitrust exemption would adversely affect the players. He argued that players would be adequately protected by the labor laws; therefore, they did not need antitrust protection. When asked if he *recognized* the recently formed NFLPA, under the labor laws, Bell hemmed and hawed but finally said, "Yes." Imagine the commissioner testifying that players such as Bill Radovich did not need antitrust protection but only protection afforded by the National Labor Relations Act while, at the same time, offering to recognize the players' union only under pressure from Congress.

Despite his "recognition" of the NFLPA at the hearings, Bell refused to negotiate for the next five months. Then, in December 1957, out of frustration, Green Bay's Billy Howton, NFLPA president, threatened Bell with a class action antitrust suit on behalf of all players in the league unless recognition was granted. (It should be noted that Vince Lombardi did not like union advocates, so he traded Howton to the Cleveland Browns.) Suddenly, the commissioner decided to recognize and meet with the NFLPA. Bell denied that the threatened lawsuit had prompted negotiations; he said he recognized and dealt with the players "because it was right."

Following the players' agreement not to file suit, some concessions were gained from Bell during 1958 and 1959, but there had been no direct bargaining with owners. Bargaining consisted of players submitting their proposals to Bell, who would listen to them and then transmit the proposals to the owners. After the owners considered the proposals, Bell would inform the players of the owners' decision. He was the broker, never the advocate.

The owners decided what they would say, and that was it. They did not negotiate.

In 1959, the NFL entered into an agreement with the fledgling NFLPA to establish a player pension fund on a handshake basis. This was the NFL-PA's first achievement . . . or was it? Before the agreement could be implemented, Commissioner Bell died in October of that year. Nothing further developed until three years later, in Pete Rozelle's term as commissioner.

Despite the owners' promise to start a pension plan, they hadn't funded one by 1963. The NFLPA again threatened a class action lawsuit unless owners honored their commitment to a pension and made a contribution. The NFL was then competing with the AFL and actually wanted a fringe benefit program; therefore, Rozelle "generously" agreed to fund the pension plan, not with owners' money but with players' licensing revenues from Topps bubble gum cards and other such programs! Thus, the players ended up funding most of their "bargained for" pension fund on their own.

Because the AFL was in full swing in the early 1960s, salaries were increasing rapidly to compete. Between 1959 and 1965, the average salary moved from $9,000 to nearly $24,000. Concerns that bothered players in the late 1950s with an average salary of $9,000 disappeared as the average player almost tripled his salary in 1963, 1964, and 1965. With their newfound riches, there was less concern about collective negotiations and more concern devoted to individual contract negotiations, per diem pay, and play-off dollars.

It would be fair to characterize the NFLPA from 1963 to 1967 as a sweetheart union. In the environment fostered by competition between leagues, there was no strike talk and few demands. At the end of the season, the player representatives, some of whom were actually appointed by club owners, would assemble in New York City to meet with owners and the commissioner. The day following a night at the theater, there would be a joint meeting of owners and player reps around a large conference table. The seating was player, owner, player, owner. At those meetings, the players would hear what the owners could afford to give them during the coming year. There were no negotiations. After all, they were all part of the NFL family.

Excused by the cozy relationship between the owners and the player reps, injustices continued in the NFL. Those who rocked the boat were cut and often banned. Some players, such as the Jets' Joe Namath, made considerable sums of money, but the run-of-the-mill player was still not doing very well. Salaries were up because of AFL competition, not because of union pressure. There was also still discrimination and inhumanity.

Most writers characterized the players' concerns about the reserve system in economic terms only, but players also made important noneconomic complaints about the system. Black players were not allowed to perform in certain positions, such as center, quarterback, guard, and middle linebacker. Anyone complaining about this fact could only go to the commissioner, which was a waste of time. Arbitrary rules were established. The only appeal was to Rozelle.

Dick Gordon, the brilliant receiver for the Bears, was benched by his coach because he wore an Afro and colorful clothes off the field. Years later in the *Mackey* trial, the owners' attorney seriously asked Gordon on the witness stand, "Mr. Gordon, if it was against club policy to wear an Afro, why did you?"

Dick glared back and responded, "It had something to do with genetics!"

Policies mandating no mustaches, no Afros, no beards, no long hair, and no late nights were not issues critical to player well-being in and of themselves. What was important was management's absolute ability to deny the right to dissent and to deny the right to seek employment with a less restrictive team. Remember, Dick Gordon couldn't quit the Bears and go to work for the Rams.

———

In *They Call It a Game*, Bernie Parrish, who played most of his career for the Cleveland Browns, wrote about the NFLPA at some length. He not only thought the NFLPA was a sweetheart union in the 1960s but actually argued that the organization was initially set up through the efforts of Browns owner Art Modell and the team's coach, Paul Brown. In his opinion, Creighton Miller, a Cleveland attorney and the attorney for the NFLPA, was less than independent. He suggested that Modell and Brown got him the job.

Creighton Miller remained as general counsel to the NFLPA for eleven years. Miller was a practicing attorney, and the NFLPA was only one of his clients. During the eleven years he was general counsel, the association had no staff. Whether Parrish was right or wrong in his suspicion about how Miller got the position, clearly Miller did not build a strong union, nor did he organize any opposition to the AFL-NFL merger that robbed players of their bargaining power. Miller was among those who believed that players were professionals and that it was against the interest of the players to be called a union. To his credit, he opposed a complete antitrust exemption for the NFL at the 1959 congressional hearings, but he agreed that certain restrictions such as the reserve clause were probably necessary in order to keep balance in the league.

Bernie Parrish was vice president of the NFLPA in 1967. He was tired of Miller's pro-management leanings. Parrish decided to talk with the American Federation of Labor and Congress of Industrial Organizations (AFL-CIO) in 1967 to obtain help in organizing the players as a union. Parrish felt that it was necessary to form a union with NLRB recognition if the players were ever to make progress. He argued that a strike, unheard of in sports at the time, should be considered. In response, AFL-CIO leader George Meany unfortunately announced publicly that players did not need a union since they were "independent contractors" who were doing quite well on their own. Meany suggested that players needed "better lawyers, not a union." (Thirteen years later, George Meany would welcome professional athletes into the AFL-CIO at the final convention he chaired. Times changed, and so did George Meany.)

Though Parrish was disappointed by Meany's rejection, he continued to talk with other union leaders across industries and was finally introduced to Harold Gibbons of the International Brotherhood of Teamsters. Gibbons, a bright, articulate union leader, welcomed the idea of including professional football players. He suggested that Parrish form an organization called the American Federation of Professional Athletes (AFPA), which, after being formed, would vote on whether to affiliate with the Teamsters.

Gibbons and Parrish traveled the country to meet with NFL players to seek authorization cards to join AFPA. According to Parrish, nearly all of the Browns, Falcons, and R******s players signed the cards. The owners heard quickly that players were organizing a real union with the Teamsters' help. In many ways, this presented a greater threat to management than the Supreme Court's *Radovich* decision. Action was required. A declaration of war, if necessary. In strong language, owners urged player reps to stay away from the Teamsters.

In the meantime, Parrish and Gibbons came up with a list of proposals, including a minimum salary of $15,000 to $20,000; preseason pay of $500 per game; a pension contribution of $5 million per year from the league; impartial arbitration of disputes; elimination of the option clause that allowed teams to retain each player's rights for a year after their actual contract with him expired; a voice in NFL Constitution and Bylaws changes; a voice in the naming of the commissioner; and film royalty payments paid into the pension fund. These demands seemed incredibly radical to many in 1967.

When Browns owner Art Modell, then president of the NFL, learned that players were seriously considering Teamsters affiliation, he wrote an unbelievable letter to Creighton Miller in which he said that "antitrust laws prohibit collective bargaining in the National Football League." Nine years later, Modell would contradict that position in testimony in federal district court, saying federal antitrust laws should not apply to the NFL because restrictions on players should be covered in collective bargaining under labor laws. Back in 1957, Bert Bell had testified that the NFL should be exempt from *antitrust laws* because players would be protected by the *labor laws*. Well, the NFL had never been accused of consistency. They would use whichever argument was immediately useful.

Modell also met with Gibbons and urged him to lay off the players. He urged Gibbons to allow players to have their own independent association. But the Teamsters persisted, and a showdown among the player reps occurred in Florida in December 1967. The player reps had to choose—be part of the Teamsters or have their own independent association. The NFL quickly agreed to recognize the NFLPA if the reps would turn down the Teamsters. The player representatives, after a tough debate, decided to remain independent, but they fired Creighton Miller and voted to hire attorneys Dan Shulman and Bernie Baum as labor counsel.

The Teamsters supporters, while disappointed, were somewhat molli-fied because Shulman was regarded as a tough negotiator who, ironically, represented a number of Teamsters locals in Chicago. Conservatives could accept Shulman because he was "better than the Teamsters." Parrish was unhappy. He viewed this as the downfall of the players and a return to the sweetheart days.

The NFL owners, anxious to avoid a recurrence of the Teamsters "men-ace," recognized the NFLPA as the players' exclusive collective bargaining agent the day after their decision to turn away from the Teamsters. They held out recognition as a carrot while players considered joining the Team-sters or remaining independent. The owners assured the players of imme-diate recognition if they voted for independence.

True recognition is a slow process when a union deals with a monopoly. In 1958, the players were first recognized by Bert Bell only because of pres-sure from a Supreme Court decision and a subcommittee of the U.S. Con-gress. Ten years later, they achieved a signed recognition agreement only as a result of the threat of outside intervention by Teamsters. Real bargaining would not come until another court decision ten years after that in *Mackey v. NFL*.

1968: The First Confrontation

At that same rep meeting in 1968, John Gordy, who had recently retired from the Detroit Lions, was elected president of the independent NFLPA.

Gordy and Shulman would orchestrate the 1968 negotiations. The demands were not great—a decent pension, some preseason pay, a fair individual contract—but there was no hope of achieving even modest goals because of the weak position of the independent union.

Following months of fruitless negotiations, the San Francisco 49ers started a three- or four-hour strike. NFL owners responded immediately by calling for a lockout of all veterans around the league. While NFL players tried negotiating with the NFL, the post-merger AFL, led by its former commissioner, Al Davis, secretly signed a sweetheart contract with Pete Rozelle concerning how AFL players would be compensated. The signing placed tremendous pressure on NFL players to sign a similar contract at a time when owners were threatening to lift the lockout, and at a time when the AFL reportedly offered to have its championship team play the college All-Stars in the annual *Chicago Tribune* game.

The AFL Players Association (AFLPA) secret deal was too much for NFL players. Negotiators quickly swallowed their pride and signed a two-year contract that merely stated in writing the benefits the players were already receiving. Rozelle remained as arbitrator of all grievances, the Standard Player Contract remained as drafted by the NFL, and the Rozelle Rule, the option clause, and the draft went untouched.

Various efforts were made to merge the NFLPA and the AFLPA in 1968 and 1969, but because of the enmity between the AFL's Jack Kemp and the NFL's John Gordy, these efforts were in vain. Kemp did not want to merge the smaller AFLPA into the NFLPA without gaining significant concessions, including getting rid of the "union militants." Kemp was working closely with the NFL owners, and they waited until they could play off one group against the other within the NFLPA, name their people to positions within the organization, and get rid of Shulman.

It has been suggested that the dispute between Kemp and Gordy was actually manufactured by Kemp in order to await the proper moment for a merger of the two organizations. The AFL-NFL merger had been approved by Congress in 1966, so there was no reason for maintaining two separate unions. However, management loved it.

The proper moment arrived in January 1970 when the two organizations met in New Orleans to establish merger terms. The AFL had formally died in January, and three NFL teams moved to the American Football Conference (AFC). Merger of the two labor organizations could no longer be delayed. At that meeting, Kemp carefully moved to find an acceptable NFLPA candidate for president who would be supported by the ten AFL teams. It was also important that the NFL person *not* be acceptable to

Gordy and the current leadership of the NFLPA, for if he were acceptable to them, Kemp felt he could not work out a deal. The NFLPA leadership was supporting defensive back Ed Meador of the Los Angeles Rams for the presidency. Kemp suggested John Mackey, the great Colt tight end as his candidate.

Kemp went to Mackey and offered him ten AFL votes for the presidency if Mackey could deliver NFLPA votes for Alan Miller to replace Dan Shulman as general counsel. Jack Kemp brought Alan Miller in as general counsel to the old AFLPA in 1969. Miller was an Oakland Raiders blocking back who attended law school in the off-season. He became friendly with Al Davis, who undoubtedly recommended him to Kemp. Kemp, as AFLPA president, always worked closely with AFL hierarchy, and under him the AFLPA bore no resemblance to a democratic institution, nor would anyone confuse the AFLPA with a union. Kemp ran it, controlled it, and, by and large, selected its officers. No one else knew what was going on. As one player put it, "Kemp ran the organization out of his locker."

Dan Shulman, by contrast, was strongly disliked by the NFL commissioner and his negotiators, largely because he knew too much. He understood how the NFL worked. He was indeed an honest, tough negotiator, so Rozelle wanted him out. It was Kemp's mistaken belief that some members of the NFL hierarchy could control John Mackey. Kemp used the reputation of John Gordy to whip the AFL player representatives into line by suggesting that, unless they supported Mackey, the "militant" Gordy would remain on the scene.

Mackey won on the first ballot, Shulman resigned as counsel, and Alan Miller, Kemp's man, became general counsel. The NFL would be safe again, league management thought. Only later would the NFL realize its mistake: Kemp's "victory" in actuality put Mackey in position to launch a major assault on the reserve system and to build a real union.

In 1968, the AFLPA Memorandum of Agreement and NFLPA Collective Bargaining Agreement expired when Mackey was elected. A new organization, with new leadership and new attorneys, would now confront the NFL management in collective bargaining. Naturally, the NFL had not made any changes in its lineup, believing this negotiation would be child's play for Rozelle, Tex Schramm, Ralph Wilson, Rankin Smith, and their famous labor attorney, Theodore W. Kheel.

Not one person on the new negotiating committee, composed of players Mackey, Ken Bowman, Ernie Wright, Pat Richter, Kermit Alexander, Nick Buoniconti, and Tom Keating, had been involved in the 1968 negotiations. No one on that committee had any familiarity with collective bargaining, nor had any of them even met Rozelle or any other owners who would appear on the negotiating committee. They were unaware of the efforts to trick the players to dump the Teamsters, the Kemp agreement in 1968, or the owners' refusal to bargain. The NFLPA did not even have a set of proposals to make to the NFL, but it did elect an outstanding Executive Committee as its negotiating arm. The first step—meet informally with Rozelle and the owners.

The first negotiating meeting in 1970 between the league and the NFL-PA took place in Hawaii at the suggestion of Pete Rozelle. The owners had their spring meeting in Honolulu, and Rozelle suggested that John Mackey and Alan Miller fly to Hawaii in March to meet with the owners' negotiating committee in an informal atmosphere.

This was typical of how the league operated. The first effort was to lull the new people into a false sense of camaraderie and impress them with the owners' wealth and power. The thrust of the Hawaii meeting was to urge Mackey to keep the arguments within the family, rather than to "hang the dirty linen in public." In other words, don't talk to the press. It was also an effort by Schramm and Rozelle to convince Mackey that both sides should keep lawyers out of the dispute. (By "lawyers," they meant outside independent counsel, as opposed to Alan Miller, whom they wanted involved.) If the inexperienced players kept lawyers out of negotiations, they would surely lose to the well-advised, experienced owners and league lawyers, just as in individual negotiations. If owners could get the players' union to negotiate without counsel, management would have a field day.

As Rozelle looked ahead to the "negotiations" in 1970, he could not have been happier. The Teamsters were gone; Shulman and Gordy were gone. Alan Miller was in; Jack Kemp just a phone call away. It was time to settle back into the sweetheart days of the mid-1960s. But Rozelle mistakenly believed that players who opposed him and the league establishment were out of touch with true sentiments of the membership and, conversely, that sweethearts like Miller or Kemp could always deliver the contract to Rozelle like some ward politician. He wanted to believe, and therefore did believe, that Shulman or Bernie Parrish or Harold Gibbons—or later me—were "opportunists," "radicals," and "troublemakers," whereas the bulk of the membership was happy with their current status.

Rozelle saw the world as he would have it, not as it really was. He could not come to grips with the fact that players would demand fair treatment and a fair share of revenues. He could never understand why a highly paid athlete would risk his big paycheck by fighting for a union or for his principles. This flaw in Rozelle's judgment would ultimately lead to dramatic changes in the power structure that had dominated players from the early 1920s to the late 1970s.

John Mackey was the first superstar to take a leadership role in the NFLPA. The other player-rep leaders had for the most part been older journeymen players. Ernie Wright, AFC vice president, was a solid ten-year AFL veteran with the Bengals; Ken Bowman, a seven-year Packer veteran; Nick Buoniconti, an eight-year vet with Miami; Tom Keating, All-Pro defensive tackle with Oakland; and Kermit Alexander, an eight-year vet with the 49ers—until he was elected to the Executive Committee, that is. At that point, he was quickly traded to Los Angeles. (Teams trading "militant" reps and officers was not new, nor would it soon end.)

All in all, it was a solid veteran committee, but the negotiating committee was not a cohesive unit. Bowman and Richter had supported Meador for president, the NFL players' first choice. They never trusted the AFL faction and, at first, weren't too sure of the Kemp-supported Mackey. Buoniconti and Keating were not overjoyed with Mackey as president, as he was "NFL," even though he was the Kemp "AFL" candidate. Keating had been the only AFL rep to oppose the AFLPA-NFLPA merger, even in 1970, just to give you some idea of his feelings about the "NFL" Players Association. Despite differences, Mackey's great leadership ability would bring the committee together. The owners' arrogance helped.

In 1965 and 1966, several player reps in the AFLPA complained bitterly about the impending merger. They also opposed a new Rozelle Rule, which they heard had been adopted after the merger, since there had been no written Rozelle Rule in the AFL. One wouldn't know that by talking with Kemp, who viewed the merger as "great for players, great for the AFL," and all the players as "delighted." Years later, Kemp would appear on behalf of the owners in the *Mackey* case to testify that football "needs the Rozelle Rule." He was one of the few to vote against the anti-blackout bill and testify against it. Old friends aren't soon forgotten—each year, Congressman Kemp and Pete Rozelle cohosted a cocktail party at the Super Bowl. Jack Kemp never seemed to have a problem getting tickets to any NFL games for a constituent.

Alan Miller was Kemp's protégé. His charge was to take over the NFL-PA and run it like Kemp ran the AFLPA. First, he would be elected general counsel. He would do such an outstanding job as general counsel that no one could challenge him for the job of executive director. He would win every grievance before Rozelle, which would build his image. Owners would tell their players that, while they didn't like Mackey or a lot of the other NFLPA people, "We can respect Alan Miller—he has class."

Miller would emerge as the players' hero, or so Kemp and league management assumed, and he seemed to fit the role—good looking, articulate, bright, a forceful speaker, a former player and then a successful lawyer. He could understand the players' problems—he had been there. All he had to do was control Mackey and the rest of the committee throughout the 1970 negotiations. Management would then help ease him into position to control the union. If Modell and Brown put Creighton Miller in charge in the 1950s, Rozelle, Davis, and Schramm would put Alan Miller in charge of the union in the 1970s.

Miller figured Keating, Wright, and Buoniconti would be automatic votes for him because he would use the "NFL boogeyman" at every opportunity. All he needed to do was gain Mackey's confidence and he would be home free. At worst, every vote then would be 4–3 in his favor. Control of Mackey shouldn't be too hard because they had all been assured by Rosenbloom that Rosenbloom could influence Mackey.

As Rozelle, Schramm, Wilson, and company met with Mackey and Alan in Hawaii in April 1970, they couldn't have been happier. Mackey never said much until he knew exactly what was happening, so Alan did all of the talking. This led them to believe that Alan was already in control of Mackey and, therefore, the NFLPA. Negotiations would be a laugher. It wasn't hard for them to believe that Alan would control Mackey—this was the natural order, they assumed. All the owners had to do now was to make Alan look good, keep militant lawyers like Shulman out of the picture, and run everything through Alan. When it was all over, Alan would take over and the league would have a generation of peace. No more Teamsters, no more Bernie Parrish, no more Gordy or Shulman—now one of their own would be at the helm.

———

John Mackey asked player reps Pat Richter and Ken Bowman, both using their off-season to study law at the University of Wisconsin, to look into the possibility of eventually finding outside labor counsel to advise the NFLPA. They immediately consulted Professor Nathan P. Feinsinger of the UW law faculty. Feinsinger, a highly respected authority on labor relations, was once the permanent umpire between the United Auto Workers and General Motors, and between Honeywell and the Teamsters. His reputation as an arbitrator was second to none. Everyone in the labor movement spoke highly of him, though he had been disabled by a car accident in the 1950s and suffered from Parkinson's disease.

Feinsinger recommended as labor counsel Leonard Lindquist of Minneapolis or Dave Previant of Milwaukee. Alan Miller wrote to both men in

January and asked for a résumé of their firms, plus a list of representative clients. Previant had been general counsel to the Teamsters International for years, and that must have been enough for Alan, since he recommended Lindquist. But because the going plan was to negotiate without outside counsel, the NFLPA would not follow up with Lindquist until later.

Following the informal Hawaii meeting, the apprehensive but eager NFLPA negotiating committee flew to New York in early April to start formal bargaining. The cast of league characters included Tex Schramm, Wayne Valley of Oakland, Rankin Smith of Atlanta, Ralph Wilson of Buffalo, Pete Rozelle, and a surprise guest, the NFL's labor counsel, Theodore W. Kheel. Since an agreement had been reached in Hawaii just a few weeks earlier to keep lawyers out of the negotiations, Mackey smelled a rat.

The owners said Kheel was only present to explain the recognition agreement, which they were going to sign. Kheel had been their behind-the-scenes labor counsel since 1963. He came into the open in 1968 to help stop the Teamsters. According to Rozelle, Kheel would help Mackey and the committee understand why it was necessary for the NFLPA to waive "in perpetuity" the union's right to negotiate preseason pay in order to obtain formal recognition by the owners. (John Mackey joked later, saying, "I didn't know how long 'in perpetuity' was, but it sounded like a long time.")

Kheel presented the recognition agreement to Alan Miller and in "Kheelese" explained that it was "no big deal." Miller agreed, but Mackey was less certain, so he asked for a caucus and then contacted Leonard Lindquist, who had given up hearing from the NFLPA and was surprised by the call. He had never talked to, let alone met with, Mackey or anyone else on the negotiating committee, but Lindquist knew Kheel when they both worked for the NLRB. He spoke with Kheel and suggested to him that the recognition question "could be worked out later," since no one doubted that the NFLPA represented the vast majority of players. He urged Kheel to put it aside and begin negotiations. Kheel seemed agreeable but, after hanging up, refused to proceed unless Mackey signed the agreement. Mackey refused, and the first formal bargaining session ended before it ever began. The players went home.

That stubborn decision by the NFL to make a foregone recognition dependent on a strong-arm deal forever waiving the right to negotiate preseason pay might have been their costliest mistake in fifty years. They were so confident of their superior bargaining position that they got greedy. That decision led to NLRB certification, Lindquist's involvement, Miller's ultimate discharge, my hire to run the NFLPA instead of Alan Miller, the *Mackey* case, and on and on.

To understate, the approach I would take would be different from Alan Miller's or Jack Kemp's. But the NFL was riding high in 1970. The merger was behind them, money was rolling in, players' salaries were down, signing bonuses for veterans had nearly been eliminated, the "union types" had been purged from the NFLPA—now they would move to eliminate preseason pay, get through negotiations, and move Miller into position. They figured all they had to do was give the players a few dollars for the pension fund and increase preseason pay, and the NFLPA might accept the deal.

But there were forces at work who believed that any gain for the union would allow it to grow stronger, so those forces chose to fight instead.

Following the abortive New York bargaining session, Miller and the business manager of the NFLPA, Mal Kennedy, flew out to Minneapolis to meet Lindquist and Gene Keating. I had joined the firm Lindquist and Vennum after finishing law school and was invited to attend the meeting. Miller and Kennedy filled us in on the New York meeting, gave us some of the history of negotiations in 1968, and stressed that the NFLPA was an "association," not a "union." Miller told us that Dan Shulman had been too tough in 1968 and assured us that the NFLPA of 1970 would do much, much better without Shulman. Here was Miller saying how successful they would be by being "reasonable," when the only reason for the visit was the owners' refusal to even sign a recognition agreement with these "reasonable men," let alone negotiate!

We advised the association to file a certification petition with the NLRB if the NFL continued its refusal to recognize the Players Association. The NLRB had recently taken jurisdiction over baseball umpires, so even though football would be the first organization of athletes to file, we were reasonably confident the board would take jurisdiction and order the NFL to recognize the Players Association. Alan Miller, the Kemp protégé, feared the union label and concluded that we couldn't go ahead without permission of the Board of Representatives. Mackey never hesitated. He immediately called a meeting of player reps.

Leonard Lindquist and I flew to Chicago for the meeting, excited to be involved. Before the meeting, we went to Mackey's room, where he confidentially briefed us on his recent meeting with Tex Schramm in Florida. Then when the rep meeting began, Mackey was in charge, but he seemed to go into his shell. Miller completely dominated the meeting. Only later would I understand Mackey's technique—he wasn't shy; he was watching for reactions, biding his time. Lindquist and I talked about certification— my role was to describe the technicalities, while Lindquist talked about labor's traditional struggle for recognition. After all of Miller's talk about anti-union sentiment, we were amazed when the vote was unanimously in favor of filing with the NLRB. We were on the way to becoming the first group of athletes to gain NLRB certification as a union!

We filed on May 9, 1970, with the NLRB, and all hell broke loose. We were immediately accused by management of the high crime of getting the government involved in sports, of jeopardizing the game; we would "lose half our members when they find out we are a union," and on, and on. Despite management's outcry, the die was cast. The petition was one of the first indications that players were not going to be pushed around and that Miller, Kemp, and Rozelle had misread player sentiment. Bert Bell's wish of 1958 to protect players through the labor laws was being fulfilled, no thanks to Bell. But the league had forgotten that pledge.

The NFL's labor attorney, Ted Kheel, responded to our NLRB filing by informing me that once we became certified, "all player contracts" would be void. Many hours of research later, we told Kheel he was full of baloney, because our position was that the union *had the right* to void the contracts but that management couldn't *force* us to. That did not faze Kheel, who felt that because his argument made sense to him, it must be the law! Even if he didn't believe it, the argument was useful to the NFL.

The NFL negotiators seized upon NLRB certification as their excuse for not bargaining with us. The NFL technique was to refuse to negotiate and, at the same time, make our players believe it was *their* fault. Gain concessions before you even get into bargaining—why wait?

The NFL insisted the NLRB hold a hearing on our petition for recognition even though they put forward no witnesses and no evidence. In my judgment, Kheel made a mistake at the hearing, attended by several Vikings players and most of the NFLPA Executive Committee. He went out of his way to embarrass Mackey on the witness stand by asking technical questions about the NFLPA Constitution. When Mackey couldn't answer, Kheel would mockingly remind Mackey that he was president of the union. Maybe his goal was to get Mackey mad at Lindquist and Vennum for not protecting him on the stand—maybe he thought he would gain some psychological advantage over us that would help him during negotiations. Whatever Kheel's motive, he did succeed in getting everyone on our side mad as hell . . . at Ted Kheel.

Enter Rozelle

In June 1970 we filed "refusal to bargain" charges against the owners, belatedly tried to organize a strike, and kept trying to get them to bargain.

Pressure mounted. Finally, the scriptwriters among the NFL owners decided it was time for Rozelle to step in. Leonard Koppett, years later, best described the commissioner's role in bargaining: "Up to the football strike of 1974, Rozelle always was able to speak for a fairly united group of owners. They would decide what was acceptable, and then let Rozelle take the credit for 'making' them do it," allowing him to appear a generous arbiter while achieving the owners' goals all along.

On the weekend of July 4, Rozelle took his white horse out of the barn and was ready to ride. He selected the extraordinarily expensive Plaza Hotel in New York as the site of negotiations. He would chair the lawyer-less negotiating sessions, while Kheel and I would supposedly try to resolve the recognition/preseason-pay issue upstairs.

As if to emphasize the difference in our backgrounds, in our first meeting Kheel quickly told me that he had been named by *New York* magazine as one of the ten most powerful people in New York City. I guess I was supposed to be impressed. Later that first day I said, "Look, Mr. Kheel, if one of the ten most powerful men in New York and one of the ten most prominent radicals from Burlington, Wisconsin, can't settle this, who can?" (I think Kheel decided then and there that I was a little nuts; in any event, it became clear that Kheel best represented the arrogance of the NFL establishment.)

Just before the committee left for New York on July 4, Gene Keating of our law firm had suggested a meeting with Don Fraser, the brilliant Minneapolis congressman and forty-fourth mayor of Minneapolis, to determine whether Congress might do something to force owners to negotiate. After all, when Congress exempted the merger in 1966, did the members believe that the owners would then use their new monopoly power to refuse to deal with the players? Fraser was quick to suggest a meeting between our top officers and the chairman of the Judiciary Committee, Emanuel Celler. Soon Celler organized a breakfast meeting with our negotiating committee and the Antitrust Subcommittee members for July 8. We were enthused—maybe this would pressure the owners to bargain.

No progress was made on July 5 and 6, but word of the breakfast got to the owners, and suddenly, on July 7, there seemed to be a new attitude. We reached agreement, and late that day they recognized the union! They agreed that we would negotiate an increase in preseason pay, that players could negotiate for additional pay, and that the commissioner's powers would be negotiated in good faith. Amazing! A dramatic breakthrough after months of legal maneuvers. We met at about 5:00 P.M. to read the outline of the agreement. Mackey read it. They agreed. Handshakes all around the room. Smiling faces.

Leonard Lindquist, who had arrived that morning, joined me in an effort to draft the agreement. In the meantime, we had arranged that John Mackey, Pat Richter, Tom Keating, Jim Tyrer of the Kansas City Chiefs, and Merlin Olsen of the Rams would go to Washington for the breakfast meeting with Celler and the Antitrust Subcommittee. Even though the owners were well aware of the congressional breakfast, Alan Miller argued strenuously that it should be canceled because the owners would find out about the breakfast and would consider our attendance to be in bad faith since several issues had been resolved. Mackey ultimately agreed that the owners would seize upon the congressional breakfast as an excuse to break off negotiations. On the heels of a preliminary agreement, the players and the public might blame our continued efforts on Capitol Hill for a breakdown in negotiations with the owners. Lindquist and I argued against canceling, but we could understand Mackey's argument. At 9:00 P.M. we called Congressman Fraser to cancel—too late to reach Celler; no telling who might show, so Fraser would go and explain.

We finished drafting the agreement at midnight and went downstairs to eat. We ran into Kheel, who was dining with some other clients. He came to our table when his associate, Dick Messina, came in with their version of the agreement. After some haggling, we exchanged copies. Kheel and Messina left, and we anxiously read over their draft. To our pleasure, it was almost identical to ours!

Leonard and I toasted each other. Possibly, this truly represented a new attitude. The midnight draft was an honest effort to record our handshake agreement. Perhaps Mackey was right in canceling the breakfast with Congress.

"You Should Have Been a Better Lawyer"

Kheel was out of town the next day, so we were to meet NFL counsel Marshall Leahy at 10:00 A.M. to work out any minor differences in our drafts. When we arrived, Marshall said that there were some changes, that a new draft was being typed at the NFL office, and that he would call when it was ready. We returned to our meeting room and waited.

At noon, a messenger arrived with the "agreement." We read it quickly, and I exploded: "Goddammit, they have changed everything! Preseason pay is now a *maximum*, and the commissioner's powers are no longer negotiable!"

Alan, who had obviously been tipped off, started defending it. "Let's not panic—it isn't so bad. We should take it."

Mackey called the Executive Committee together. Miller spoke first. All morning, before we received the new draft, he had been totally preoccupied with multiplying preseason pay and per diem increases times the number of players in the NFL times four years. (Obviously, if you multiply by enough figures, the total sounds impressive.) He said to the committee, "This package is worth four million dollars. Are you going to blow this out of the water because of a few words!" He was shouting: *"This is a great package—don't blow it!* Take it! Then we can negotiate pensions!" (Four million dollars over four years is the equivalent of $700 per player. That sounds a little less impressive than $4 million.)

Mackey called on me. I said, "The issue is simple. They agreed with us yesterday, we shook hands, we canceled our breakfast meeting with Congress, and now they are going back on their word. If you let them get away with this, negotiations are over—go in and ask what they will give you on all issues and take it."

Alan was beside himself. He had lost his cool in front of the committee, and he had lost the argument. The committee unanimously rejected the "agreement."

On the previous day, Rozelle assured us that a majority of owners had accepted the interim agreement. He tried to explain the new version by blaming Art Modell, who, according to Rozelle, called the owners who were not on the committee and got a majority to reject the agreement. Only they know what really happened, but it's impossible for me to believe that an absent owner would care enough about recognition to kill a deal. What probably happened is that Rozelle killed it because his powers were going to be negotiated, and then blamed Modell.

The players were furious. It was now only four days from the opening of training camps. The committee moved into another, less expensive hotel. We told the owners that the players were fed up and many were on their way home. They would come back if the owners agreed to the original draft.

Alan Miller and I remained. Mackey and Bowman grabbed me before leaving and warned me to keep Alan within my sight. Marshall Leahy called, and I told him that the players had left but assured him that Miller and I had authority to bargain. Within minutes, Tex Schramm called Miller—then Pete Rozelle called, and suddenly, Alan Miller was bolting for the door. "Where are you going?" I asked.

"I've got to meet Rozelle" was the response as he was halfway down the hall.

Just then the phone rang. It was Mackey: "Where is Alan?" I told him that he had raced off to meet Rozelle. To say the least, Mackey was not happy, and he said he was on his way back.

Before Mackey, Bowman, Alexander, and Richter could return to the Plaza, Miller burst into the room with "great news." In order to get the players back to the bargaining table, Miller had "convinced" Rozelle to step aside as arbitrator of injury grievance—a grievance that arises when a player is cut by his team and the player believes that he is injured. The team claims he isn't injured, he just isn't good enough. After doctors examine the player, arguments are made to an arbitrator, who for years was Rozelle. But Rozelle didn't like the role because the clubs got mad as hell when they lost—after all, their employee, Rozelle, had ruled against their handling of a former player employee. Thus, we were to have an impartial arbitrator for injuries.

You can imagine how much "convincing" Miller did during this ten-minute meeting with Rozelle, which was clearly part of the setup to make Miller look good. But the players returned to the bargaining table, and Lindquist and I were once again expelled as the "no lawyer" rule went back into effect.

Back to the bargaining table, back to more drafts. Finally, on July 10, a tentative agreement was reached on preseason pay, recognition, and impartial arbitration of injury grievances. It was less than we had achieved before the switch, but it wasn't bad.

The agreement was typed at the NFL office. When it was presented for signature, I turned to John Mackey and said we should proofread the agreement, which had just arrived. Miller dissented: "No problem, let's sign." Before Mackey did, I asked Kheel and Schramm, "Are there any changes or problems with the recognition agreement?" None at all, they assured us. John and Tex signed. A step forward—now we would see if they were telling the truth about desiring negotiations on pension and insurance, once the preseason-pay and recognition questions were out of the way. Maybe, just maybe, good faith negotiations were about to begin.

Oh yes, there was a problem, as we learned *after* the signing. One page of the recognition agreement had been retyped and significantly altered, despite their assurances that our version had been left untouched. Furious, I brought this to Kheel's attention. In my naivete, I actually thought he would agree to change it back to the way we had drafted it—the way we had agreed to it.

He looked at me and said, "You should have been a better lawyer. You should proofread agreements before your clients sign."

I was beginning to understand the ethics of the NFL.

The Lockout

The owners had held out the carrot of a pension offer for several months: Withdraw your certifications petition, and we will tell you our offer. The first NFLPA pension proposal had been made in May. The owners grabbed the figures, costed it out, showed how much a twenty-year veteran would get at age sixty-five (even as the average career in the NFL was 4.6 years, well short of 20), including Social Security benefits, and started spreading the word that the NFLPA was seeking an annual pension of $50,000 to $100,000. The press jumped on those numbers and made us look stupid or greedy. Players around the country were upset. Some bought the owners' line that the NFLPA "advisers" were out of touch with the realities of NFL economics.

Finally, on July 10, all of the so-called obstacles had been removed, and the players looked forward to the offer. The next day, the NFLPA was asked to give its pension proposal first, and then the owners would tell the committee their offer. By then we had substantially reduced the proposal, and our actuary had come up with a novel idea: If, for some unforeseen reason, revenues would dip during the next four years, we would agree to reduce the pension contribution one dollar for every three dollars lost. After the presentation was made, the owners asked for time to consider the proposal. Their ridiculously low proposal, an intentional insult, came on July 12. There were a number of caucuses that interrupted negotiations, and, after each one, Tex Schramm would nervously pace back and forth while explaining why the league couldn't afford any more money.

While some owners pretended to be negotiating on July 12, others supposedly held a secret meeting in Chicago. (My guess is that they didn't meet; at best, they held a conference call). Following the "meeting," Lamar Hunt, president of the AFC, and George Halas, president of the NFC, announced a lockout. They said an impasse had been reached because of our unreasonable demands and all training camps would be closed to veterans; however, camps would be open to rookies. Notice of their decision came by messenger at midnight via a letter from Schramm informing Mackey of the decision.

The committee was surprised and angered. It was extremely bad faith on the owners' part. Miller's prediction was falling apart. Being "reasonable men" wasn't enough.

Soon we learned that the club's definition of a "rookie" was any veteran who had been on a taxi squad in addition to the legitimate first-year men.

We had no way to check who was in camp. As players started reporting to camp, pressure mounted on the "striking" veterans, who were, in fact, locked out. After all, the rookies were there to take the veterans' jobs. The press played up the performance of the new men, and coaches publicly said, "If I were so-and-so, I'd sure want to be in camp because this rookie we got is looking good." The papers played management's game.

Even though the veterans were locked out, we had players calling us daily asking when the "strike" would end. They wanted to go in to secure their jobs. To make matters worse, the press never made clear to the public whether it was a strike or a lockout. Most writers assumed it was a strike and blamed us. We were "unreasonable" to "strike" for a $50,000 a year pension.

This was a clever move by the owners. They had taken and held the initiative throughout the negotiating period in 1970. They then refused to recognize the Players Association until concessions were made; refused to make a comprehensive offer until preseason pay was settled; refused to bargain; and then locked out some of our people. Better to pit players against players than to have them united against the owners. All the pressure was on us, and with Miller's help, the owners even selected the key bargaining issue: pension. Not the Standard Player Contract, reserve system, minimum salary, or preseason pay, all of which would be of immediate benefit to the players newly trying to organize, but a pension that players would look to forty years down the road. Twenty-four-year-old players are not focused on a pension at age sixty-five.

Within two days of the announced lockout and the owners' refusal to meet and negotiate, we asked the Federal Mediation and Conciliation Service (FMCS) to enter the dispute. Rozelle was furious. After all, wasn't Pete the neutral mediator? That's the way he described his role to the press. He argued with us that the owners (not Rozelle himself, of course) would be extremely upset by more "government interference" in football: "Isn't the NLRB enough?" He pleaded that we give him a chance to get the owners back to the table before calling in the FMCS. We agreed to a two-day delay. Whether he tried or not I don't know, but the owners did not come back to the table, so we moved our "strike headquarters" to Washington in order to be available for the federal mediators.

The NFLPA Executive Committee was delighted to be out of New York. After all, the negotiators were active players who had to be ready for the season or they might get cut. The players would work out at Georgetown University in DC—no more running up and down the stairwell at the City Squire Hotel to get in shape for the season. Pressure on the negotiators increased as opening day neared.

FMCS called for a 6:00 P.M. session at the Department of Labor. Ten minutes before we left the hotel, a news bulletin appeared on television, quoting F. Curtis Counts, the FMCS director, saying in effect that "both sides had failed to appear" so the session had been canceled. We were angry! We appeared at 6:00 P.M. anyway and demanded retraction from FMCS. After a rather stormy session, the mediators retracted the statement and told the truth: It was the owners who had failed to show. Then they reset the first session for Baltimore because the owners wanted no part of "political" Washington. After some bantering back and forth, the next day the owners refused to go to Baltimore because "it's too close to Washington" but finally agreed to go to Philadelphia.

After all the haggling, the owners showed up in Philadelphia only to announce at the first session, "We will not tolerate any recommendations by the mediators, either privately or before the group."

That statement effectively killed any chance of making progress. The essence of bargaining is compromise. When parties refuse to bargain, they refuse to compromise. If mediators cannot explore compromise, they cannot do their job. Rozelle made sure the mediators would get no credit. Two days later, the owners walked out, claiming, "Mediation had failed." The fact is Rozelle wouldn't let it succeed. There would be no further negotiations until the "players become more reasonable." The kept press believed the owners. As a matter of policy, the mediators could not comment. They would not return.

The NFL's behavior had been totally unreasonable and unethical—but effective. They changed pages in agreements, lied to get us to cancel a congressional breakfast meeting, refused to bargain, insulted the mediator, and lied about our bargaining position, our leadership, and our advisers. They even started a rumor that we were using "Black Panther tactics" at the bargaining table. But success at the bargaining table doesn't go to the most honest—it goes to the most powerful.

We were almost out of money. There was no staff, no way to communicate effectively with our members, and no way to get fair treatment from the sports press. The NFL controlled the message.

After the owners walked out of the FMCS sessions in Philadelphia, Mackey agreed with Rozelle to call for a meeting of "superstars" in Chicago. Not much discussion went into the decision to hold the meeting, but hold it we did. Four or five star players from each team flew in, almost all of whom management had selected. The idea was to test our strength. In retrospect, the starters would be the ones making good salaries, and they would be less concerned about insurance, disability, and pension benefits.

The $15,000-a-year player would fight for fringe benefits, but not the stars. The wrong group was there.

Over a hundred players arrived, including Bart Starr, Billy Ray Smith, John Unitas, Daryle Lamonica, Tim Tyrer, Merlin Olsen, and Ben Davidson. The meeting "for players only" lasted for four hours. Everyone had a chance to speak. At 1:00 A.M., the vote was taken. Surprisingly, they overwhelmingly authorized a strike—a triumph for Mackey. He had put their feet to the fire, and they had responded. Management had planned on players capitulating, but players heard about the owners' dirty tricks, and even the pro-management players became angry.

Bart Starr played a key role. He was so angered about Rozelle's attempt to use Vince Lombardi against the union that Starr urged a strike to benefit "the lineman, the 'little guys' who made it possible for me to make a living." Rozelle had told Mackey the previous week in Philadelphia that if the seriously ill Lombardi died while the strike was on, "Everyone will blame you, John, for the coach's death." He said, "The owners will call off the season if he dies, so I advise you to take the owners' last offer."

Rozelle said this to Mackey when the mediators were trying to get the parties to negotiate in Philadelphia. The tactic didn't work (and for the record, when Vince Lombardi died a little more than a month later, in September 1970, the NFL office remained open for business and the season was not canceled).

Two-Day Strike

We announced the strike the next morning, but league management had sent telegrams to all veterans the previous day announcing that the lockout was ending. The telegram said that since no strike was called, players had a *legal obligation* under their Standard Player Contract to report at 10:00 A.M. Saturday. The All-Star Game was scheduled for 8:00 P.M. the following Friday. Coach Paul Brown told his Bengals rookies to avoid the doorways: "The vets will be streaming in here and anyone in the doorway could get hurt." It didn't happen that way, but Paul Brown understood our weaknesses. The vets wanted to play.

After announcing the strike at a hastily called press conference, we looked forward to the headlines. This was our first bold move, and we anxiously awaited the media's treatment of the announcement. This was the first real strike by NFL players. As we grabbed the papers, the headlines read: "NFL Players to Strike: Cowboys to Go In."

I couldn't believe it! Before we could even get a response, Dallas quarterback Craig Morton announced that the Cowboys players would not strike—they would defy the association. Where were such statements during the owners' lockout? Why didn't Morton speak out then? Anyway, goddammit, hadn't the Cowboys players at the Chicago meeting voted for a strike? What effect would the strike have? No one knew. Because the press played up the Cowboys statement, the public's focus would be on union weakness, not strength. We would concern ourselves about the Cowboys rather than the Packers, who promised to stay out until a decent package was offered, even if the strike went into the regular season.

By late afternoon on the first day of the strike, everyone was nervous. Geography divided us. Strike headquarters remained in Washington under the guidance of Len Hauss, John Wilbur, Bill Curry, and several R******s players. The negotiating committee was isolated in Chicago. Part of our day had been spent reassuring Washington about the previous night's events. Communications were breaking down because of management's false rumors. We spent more time reassuring our own people than planning strategy.

On Friday morning, we were sitting around a large room discussing alternative pension proposals when the phone rang. I happened to be closest to the phone, so I answered. It was none other than Jack Kemp calling for his old friend Alan Miller. I gave Miller the phone; he carried on a short and seemingly innocuous conversation and quickly hung up. He bolted for the door, and I headed out after him.

"What did Kemp want?" I asked.

"He wants me to call him back; he has some developments he wants to discuss privately. I'll tell you later."

I went to my room, suspicions mounting. Before long, Kermit Alexander and John Mackey were at my door. They said Rozelle had called Mackey and suggested that he and Miller come to New York City to discuss settlement. I told them of the Kemp-Miller phone call and of Miller's comments. We concluded that Kemp had set up the meeting. I recommended against the trip because John would be up against Rozelle, Schramm, *and* Miller: "Let's face it, John, Alan is with them. He wants a settlement at any price. He is in Kemp's corner."

Mackey said he agreed but felt he should grasp at the straw because players were getting anxious. He promised to be careful and to stay in touch. Mackey and Miller left for the airport with reservations made in false names at Rozelle's suggestion. Rozelle's limo would meet them at La Guardia and take them to Rozelle's apartment on Sutton Place. Rozelle understood psychology. False names, limousines, and the crisis atmosphere would place additional importance on his role in orchestrating it all and put more pressure on Mackey to settle. The trip would also rob us of Mackey's leadership at a critical point. The committee would be divided and isolated.

Mackey and Miller were welcomed into Rozelle's home to watch the college All-Star Game with Rozelle, Schramm, and Rankin Smith. During the game, Rozelle would call the broadcast booth to ask ABC to do something or to stop referring to the All-Stars' colleges and start referring to their new teams in the NFL. Here is where the power of Rozelle was best exemplified—his control of the media: If you don't like the coverage, call and change it. The group watched the game, talked about the need for a settlement, and then started in on Mackey. They told him he was alone in the NFL, that none of the players really understood the issues or even cared about them. He was told repeatedly that many reps had been calling their owners and informing them of their desire to go to camp.

Rozelle told Mackey that his only hope was in the room. His only friends were Schramm, Rankin, and Rozelle. They didn't want him to be embarrassed. They had come to respect him for his toughness and honesty. But they warned that he would be remembered as the man "who destroyed football" unless they settled, and settled now. Miller remained silent. Mackey was surrounded.

Miller and Mackey slept at Rozelle's apartment that night but moved to the City Squire Hotel the next morning. They were to talk again on Saturday, and Rozelle promised to force an offer out of the owners that day. John said he would bring the committee in from Chicago if a worthwhile offer were put on the table. But Saturday was not the day. While this was happening, the lockout had ended, and the coaches and general managers were pressuring veterans to report. Rozelle's timing was perfect. Very few veterans went to camp, but Rozelle would tell John they were "on the way in." We had no way to check because we lacked staff and phone numbers.

By Sunday afternoon, pressure mounted. Would there be a new offer? Would players break ranks and go to camp? Mike Curtis, Mackey's Colts teammate, had announced very early that he couldn't wait to "run through the picket line." Others would sneak across.

Summoned to New York

Most of the players working with me at the NFLPA were training outside when I received a call from Miller late Sunday afternoon: "John wants you all on the next thing flying."

"Is it a good offer?" I asked.

Alan responded that we would get the offer when we arrived. Mal Kennedy, NFLPA business manager, made reservations for 7:00 P.M. I started packing. Players gathered their belongings. Tom Keating was across town seeing his parents, but someone reached him; he would meet us at the airport. The scene was somewhat comic.

Kennedy had been selling homemade ties on behalf of a former player's wife, and he eventually showed up with at least ten ties draped around his neck and the rest in an overflowing box. We all laughed as he forced his way into the car. We were in good humor. Everyone anticipated a good offer. Several said, "John wouldn't have called if it was lousy." We started guessing the amount of the pension offer. They had offered $19 million for four years in July before the lockout. Would it be $21 million or $23 million now? Most were betting on $21 million.

We barely made the plane. On the flight, I reworked some draft language on our pension proposal and talked about it with Pat Richter. When we arrived after 10:00 P.M., two of Rozelle's chauffeurs met us at the baggage area. One started to tell us who could go in which car when Ken Bowman told him that *we* would decide, not Rozelle's chauffeur. The NFL had planned it so precisely that Rozelle had even decided who should ride in each car!

We were driven to the Sheraton La Guardia, where Miller and Mackey waited in a cramped little room. Why didn't the drivers take us all to the City Squire only twenty minutes away? Presumably to keep as much distance as possible between Rozelle, the owners, and us. There was no reason to meet at the airport, but there we were. Mackey greeted everyone, and then Miller read the offer, which, he informed us, *must* be accepted by 1:00 A.M. or it would be withdrawn, the first preseason game canceled, and all economic offers reduced. That gave us exactly two hours to consider it and negotiate. No time to call reps. This was it: "Take it or leave it."

Ken Bowman and Nick Buoniconti exploded. The offer was almost to the penny the amount offered July 13: $19 million for four years for pension, and the minimum wage would stay at $12,000. What had the strike accomplished? Not one damned thing! Ken Bowman demanded to know why John had asked us to come to New York for this nonsense!

Mackey reported that several reps had called him saying their players were ready to break the strike. He then posed a question to the committee for a vote: "Will your players accept this package?" The answer had to be "Yes, if we tell our players this is all we can get." The better question might have been "Will your players stay out on strike for something better than this?" But that question was not asked, and the decision was to accept. Mackey knew the time was right for a deal. Building the union would come later.

Mackey asked for my comment. I said, "Look, this is the time to negotiate. We have waited all summer for this opportunity, so let's make them negotiate. Even if both sides know the players will accept it, they don't know whether or not *we* will reject it. If we say no, we can still threaten the first preseason game. Tell them we reject the offer but that we want to negotiate now. Then we can try to win six or seven more things before accepting."

Everyone rallied to the suggestion except Miller, who was incredibly nervous. He kept saying, "We have to let them know by one o'clock or they will cancel the game!" Mackey ordered Miller to calm down and to call Rozelle in our presence, reject the offer, and demand negotiations. Miller called, Rozelle agreed to meet, and we headed for 410 Park Avenue at 1:00 A.M. to meet the owners. The bluff was working.

The owners' desire to beat us was obvious. They wanted to punish their "children" for getting out of line. The reason for keeping the pension contribution the same was to let us know that the great NFL would not be intimidated, nor would it tolerate collective action. Rozelle had successfully taken on the Congress, the AFL, and the press. He would not be defeated by the players' union.

We arrived at 410 Park Avenue at 1:30 A.M. This was my first visit to the "Taj Mahal," as it was called by some owners. The temperature was near 90 degrees. The buildings were steaming. We went to the twelfth floor, only to find that the air-conditioning in the building had been off since 5:00 P.M. We were put into a little windowless conference room and told that the owners were upstairs. (Whether they were or not we will never know.) Kheel greeted us as we entered: "Welcome to New York" was his sarcastic reminder that we had steadfastly refused to return to New York in July because of the expense and lack of workout facilities. Kheel was rubbing it in and making sure we understood that he was running the show.

We sparred for two or three hours on the length of the contract. We demanded a two-year deal. They insisted on four. They won.

We insisted on an agreement on a minimum squad size. We lost.

We insisted on protection against theater TV. They refused.

We won two things in that all-night session: A dental benefit and earlier payments in the pension fund. (Later, they would refuse the early payments for "tax purposes" on the basis of an absurd memo from lawyers at Covington and Burling.)

As always, there were some humorous moments: Rozelle always entered and left with the owners. At one point, Mackey said, "Hey, Pete, if you are the neutral, how come you never meet with us?" Later, Mackey was engaged in discussion and forgot his earlier chiding of Rozelle, who was now in our room. When he looked up and saw Rozelle, he said, "Hey, Pete, we want to get some work done. Could you get the hell out of here?" Not only did he expel Pete, but Mackey also ordered Tom Vance, our PR man, to sit outside the door to make sure Pete was not listening.

Hours passed. Heat increased. Everyone got sleepy. Lindquist and Tom Keating were stretched out on the floor. Finally, at 7:30 A.M., the owners came in with their response to the few remaining items on our list. They accepted our three minor points, and "agreement" was reached.

Kheel expected handshakes and smiles, but there were few. He knew we had been beaten. There was agreement, but it was on their terms. We had gained very little; no one was in the mood for smiles and handshakes.

That night, Mackey, Richter, Alexander, Bowman, and I agreed that we would use the four years to build an organization. We vowed to get back at them for their humiliating treatment by building a union with the strength to force them to bargain. They beat us in 1970, but we knew this was the beginning, not the end. We had learned from the experience, and we would not soon forget. One of us said, "It's the players as losers; that is how they see it, and we have to change it." We knew they would try their damnedest to get rid of all of us, as they had with Shulman and the Teamsters. But we vowed to make it a fight.

Before we could leave, Rozelle's PR machine was at work. I heard one of them calling in the press release to the wire services, saying, "The commissioner moved from group to group as a mediator . . . agreement coming after an all-night session." Nonsense! Then I fully understood their behavior. The *commissioner*, not the FMCS, would "mediate" the dispute! The *New York Post* declared, "Rozelle Ends Strike."

For years, sycophantic writers would talk about Rozelle:

"Rozelle locked them in a room until they agreed."

"The iron commissioner found a solution."

"Rozelle the mediator, the good, the humble."

He mediated nothing. He watched while the owners stuck it to us and humiliated the union. He would never again be involved in negotiations.

But the strike that had begun at 10:00 A.M., August 1, was over at 9:00 A.M., August 3, ending with one or two people shaking hands forty-seven hours later. Pete and Ted had earned their bread. Cost of the new contract to the owners? About $1,000 per player. The NFL lawyers received more than the players.

Sign It or Else

We returned to the City Squire and said goodbye to the committee. It was a strange feeling—after this intimate, highly charged period of time together, it was suddenly over. Mackey left first and headed for camp; practice was scheduled for that night. Ernie Wright, Tom Keating, and Kermit Alexander left for California, Nick Buoniconti for Miami, Pat Richter for Washington, and Ken Bowman for Green Bay. Suddenly, only the lawyers were left. What was the mandate? What had really been agreed to?

The next day we started to draft an agreement. Three days later we met with Kheel and the other lawyers and exchanged drafts. We agreed to meet in Minneapolis in late August to continue working on the drafts. Soon we would learn that the owners would try to win by drafting what they had forgotten about in bargaining. Perhaps they were so confident of Alan Miller's ability to control the drafting that they weren't worried. They did not anticipate that I would be at every drafting session and that I would fight long and hard to avoid more concessions. After all, we hadn't won anything of substance in negotiations. I would be damned if we would lose issues in drafting.

One meeting led to another, each more acrimonious than the previous. When it dawned on the owners that we weren't going to be beaten into submission, they became increasingly difficult to deal with.

The best example was their insistence on a so-called zipper clause, which was their demand that we waive our right to bargain on everything until 1974. Imagine! Every player must sign the owner-drafted Standard Player Contract. The Constitution and Bylaws are incorporated into those contracts, and, therefore, the owners, without any bargaining with the union, could amend either document by majority vote. If we gave up our right to negotiate on all issues for four years, the owners could do anything they desired to the players without opposition from us by simply amending all player contracts. To make matters worse, if we charged that a change violated the agreement, guess who would decide? That's right: Pete Rozelle! To give up our right to bargain for four years under those circumstances would be suicidal.

After months of bickering and inconclusive meetings, we agreed to meet at the Summit Hotel in New York City for a final session on February 27, 1971, to resolve the differences. Alan Miller had been fired the month before in San Diego, so Leonard Lindquist and I headed for New York.

I met with Rozelle before the Summit Hotel meeting to discuss a number of issues, but primarily to urge him to exert some leadership with the owners. I suggested that nothing would be resolved unless he tried to convince owners to compromise. Rozelle, still smarting from Miller's dismissal by the NFLPA, couldn't contain his temper. Instead of offering help in concluding the agreement, he said, "The owners will never respect the players as long as they have their feet on the table."

I could not figure out what he was talking about and asked what he meant. (I had visions of Nikita Khrushchev banging his shoe at the UN!)

He said, "When the owners come into bargaining sessions and Tom Keating has his feet on the table, we can't have respect for you."

I laughed as I then recalled the 3:00 A.M. sessions in near hundred-degree heat on August 3. I couldn't even remember whether Keating's feet had been on the table, but could they really care about that? But this was the mentality of Rozelle and Schramm.

By late afternoon on February 28, we had achieved complete agreement on all but one issue: postseason pay for players cut by the team prior to the playoffs. Rozelle was adamant on the issue because he did not want Lance Rentzel to get a Super Bowl check. We stood firm, and Rentzel received his check. They had actually put forth an effort to compromise, leading to another (reluctant) handshake. We had finally settled, and this time there were a few concessions from the owners.

Mackey joined Leonard Lindquist and me for a drink to celebrate. Finally! The battle was over. Now we could get on with plans to move the offices, build a union, and hire staff.

The agreement was now in writing. Marshall Leahy, for the NFL, and I, for the union, placed our initials on every page of the agreement so there could be no argument. On March 5, the league insisted on a joint press release by Mackey and Schramm stating that final agreement had been reached. The release went out.

I returned to Minneapolis and had the agreement typed and signed by Mackey. We sent it to Schramm for signature and waited to receive the executed copy.

Attorneys for management assured me that there would be no problem, but weeks passed without a return. The owners were to meet in Bal Harbour, Florida, toward the end of March. Prior to the meeting, Rozelle and Tex Schramm went on a cruise on Pete's yacht, the *Triple Eagle*, with the agreement.

On March 30, I received the signed agreement, but it was not the one Mackey had signed. Kheel's cover letter suggested that John sign it and send a copy back to them. There was no indication of changes, but I remembered Kheel's statement the summer before: "You should have been a better lawyer."

Needless to say, I proofread the agreement. I was shocked! They had changed over fifteen pages to suit their position! This, after months of effort, the Summit Hotel meeting, the initialing of pages, and the joint press release! Subsequently, I learned that the "new agreement" was typed at "neutral" Rozelle's office. The "mediator" was tipping his hand: "Mackey will sign the revised agreement, the payment will go through, but if not, I have been instructed to stop payment on the check."

I was furious! There was no need to consult Mackey. I told Rozelle to do whatever he wanted to do with the check; in fact, I gave him a suggestion, and then said, "We will not submit to blackmail!" I hung up, immediately fired off a telegram to the Executive Committee, and prepared to file charges against the owners for refusal to execute the agreement.

Kheel called back late at night and said, "Your arguments were so persuasive we decided to make the contribution." We filed charges on April 2 anyway, and as the NLRB was about to issue a complaint, the owners finally signed the original agreement on June 17, 1971, following yet another all-night session.

Throughout the 1970 negotiations, the owners set the stage for the longest struggle in professional sports history by trying to outmaneuver the union. In 1974, they would try to break the union. Through it all, the NFL owners and Rozelle wanted to deliver a body blow to the union and its leaders. Rozelle had a teeter-totter mentality when it came to the union. If the union's status rose, his status went down and vice versa. Any concession was an admission of defeat.

Next time it would be different, or so we thought in June 1971. We would have three years to build, three years to prepare. We would take them on. Next time no handshakes, no naive belief in the goodness of man.

4

No Freedom, No Football—1974

A s I headed for the Illinois Tollway on my way to Burlington, Wisconsin, to visit my parents, I had time to think about what had gone wrong. It was August 28, 1974, a couple of weeks before the start of the regular season. Player reps had voted to play the season without a collective bargaining agreement after rejecting the owners' last offer. The owners beat us just as they had in 1970, or at least that's how the media and most objective observers viewed it. For psychological reasons, I felt then that it was important to stress internally that we may have lost another battle but we were not beaten. For now, it was a standoff. The pressure on our people had been tremendous. The power of the NFL was awesome. This was not the best time to evaluate our performance.

Two weeks later, Pettis Norman, a twelve-year veteran tight end with Dallas and San Diego, would convince me that the only way to approach the coming season was to admit defeat because "players understand defeat but not a tie."

For most of us, "defeat" is a very tough pill to swallow, so I put it out of my mind and focused on what had gone wrong and what had gone right.

The strike of 1974 had not worked, but it had cost the owners millions of dollars and had exposed the reserve system to the public. For the first time in fifty-four years, a labor dispute had hit owners where it hurt—in their pocketbooks. In 1970, they saved money by locking out the veterans. This time, hundreds of thousands of fans refused to attend preseason games played by scabs. I knew that casualties would start to mount, as the NFL machine would punish those who had led the strike and cost the owners money.

The totalitarian society would not tolerate costly dissent. Even players who had not been leaders, those who had been on the picket lines at all would not be forgotten by owners. Film had been taken of all the picket lines, and the names of participants were on file. The "No Freedom, No Football" T-shirts with the clenched fists, the bumper stickers, the picket signs had been important in holding the strike together, but they also symbolized the cutting of the umbilical cord between players and owners. The owners would never forgive us, and they would now go about punishing their "boys" who had gotten out of line.

As I headed for Wisconsin, I had to ask the tough question of whether the union could survive without an agreement because it was clear that management would move to disrupt our leadership and make life difficult in every way possible. We were dealing with people who would go for the jugular. The totalitarian minds would spare no effort to return to their "normalcy." It had cost them money, but with the union in a weak posture, maybe they could finally break us.

Priorities Developed

I repeatedly reviewed the three years leading to the 1974 negotiations. From June 17, 1971, when we signed the second collective bargaining settlement in NFL history, until January 1974, Rozelle tried to forget that there was a union, a Mackey, a Garvey, and a collective bargaining agreement. There was no cooperation whatsoever.

In order to shield Rozelle from our questions, arguments, objections, and demands, the owners had established an office for their collective bargaining arm, the Management Council. The council was no different from the league, but in order to confuse the press and the NLRB, they maintained that there was a big difference between the two. The same twenty-six clubs (at the time) sitting in the same room and voting as a league at 10:00 A.M. also voted as the Management Council at 11:00 A.M. What conceivable difference could there be between the two? But with the Management Council on the scene, they could place Rozelle "in the middle"—between the Management Council and the NFLPA, and Rozelle would at least pretend that he was neutral. The Management Council would give him an excuse to dodge tough issues.

They created this sham organization and opened an office in 1971 on Madison Avenue. John Thompson, who worked for Rozelle, was named executive director of the Management Council. Thompson's job was to hold me off, keep track of our activities, frustrate the union at every turn, and coordinate the efforts to break the union in 1974. Discrediting our leadership was a top priority. He was given no authority to work out problems with the union and probably wouldn't have known what to do with it if he had the authority.

Thompson's background qualified him to head the Management Council only as much as Rozelle's qualified him to head the NFL. Thompson, too, had been a PR man, only he worked for the Vikings, not the Rams. He proudly wore the championship ring of the Vikings, won by Joe Kapp and the other Vikings players in the 1969 season. The ring gave Thompson his identity, his link to the players. After handling PR for the Vikings, he became assistant general manager under Jim Finks and was later hired by Rozelle to work at the NFL office in a nonexistent job as assistant to George Halas, the president of the National Football Conference (NFC). Halas was almost never at the NFL office and clearly had no league-wide responsibility, so one can imagine the depth of Thompson's job. During the 1970 negotiations, Thompson literally served as Rozelle's messenger, even serving coffee during the bargaining session.

In early January 1972, Mackey invited Thompson to speak at the Board of Representatives meeting in Key Biscayne in return for an invitation for me to speak at an upcoming owners' meeting in New York. It was clear that Thompson had no idea what his job was about. Other than one-on-one contract negotiations or social situations, I doubt if Thompson had ever talked to players before, and certainly not to leaders in a group. He was scared. It's one thing to talk to a sportswriter and explain that your job is to engage in collective bargaining, but it's another thing to talk to people who know what's going on and try to answer questions about your role for over an hour.

When Thompson was finished, Andy Russell of the Steelers, the most conservative rep on the board, asked, "Why should Ed waste his time talking to you when you don't even know what your job is?"

Thompson responded, "You're right, Andy. I'm going to go back to the owners and clarify my job description."

Everyone laughed, and the meeting ended.

But Thompson had done what he was supposed to do. He stalled and moaned and complained and tried to keep us off Rozelle's back. For three years, every question asked of Rozelle was channeled to Thompson or his newly hired Cleveland attorney, Sargent Karch. If we asked a question of the league, Rozelle would refer it to Thompson. If, on the other hand, the question was too hot for the Management Council, they would ship it back to the league, and the league would ship it back to the Management Council, and the whole thing would get lost somewhere in between. The result was that we would not get an answer. Trying to get PR types to respond on the record to difficult questions is, to quote political icon Al Smith, like "trying to nail a custard to the wall."

Perhaps Thompson never had a chance to accomplish anything since his role was designed to be totally negative. Rozelle may, in fact, have had a tough fight the night of August 3, 1970, when the owners "accepted" the collective bargaining agreement by a 14–12 vote. Rozelle later said that the vote was 13–13 but he intervened and convinced one person to change his vote. If that was the case, then it would seem that those who were holding out against the contract believed that if nothing was settled, the union would collapse. It would then take players several years to rebuild the union, during which time owners would have free rein to do what they wanted or to start a company union. Those urging acceptance undoubtedly argued that total destruction of the union would give the league a bad reputation and might actually invite outside interference from the Teamsters or Congress. Few doubted that in 1970 the owners had the power to break us.

According to Ralph Wilson, Buffalo Bills owner, a decision was made following the 1970 contract that only those who voted *against* the settlement in 1970 could be on the Management Council negotiating committee in 1974. I believe they had decided in 1970 that next time they would get rid of the union's leadership or bust the union completely. If Alan Miller would take over, that would be acceptable to the owners, but if not, the owners would break the union. Thompson's role, therefore, was quite simple: Do everything possible to make union leadership look bad and make certain that the union could not take credit for anything. He would set us up for the kill.

During this time span, the league wanted desperately to belittle the union. Dealing openly with the union or reaching agreement with leadership would give special credit to me, Mackey, or Alexander. It would confer importance, which is exactly what the league opposed. Rozelle wanted to avoid questions about the union at his annual press conference, in part because he was afraid that by referring to us he would make us newsworthy and in part because we were raising all the tough questions. He wanted to create the impression that we were simply like gnats—an annoyance but certainly not a threat or even an effective voice. He was telling the press to follow his lead.

From Rozelle's perspective, if he never agreed, never gave the desired information, never compromised, and always forced the union to turn to the courts, Congress, or the NLRB, he accomplished several things.

First, he made the union appear to be a quarrelsome outfit out to cause trouble at every turn. If the union were busted it was their own fault.

Second, the union leadership's competence was undermined because it would have to keep explaining to the membership why it could not accomplish anything.

Third, he gave enough material to favored sportswriters to paint the union as unreasonable militants out to destroy the league.

Fourth, at his press conferences, if forced to comment on the union, he could accuse the union, and particularly me, of always running to Congress or the NLRB for publicity purposes. This became one of Rozelle's favorite attacks. If we accused the league of illegal activity at the NLRB, that was "running to the NLRB." If we sued to stop antitrust violations, we were "running to court." He tried to make it appear downright un-American to pursue our legal rights and the only recourse that got us results.

Apparently, only cowards exercised their power to seek redress of grievances! The impression given to the public and the players was of a feisty, cantankerous, publicity-seeking Garvey who preferred confrontation to compromise, publicity to progress.

Finally, their strategy made intelligent bargaining impossible. If they refused to provide any information or starting points prior to bargaining, the owners could look at the proposals from the union and argue that our collective demands were "outrageous" because salaries increased by $10,000 over the previous two years. Their negotiators could say that their injury data proved that synthetic turf is "as safe as grass," which we knew was untrue, but we could not prove it because we could not see the injury data.

A very important side effect of forcing the union to use the courts and the NLRB was to force the union to spend its resources on legal fees, transportation, and associated expenses, which all required considerable time. Players are young and have a short career. To tell a player that the NLRB would decide in three or four years was frustrating as hell for athletes who were used to quick decisions.

Thompson successfully denied us the information we sought from him and carried out Rozelle's policy of making cooperation impossible. As we got ready for bargaining in 1974, we knew that we could expect no cooperation whatsoever from him, so we started preparing early in May 1973 even though, predictably, the NFL refused to give us any information.

We knew we were in for a tough battle, but when we tried to assess our strengths, we were haunted with questions from 1970, when owners had seized the initiative by locking out the players. When they lifted the lockout, the pressure was on the union. Would the strike work? Were the players as eager to go to work as those who called daily? How long could we keep them out? Even our strongest members were unhappy about the probable answers. The result, according to Ken Bowman and others, was that we had allowed a few weak teams to control the union in 1970. This argument was sound. We were afraid of the domino effect if some players crossed the line. Later, the strong players argued that even if only five teams stayed out, the owners could not carry on the season; therefore, why should we worry about three, five, or even ten teams going back to work? All we needed was a few teams because the NFL was dependent on all teams working at the same time.

As we looked into our crystal ball for 1974, we would follow that philosophy. We felt that we could overcome our deficiencies exposed in 1970 by stressing that we were as "strong as our *strongest* link" and not our *weakest*, and by educating the players and involving them in the process of establishing priorities for bargaining. If players fully understood the priorities and participated in the process, we believed they would support the negotiating committee and be prepared to strike if necessary. If we called a strike, rather than waiting for a lockout, then we would control the flow of events by being in a position to end the strike and by discovering at the outset whether it would work. Pressure would then be on management rather than on the union. The element of surprise was in our control, not theirs.

Convention

In September 1970, John Mackey asked me to write a memorandum to him on the future development of the association. In it, I stressed that the NFLPA should have an annual convention bringing together 30–50 percent of the membership to discuss the future. We could become the most democratic and, in many ways, the most effective union in America. Few unions have the luxury of bringing a substantial percentage of the entire membership together at one time to discuss future policy, but because of our small number and relative affluence, I maintained that such a gathering should be possible. We realized that goal in June 1973 when the first NFLPA convention was held in Las Vegas. The primary purpose was to outline goals for collective bargaining and to involve the membership in that process. Approximately two hundred players attended and became intimately involved in the work of the union, forming the backbone of the union's efforts to achieve agreement in 1974.

The convention went well as the players slowly began to get involved. The emphasis was on the Rozelle Rule, Rozelle as arbitrator, the draft, and the unfairness of the Standard Player Contract. The theme "a contract is a contract" took hold as Oakland's Tom Keating best articulated the position, saying that we could achieve no greater benefit than to force owners to give players a real contract—a guaranteed contract, rather than a document that gives away a player's rights while providing little in return.

We departed Las Vegas with a good feeling. Bringing players together was a big deal at a time when the commissioner had a nonfraternization rule, saying players weren't supposed to shake hands after a game or have dinner with opponents the night before a game. The purpose was to stress the team, not the league or the union. But this had been our first convention, and there was a new sense of unity among the players as we approached the 1973 season.

I looked forward to the team meetings because I felt there would be a base of leadership to discuss issues with players and that even more players would become involved in the bargaining process. We were confident that this union would be significantly different from the one the owners had faced in 1970. In a real sense, this would be the first set of negotiations. No more nonsense about how the owners would "give us" millions extra in the pension fund if we were reasonable. This time the union would be ready. We had built a strike fund of over $200,000, held over fifty team meetings, held the Las Vegas convention, and established outstanding player leadership.

We would have more team meetings and a second convention in Chicago in March 1974 before presenting owners with our list of demands. If they refused to deal with us, doing so would cost them some money.

A blow we had not anticipated was the sudden resignation of John Mackey in July 1973. In part, we looked forward to the 1974 negotiations because Mackey, Alexander, Bowman, and Keating—the heart of the 1970 negotiating committee—would be back to look across the bargaining table at Schramm, Rozelle, and others. We would miss Pat Richter and the others, but four out of seven wasn't bad.

Few organizations have been blessed with the kind of leadership John Mackey provided. On that night in July, Mackey told me that he was finished with football. He was no longer going to live with assistant coaches screaming at him about what time to go to bed, which was the case more often before preseason games than regular-season games. People laughed at our objection to curfews because the popular image was of the professional athlete hanging out in bars. Mackey finally said to hell with it. The next morning, he woke up and explained to his teammates that he was leaving, and he did.

Mackey's impact on the union would never be forgotten. Immediately after the 1970 negotiations, league management told the press that Mackey "had lost a step" on the field, part of its systematic response to those involved in negotiations. He was benched and finally waived, the NFL's way of treating the greatest tight end who had ever played the game. John had asked, "Why?" too many times.

Bill Curry, as first vice president of the union, took John's place as president. Curry was a two-time Pro Bowl center who had played alongside Mackey for years with the Colts before being traded to the Houston Oilers and later the LA Rams. Even without Mackey, we flew into the negotiations with a strong team. Curry, Alexander, Bowman, and Keating had been intimately involved in 1970. Four newcomers would add more strength: Alan Page of the Vikings; Willie Brown of Oakland; Brig Owens of Washington; and Ed Podolak of Kansas City. We were ready.

One thing was clear: Everyone wanted freedom that could only be achieved by eliminating the Rozelle Rule and removing Rozelle as arbitrator of grievances. It was the strong belief of the players that we could no longer tolerate a reserve system in professional sports. We were going for all the marbles, and we knew that a strike might be necessary to help reach our goals.

The All-Star Game

The delegates to the convention made an important decision: To cancel the annual Chicago All-Star Game scheduled for late July between Miami and the college All-Stars if a strike was on. Doug Swift, an exceptionally strong leader for the Dolphins, warned convention delegates that his teammates wanted to play and probably would play no matter what the union decided, since players would receive between $3,000 and $7,000 each for that game.

At first, delegates leaned toward leaving the decision of whether to play or not up to the Dolphins, which, in effect, was no decision because we knew they would play. Ultimately, however, players such as Rosey Taylor carried the day. Taylor argued that this was a union decision, not a Dolphins decision. He noted that everyone, not just the Dolphins, would suffer if there were a strike, but if we were to allow the Dolphins to play, only the Dolphins would make money during the strike. This would be unfair. Merlin Olson argued that playing the game would make other players eager to play football; it would help to create the "football atmosphere" at a time when we could be trying to keep people out of practices and on strike. Others said it would signal management that we weren't serious.

By the time the vote was taken, nearly everyone had been convinced: Shut down the game if we were on strike! Everyone there knew that the burden would fall on the shoulders of the Dolphins' player representative, Doug Swift, and a few other Dolphins who had the guts to support the union leadership. In many ways, this was the first time the NFLPA started to act as a union of *all* players, rather than twenty-six locals.

In 1970 the Kansas City Chiefs had played the All-Stars against the wishes of the union. We had urged them to boycott the game, but we had said it ultimately was their decision, not the union's. Just short of fistfights in the Chiefs' last meeting, the players voted *not* to play the 1970 game. Later that night, certain players were lied to by management. They were told that a new vote had been taken and that the decision was to play the game and then join everyone else on strike. The game was played before the players could figure out that there had not been another vote. So in 1974 we had to face the fact that the Miami Dolphins were a weak union team and would want to do the same thing the Kansas City Chiefs had done in 1970. Go in, make the money, then strike. Management would be pushing them to play. But this time, the union's decision and its orders were clear: I had to shut down that game if at all possible.

On the last day of the convention, Roy Jefferson of Washington gave a stirring speech, urging all players to commit to one another that at the "next convention we will join together as free men. . . . Nothing," he said, "should stand in the way of achieving that goal." (It should be noted that Jefferson had been the Pittsburgh player representative in 1970, but following the strike, Steelers management said they didn't need "militant trade unionists on their team." He was traded to Baltimore and then to Washington.)

Winston Hill, the gigantic tackle for the New York Jets, stood briefly and said it all: "We are not doing this simply because we want our dignity; we are doing it because it is right for us to protect future players."

Before the session closed, I asked from the chair whether the convention was committed to the freedom issues. Specifically, I asked, "All those who believe the Rozelle Rule must be eliminated before there can be a settlement, raise your hands." Every hand went up.

Bill Curry then stepped forward and dramatically said, "This is the most important vote in the history of the Players Association. I want to make sure that everyone here understands. I interpret your vote as a mandate to achieve freedom and to reject any contract offer with a Rozelle Rule in it. Now, all those in favor, please stand." Everyone in the room stood up, and there was spontaneous applause. That applause rang in our ears as we headed into negotiations. It was a heavy mandate. We would meet again as free men.

———

On March 16, 1974, just ten days after the convention, the owners' negotiating committee came to the NFLPA office to begin collective bargaining. The process started that day and would not end for three years. Even the most cynical among us could not have predicted the intensity of the struggle ahead. We were foolishly confident of an early settlement, in part because this was the first year of operation for the World Football League (WFL), which we hoped would have a competitive effect in the labor market as the emergence of the AFL had years earlier, and also because we felt that we had strength for the first time. The fact that the owners were coming to our offices rather than arguing endlessly about where the sessions were to be held seemed a concession to recognize the union.

The first session was attended by Wellington Mara, New York Giants owner and chairman of the committee; Rankin Smith, Atlanta Falcons owner; Ralph Wilson, Buffalo Bills owner; Art Modell, Cleveland Browns owner; and Joe Robbie, Miami Dolphins owner, along with Ted Kheel, their trusted labor counsel for the past decade; Thompson; Karch; and Terry Bledsoe, management's PR man. From our side the entire committee was there: Bill Curry, Kermit Alexander, Tom Keating, Alan Page, Jim Brown, Ed Podolak, Brig Owens, Ken Bowman, and our attorneys Leonard Lindquist, Gene Keating, and Dick Berthelsen.

The session began as usual—friendly smiles and handshakes all around. Bill Curry made opening remarks about our hopes to achieve an early agreement and our desire to avoid discord if possible. Mara responded with some inane comments that essentially indicated their agreement with that sentiment. I then read the introduction to the demands, which one law professor from the University of Minnesota characterized, in a Minneapolis *Tribune* interview, as straight out of the 1930s. In part, it said:

> In terms of labor management relations, the players accuse you of taking freedom from the players with no justification beyond hollow phrases such as "competitive balance." We accuse you of ignoring the injustices occasioned by head coaches and general managers who fine indiscriminately and who threaten disciplinary action if players exercise their first amendment freedoms. You are guilty of indifference to societal changes, which have occurred since the early

'60s. You have perpetuated an unjust system of control over the athletes headed by those who have demonstrated disdain for the constitutional rights of the athletes. . . . It is time for change in the NFL. It is time to end the suffocating paternalism and the suppression of constitutional rights in the NFL. It is time for freedom.

To say that the owners were upset with the language and demands would be a profound understatement. We were demanding elimination of the entire reserve system. We were setting the record straight about our attitude toward them in their efforts to dominate the union and dehumanize players. We were declaring war. Our first four demands were to eliminate the Rozelle Rule; the option clause; the waiver system; and the commissioner from any role in grievances.

The owners announced that they were going to stop group insurance, which covered the families of players for any medical costs they might incur, and we responded that was hardly the way to commence collective bargaining. Kheel nearly shouted a non sequitur that they "should not subsidize a strike" and that players could get their own insurance. The vehemence of their position was clear: Punish the players for even thinking about freedom. This was the warden's mentality, the Gulag approach.

The session was brief, ending with solemn looks and an argument about whether to give the demands to the press. We had suggested the press be invited into the negotiations. Naturally, the owners had refused. Before leaving our offices, they agreed to come back in ten days to ask questions and to seek clarification from us.

The press begged us for the proposals after the session, but we told them that there had been an agreement that the proposals would not be released. We returned to the other end of the hall, sat back, and discussed the day's events. Before long, a local reporter called to inform me that Terry Bledsoe had just delivered our demands to the wire services. Soon, two other reporters called to say Bledsoe had also reached them.

This is how it would be. We had no right to be surprised by their perfidious conduct, but we were. (Had we forgotten 1970 already?) Later the owners denied releasing the demands to the press, but it became obvious who had done it. Then they said they only did it after we gave the "introduction" to the press.

From March 16 forward, we would never beat them to the punch in the press. We could have the most clear-cut press boycott, but Bledsoe would call the story to his office, and his office would send it to all the clubs, and the clubs would then release the information. When confronted, they simply said it was difficult to keep information out of the press when so many people were involved.

But at least we were underway.

Anarchy, Chaos, and Kheel

"Mr. Chairman, I am Mr. Kheel, Theodore W. Kheel. I have been the counsel to the Management Council in collective bargaining since 1968, and I think I can address myself to the question that Mr. Seiberling asked."

It was October 1975, and hearings chaired by Congressman Peter Rodino before the House Subcommittee on Monopolies and Commercial Law had nearly concluded when those words were almost shouted from the back of the room. In a bizarre ending to the hearings, Ted Kheel could no longer suppress his desire to have his presence noted for the record. Earlier that day Kermit Alexander, Ed Glennon, George Burman, and I had testified in favor of the Seiberling Bill, which would outlaw the Rozelle Rule. We were followed to the stand by Rozelle and attorney Ham Carothers. But Kheel would not be denied. He would, uninvited, stand and lecture Peter Rodino and the subcommittee on the value of collective bargaining, saying, "Congress and the courts have no business interfering with the bargaining relationship!"

Rodino slammed the gavel and adjourned the hearing.

Kheel was not to be heard that day, but he was the man we had dealt with for years, the man known unbelievably as "a friend of labor" throughout his career as a successful mediator and private practitioner. Kheel was executive secretary of the Institute of Collective Bargaining in New York City. The institute urged the use of collective bargaining to solve every type of societal problem from rent strikes to racial problems—but apparently not in football. As a member of the National Academy of Arbitrators, Kheel had a reputation for championing the cause of impartial arbitration to settle disputes. But in the NFL, he vigorously opposed "impartial" arbitration. While receiving awards from labor groups, he was the chief spokesman for the most backward labor management system in the United States, the NFL—a system that stood as an insult to the words "due process," a system that was the very antitheses of impartial arbitration. He became one of the architects of the play to bust the union.

Many labor people found it difficult, if not impossible, to understand how he could represent the NFL and its one-sided system. For many years people were misled to believe that Kheel was a mediator selected by players and owners. A broker, so to speak, and friend of the players in the best tradition of the commissioners.

Kheel had been hired by the NFL in 1963 at the same time the Rozelle Rule was unilaterally implemented by NFL owners. He said the NFL hired him solely to advise them on pension matters, a rather startling admission because in that year the NFL decided that any veteran playing out his option and signing with an AFL team would forfeit all of his vested pension credit! Hard to believe that a "friend of labor" would tolerate or recommend such a provision.

But Kheel defended the reserve system vigorously over the years. He even defended Rozelle as arbitrator in a debate with me in 1971 before a meeting of the National Academy of Arbitrators in Atlanta. Kheel talked of the need to preserve the "integrity of the game" and argued that the "commissioner form of self-government" is a wonderful example of "democracy with restraints"! It became increasingly apparent to me that Kheel had concluded that if he believed it and advocated it, then it must be the law and therefore it must be acceptable. The fact that Kheel would argue before his peers at the National Academy of Arbitrators against the union's right to a voice in selecting the arbitrators says a lot. Most of the arbitrators were appalled by his position.

Kheel vigorously denied that he was the architect of the NFL's strategy of union busting, refusal to recognize the union, character assassination of union leadership, and efforts to influence the NRLB to delay and frustrate the union at every turn. I assume he was right in that Rozelle was the quarterback, but Kheel was their chief spokesman and defender.

I suspected that Kheel believed with Nixonian certainty that he was above the law—he knew what was best for players as well as for management. No need to research the law; he would simply make pronouncements, and everyone within earshot was supposed to believe that what he said was true because he said it was true. He seemed to forget that other people might have contrary views with merit and might actually back them up. But for Kheel, the fact that players were demanding freedom in 1974 was tough to handle. The fact that he was now clearly management's spokesman *against* freedom and not a mediator brought additional pressure on him because he must now publicly state his position for the record.

To his credit, Kheel did not shy from the task. He rushed into print at the first opportunity to state in the *New York Times* that if the freedom issues were granted it would mean "chaos" within the NFL. He would compare the reserve system to stoplights and speed limits on the freeways of

America and maintained that granting the NFLPA proposals and bargaining would bring about "anarchy."

Red Smith wrote a particularly memorable column after Kheel's charges of anarchy, saying that when Kheel claimed that we were demanding the elimination of all restraints on employees, he was ignoring the considerable restraints that every employer has on employees to subject them to discipline, suspension, and firing if they do not obey proper management directives. Smith added, "When the rich gather to concern themselves about the business of the poor, it's called charity. When the poor gather to concern themselves about the business of the rich, it's called anarchy!"

To listen to Kheel was to believe that we were seeking some sort of bizarre workers' paradise where players would vote on whether to punt or pass, play in the cold or stay in the locker room, continue the game or take a beer break. Kheel claimed that the NFL would collapse if athletes were given the same freedom as the NFL's coaches, trainers, general managers, or lawyers. He said it in print, and he said it at the bargaining table repeatedly. By early April, it was clear that there would be no negotiations and there would be no concessions until the strike became effective. It was the 1968 and 1970 script with a few alterations.

Owners, through Kheel and Mara, said time and again that they would never agree to the elimination or modification of the Rozelle Rule and would not bargain on any subject until we removed that demand. Our position was best summed up by an article in the *New York Times* authored by John Mackey that ran alongside an article by Kheel. Mackey wrote, in part, "Make no mistake. NFL players are not asking for freedom—they are demanding it, and they will have it—don't loosen the cuffs, take them off."

The biggest battle in the history of professional sports was about to get underway, a battle that would touch the lives of everyone associated with professional football, a battle that would affect the lives of people in all professional sports. We would fight the fight for basketball, hockey, and baseball, as well as football. We would work closely together, while others remained aloof from this battle.

Pickets and Clenched Fists

Long after the demands had been made, my phone rang at home one Saturday morning in May. A reporter wanted my comments on a quote from Richie Petitbon, the new assistant coach of the Houston Oilers, that said NFL teams would "play preseason games with rookies if there were a strike of the veterans." I confidently predicted that no games would be played if there were a strike.

"How could they put games on?" I asked. "Who would come? Besides," I argued with considerable confidence, "with the World Football League starting to play for the first time, the NFL could never put on sandlot football games—they would make the WFL look good, which is something they do not want to do."

We all believed that they couldn't do it. It was a bluff. Or so we thought. Mistake number one.

Negotiations had gone nowhere after we presented our demands. Over the next three months, there had been a few meetings with some sparring, but no progress was made, and the owners refused to put forth an offer. The only item of interest that occurred during April, May, and June was the entrance into the dispute of William J. Usery, director of the Federal Mediation and Conciliation Service (FMCS). Usery, who was building a reputation as a "wonder mediator," was delighted with the prospect of settling every dispute he personally entered in forty-eight hours or less, and he was clearly looking forward to settling the highly visible football dispute.

In 1970 the NFLPA had requested FMCS to intervene, over the strenuous objection of Rozelle, who argued that he alone should play the role of mediator. The roles were reversed in 1974, with the owners inviting the FMCS to intervene instead of Congress and with the players objecting. Given our paranoia about the owners' influence with the Nixon administration, there was an automatic assumption that Kheel had a special relationship with Usery or someone else in the service. We told Usery we would be happy to invite the FMCS to intervene after bargaining had progressed but that it seemed premature, at best, to involve the service in May, when the owners had not yet put an offer on the table.

Nevertheless, we acceded when Usery indicated that he would like to involve himself in this dispute. Quite possibly, that was mistake number two.

In order to demonstrate his worth to us, Usery immediately "convinced" owners to reinstitute the group health and accident insurance that had been cut off at the end of March. They agreed to pay the insurance premium until such time as a strike occurred, and then it would fall back on the union. Usery then imposed a press boycott on statements made about bargaining sessions. We fell into the trap of agreeing to that, and Usery would make statements about "progress being made" and keep us from exposing the owners, who refused to put forward a complete proposal throughout the 1974 negotiations.

By mid-June, three things were obvious to our committee: Owners would not bend on the freedom issues; they were planning to play preseason games with rookies; and they had decided to break the union. Because it was apparent by late June that they would try to play preseason games, we made a last-minute decision to set up picket lines at training camps.

We naively hoped that some rookies would honor the picket lines and not report to camp. Even if rookies did report to camp, we hoped we could shut down games because other unions would honor our picket lines. Our members would walk the picket lines and thus build a commitment for the issues, which we felt would be a useful method of communicating to rookies and the public that we were serious about our strike. Finally, we thought the picket lines would make it more difficult for veterans to go into camp. How could they walk past their teammates and break a strike?

So in June we ordered picket signs. At the same time, it was suggested that we should have some T-shirts that would easily identify anyone walking the picket lines as an NFL player. Two of our people designed the T-shirts while the rest created slogans for the picket signs, including lineman and long snapper George Burman's famous quote, "Up with Oligopsony," an ironic observation about the NFL's monopolistic power to control the labor market single-handedly. There were others, such as "Rookies Are People, Too" and "End Commissioner Dictatorship." (Given the San Diego 8 situation, one suggested picket sign read, "There Is a Narc at 410 Park." We killed that idea.)

Those who designed the T-shirt came up with "No Freedom, No Football," which became our slogan for the entire strike. The slogan went a long way toward convincing the fans that players were serious about the freedom issues above and beyond economic improvements. A clenched fist was featured on the T-shirt to demonstrate the association's defiance. When I saw it, I realized that many people were going to be very upset, so I suggested a T-shirt with the Liberty Bell that would also carry the slogan of "No Freedom, No Football." We ordered bumper stickers, picket signs, and hundreds of T-shirts to be distributed to the players at the campsites. There was great excitement at national headquarters.

Owners were convinced that we would never have picket lines because it would be "degrading" for a player to carry a picket sign. They wouldn't accept the fact that the NFL "family" would act like a union. But on July 1, 1974, we held a press conference to announce that the NFLPA was on strike and that, "yes, there will be picket lines." We confirmed that San Diego would be the first site for picketing.

But first, following the press conference, Bill Curry and I caught a 4:00 P.M. flight to Cincinnati because Pat Matson, the Bengals' player rep, had urged us to try to build enthusiasm for the strike with this traditionally management-dominated team. When we arrived at the meeting place, we were surprised to find that in addition to the players who were present, Mike Brown, a Bengals executive and son of team owner Paul Brown, was there, along with a few fans carrying anti-Garvey signs in the parking lot. Mike Brown indicated that it was the NFLPA position that *we* would not bargain on any issues until the owners had agreed on the freedom issues. We told him, and the players, that was nonsense. We explained that the *owners* refused to bargain on *any* issues until *we* withdrew the freedom issues from the bargaining table.

Some of the Bengals players who would break the picket lines in order to please Mike and Paul Brown were quick to ask whether we were telling the truth! This shocked us because we worked for them and Bill Curry was risking, and would ultimately lose, his football career by being president. Was it possible that they would believe management instead of their own people?

The meeting went from bad to worse as many of the players indicated that they were "no longer interested" in the freedom issues because they had signed long-term contracts. Later we would learn that in addition to signing players to new contracts to keep them from going to the WFL, Paul Brown offered bonuses to players if they would report to training camp on time and not participate in any strike activity. We left Cincinnati for San Diego feeling less confident and slightly confused. The evils of secret individual negotiations were beginning to divide us at the start of negotiations.

Our spirits improved when we arrived in San Diego, where there was an air of excitement about the strike. We met with forty-five to fifty players who were deeply committed to the elimination of the reserve system. They believed in the freedom issues, and it did not take a speech to convince them. We met with more than fifty players the evening of July 2 to review plans for the picket lines, to instruct everyone on how they were to behave in order to avoid violence, and to get ideas about the best way to carry out our mission.

Earlier that day several NFLPA supporters and I met with officials at the U.S. International University (USIU), where the Chargers were training, to discuss where we could picket. The college had said it would be acceptable to picket on campus because picketing the Chargers would not interfere with college activities. But by the time I got there, the university officials had suddenly changed their story. We were told that we must stay off the campus. Instead of being where the rookies could see us, we were relegated to a gate at the bottom of a hill several hundred yards from the training area.

We carefully avoided making any commitment to remain in the designated area because we needed to research California law to determine whether they had the right to keep us off the property. We prepared to go to court if necessary. We did assure them that we would avoid any violence and interference with classes or other campus activities. Jerry Magee, of the San Diego *Union*, "assumed" that we agreed to stay off campus because that is what management told him. The fact that we did not agree seemed of little interest. His colleague, Jack Murphy, wrote on July 5, "The union leader, Ed Garvey, previously had pledged he and his men would respect the University's wishes and would not trespass on private property. Then they reconsidered and went up the hill until Fields and Sullivan stopped them. Garvey wrapped himself in the flag and declared himself a man of peace. 'There was no demonstration of force. We were here to maintain peace and order. It's Independence Day and I think it's a sad occasion when the veterans aren't allowed to talk to the rookies.'"

Murphy had accepted the "fact" that we were violating the law by "trespassing," in addition to the faulty assumption about a "pledge" to stay off campus. There was no pledge, and we were not trespassing.

We met with forty-five to fifty players and urged them to stay within the picketing area, to keep moving, and to avoid arguments. Though no promise had ever been made to stay off campus, we decided to stay at the bottom of the hill for a while rather than risk arrest. Our purpose was to educate and, hopefully, stop people from crossing those picket lines, not to start any fights that would quickly use up our reserves. We would see if it worked. There was a great spirit in the room because everyone felt excited about the possibility of shutting down the camp. We would meet at 9:00 A.M. the next day to head to the USIU campus.

We were staying at the Town and Country Motel in San Diego, and the morning of July 3 started with coffee being served in the motel's large parking lot. There were two vans, which were quickly dubbed "freedom vans": One that Dave Elmendorf drove down with the seven Rams teammates from Los Angeles and one owned by Joe Beauchamp of the Chargers. Players began to arrive with a lot of humor and excitement about being on the first picket line. A caravan of about twenty to twenty-five cars plus the two vans headed for USIU. We arrived, got out of the cars, lined up, and distributed the picket signs. My sign read "Freedom—Not an Issue but a Right," and I proudly carried it to the head of the first picket line in the history of pro sports, along with Bill Curry, Alan Page, and Kermit Alexander. For us, it was a thrilling moment because the pickets clearly demonstrated the players' commitment to freedom. No one seriously thought that players would ever walk a picket line. Yet here were fifty-five to sixty players carrying picket signs in the hot sun.

Reporters were all over the place. Gene Klein, Chargers owner, was standing on the other side of the line with Stacey Sullivan, his lawyer. We would occasionally fake-march over the line, but the mood was almost jovial. The owners acted as if it was war—we didn't, which was another mistake.

When Jim Hill, Packers defensive back who had NBC credentials, went up the hill to interview rookies, owners reacted as if their lines were being infiltrated by the enemy. And when Pettis Norman went up the hill to see the team doctor, Sullivan screamed at him that it was a trick and said that he couldn't go. Few people could out-argue Norman, nicknamed "Rev. Ike" by his friends, and Sullivan eventually stepped back, and Pettis went up the hill. That was as close as we came to an incident until about 1:00 P.M., when Jesse Freitas, one of San Diego's top draft choices, crossed the picket line. Some of the players wanted to stop him, but we urged them to let him go.

There were other exciting moments, like when Teamsters drivers refused to cross the picket line to deliver products to the Chargers and great cheers erupted as their trucks turned around and left. Later, in another example of the owners' war mentality, Klein said that he would order an "airlift of supplies" if he could not get people to cross the lines. Klein was probably a frustrated "general" who always thought that he could do as well as Patton and longed for the opportunity.

Storm the Hill

We returned to the hotel at about 5:00 P.M. to assess the day's activities. Passions ran high as the players felt the extreme frustration of walking a picket line with no results. It was almost fun, but it hadn't worked. Nearly all the rookies were in camp before we could set up the picket lines, and those few who weren't were hustled through the picket lines in vans by nervous Chargers officials.

Pettis Norman was one of the first to speak: "No cause is worthwhile unless it is worth going to jail for." Soon everyone in the group felt the same way, and by the end of the meeting, we voted to "storm the hill" the next day. The meeting broke at about 9:00 P.M.

At about 6:15 A.M., Bill Curry called me to say he hadn't slept all night and would like to talk about the decision to storm the hill. He felt it was a

mistake, and I agreed. Before the group meeting, the Executive Committee met, and we agreed to convince the group not to go forward with the
plan. It might be illegal, it would be bad PR, it probably wouldn't work, and
it would have an adverse impact on pickets in other camps. If our people
were arrested, Oilers, Dolphins, Cowboys, and others would be reluctant to
picket. Another concern was that owners were doing everything they could
to invoke racial prejudice against our protest and storming the hill would
give them a chance to label us as "Black militants."

We then headed to the meeting, where everyone was ready to go. We
presented our recommendation, and I explained that owners would try to
exploit it as a Black militant effort and that we would be playing into their
hands. After considerable discussion, the vote was unanimous to hold off.

As an alternative to storming the hill, we decided to make the Chargers
tell us once and for all whether or not they would arrest us if we peacefully
walked onto the campus. Rather than go up the hill, we would march forward deliberately until we were told to turn back or face arrest. We believed
we had the legal right to go onto the campus. This was, after all, Independence Day. There could be no disruption of the campus activities since the
students would not be in school, and therefore we had every right to go on
public property.

When we arrived to picket, none of the lawyers or any Chargers officials
were present. Only a friendly guard was sitting at the gate. He shook hands
with us, and we kept on walking. The players started singing "God Bless
America" as we marched forward and continued beyond the gate and up
the hill. Suddenly, the Chargers van came roaring down the hill, and Stacey
Sullivan, Chargers attorney, jumped out and started shouting, accusing us
of being on private property.

Since he was the attorney for the Chargers, not the university, I asked,
"Are you going to have us arrested?"

He refused to answer directly, but the implication was clear that they
would call the authorities. I urged him to let us, on this July 4, go up and talk
to the rookies. He started to panic. Obviously, he had overslept or something and hadn't been at his post to stop this from happening, and now we
were on "his" property, and he didn't know what to do about it. He shouted
that we were breaking agreements. I tried to calm him. To avoid a major
confrontation, I decided to ask the players to go back down the hill, and Curry, Beauchamp, and I would continue on up to talk with the rookies. Probably another mistake.

The veteran players turned around and unenthusiastically walked away
while Curry, Beauchamp, and I went up the hill. When we arrived at the

meeting room, we were surprised to see head coach Tommy Prothro and his staff there. When I asked them to leave, they refused. Finally, I convinced them that they should leave during the question-and-answer period since some of the players might feel intimidated if they were in the room. Prothro agreed. Management tried in vain to order him back, but he stayed out.

Curry addressed the rookies on the importance of the strike and gave them some idea of the issues. Beauchamp talked about the need for them to work with the veterans and to join us in the strike. Finally, I urged them to walk down the hill and meet with the veterans so they could decide for themselves. This appealed to a number of players, and they asked us to leave the room while they voted on the issues.

When the three of us walked out, Prothro was going wild wondering what was going on inside. When we told him, he bolted for the door. We went back in with Prothro to learn that the rookies had voted to go down the hill. Prothro then insisted on a twenty-minute limit, and I foolishly agreed to that limitation, since I thought even twenty minutes with the veterans would convince the rookies to leave camp.

The veterans were jubilant when they saw the group coming because they thought the rookies were walking out of camp and joining the strike. When we arrived with the rookies and explained the circumstances, the veterans were less happy but nevertheless went to work talking to the rookies and urging them to join us on the picket lines. Pettis Norman, in a dramatic moment, joined me on top of a car to talk to the players. Pettis said, "If they can enslave us, and they have, then *they will enslave you*! The only way to have your freedom and dignity is to join with us to gain freedom for all athletes."

Clearly, Norman's speech had an effect on some of the rookies, and our first player went back, packed his bags, and came down the hill. His name was Coleman Zeno, a wide receiver from Grambling State who had played with the New York Giants during the 1971 season and was briefly with the Bears and R******s and ended up with the Chargers.

Zeno told the press, "I agree one hundred percent with the veterans. We need to have a change; we don't have the freedom to do what we want to do." Some of the press referred to Zeno's joining his fellow workers as making him a "defector," a term that doubtlessly influenced the thinking of rookies still in camp who were considering joining the veterans on the picket lines. It's hard to say whether it was a lack of talent or his participation in the strike, but Coleman was never heard from again in the NFL.

As we gathered at the hotel with the picketers that night, everyone felt a little better because we thought increasing numbers of players would leave camp and join the picket lines. There was an air of enthusiasm. The only other time I had felt so much solidarity was in the early 1960s in the Civil Rights Movement. We knew that we were right and that because our cause was right, we would ultimately prevail.

We were moving. The strike had begun. The players walked the picket lines. The owners would never forget.

On July 5, Kermit Alexander and I flew to Miami to meet with the Dolphins to discuss the All-Star Game. Both Kermit and I felt that the picket lines would ultimately work. The pickets were building morale and getting some decent press coverage of our issues. When we arrived in Miami, the television crews were at the airport to ask us the key questions: "Will the All-Star Game be played? Will the Dolphins vote?"

We stressed that the NFLPA was a union and that the union, *not* the Dolphins, would make the decision on the All-Star Game: "If we are still on strike, the game will not be played."

When we arrived at a Howard Johnson's for the Dolphins meeting, the players were so uptight they would hardly talk. We tried to get the Dolphins to make individual commitments, but only Ron Sellers joined Doug Swift in pledging that he would definitely strike no matter what happened. Bob Griese suggested that it would help them out if we could get the All-Stars to strike since that would take the public relations pressure off the Dolphins to play in this "charity" game. I told Bob it was a good suggestion and that I would be in Chicago when the All-Stars arrived to convince them to strike.

After the meeting, we received a call informing us that Don Goode, first-round draft choice of San Diego, had walked out and joined the picket line. It could have been the beginning of an avalanche, but Gene Klein promptly announced publicly that if Goode were not back in camp within twenty-four hours he would forfeit his $90,000 signing bonus. Goode asked us to guarantee his bonus, but I did not think the union could take on the potential liability of a $90,000 signing bonus despite the obvious breach of law represented by Klein's threat. Now this tactic would be used to scare rookies and keep them in camp. We felt helpless to counteract this move because of the large amounts of money involved.

While we were meeting with the Dolphins, Bill Curry went to Kerrville, Texas, where his team, the Houston Oilers, was in camp. Curry would set up the picket lines in Kerrville. Dick Berthelsen went to Thousand Oaks, California, to help Gene Upshaw, Calvin Hill, and Willie Brown set up picket lines for the Cowboys. Gradually, picket lines would be set up at all twenty-six sites. Another mistake? We had possibly spread ourselves too thin, but we believed then that teammates would convince other teammates and that every camp must be covered.

On Sunday, July 7, I left for Chicago to meet with the All-Stars. It had been almost four months since our demands had been presented, yet the NFL had still not given us an offer! John Mackey met me at Chicago's O'Hare Airport, and we took a cab together over to the All-Star headquarters, the Orrington Hotel in Evanston. There we met with Bobby Douglass, then of the Chicago Bears, Dan Dierdorf of the Cardinals, and his teammates Conrad Dobler and Bob Rowe. From the Bears, in addition to Douglass, we had Joe Moore, Rich Coady, George Seals, and Ike Hill. Alan Page flew down from Minneapolis and Ken Bowman from Green Bay.

At 4:00 P.M., we met the All-Stars in a large meeting room and talked for an hour about where we were in negotiations and why they should strike. I told them about Griese's comment that a strike by the All-Stars would make it easier on the Dolphins. Mackey gave a speech on why they should join the strike and told them not to worry about their bonuses since our legal advisers had convinced him that the owners could not take back the signing bonus. George Seals stood and said simply, "Be a man." Alan Page explained that many veterans had been where the All-Stars were now and urged them to join us in order to make this game worthwhile for their futures. Dan Dierdorf told them that this was the first time they could make their own decisions as professionals and urged them to join us.

Mark Markovich, an All-Star from San Diego, said it wasn't fair that there was no one from management "to present their side." I quickly agreed with him and suggested a debate with Jim Finks, who was scheduled to talk to the All-Stars the next day. Markovich had inadvertently given us a great idea: We would confront Finks in front of the players. If he refused, he would lose by default. If he agreed, we would win.

The next morning, we informed the press that we were confident "Finks would accept our invitation to debate." As the lunch hour approached, Alan Page went into the All-Stars dining room and announced that I would be there to debate with Finks at 1:00 P.M., when he was scheduled to talk to the players. We were setting the trap.

As we arrived at the meeting room, there were plenty of press and television people around. I shook hands with Finks, the cameras turned on, and a microphone was put between us. I asked, "Jim, are you ready?"

"For what?" said Finks.

"The debate?"

Finks quickly said, "I won't debate with you in front of the rookies. I'll talk with you and Alan later."

Rick Middleton, an All-Star, was standing there listening. He innocently asked, "Why not? How will we know who is telling the truth unless we hear both of you?"

Finks wheeled around, put his finger on Middleton's chest, and demanded, "What's your name, young man?" Middleton told him his name, and then Finks said, "You will have to make up your own mind."

The All-Stars booed, and Finks had blown it from the get-go for the reporters and any of the players who were listening. He symbolized with one gesture what the fight was all about: Management doesn't like it when their property talks back by asking, "Why?"

"I will tell you what to believe" might well have been the management's response, or "Do as you are told."

Finks, angry and nervous, quickly turned and went into the room. The All-Stars filed in. I was not allowed in. In anticipation of our efforts to get the All-Stars to strike, each team had sent at least one scout to babysit their players in the All-Star Game. They guarded entry to the room as if Alan Page, Dan Dierdorf, Dave Rowe, and I were somehow going to break through and drop large doses of truth in the room or kidnap the players. The scene was comical. The babysitters glowered at us. We were the enemy. The anarchists. The commies.

Finks had been talking to the All-Stars for about an hour when, suddenly, the door opened and rookie John Hicks of Ohio State stepped out and said, "We would like Ed Garvey to come in and debate the issues with Jim Finks in front of the whole group."

Finks was now trapped. He couldn't refuse because the media were there. He came out, grabbed some more cigarettes, and went back in with me. I started the discussion. After explaining a few issues, I said I thought it would be most helpful to hear from the All-Stars on matters that Finks had raised. They started talking to me, and after I corrected some of Finks's misstatements, he started lecturing them on their "moral and legal commitment" to play the game, saying, "You could be jeopardizing your career because you cannot play in any preseason game if you do not play in the *Tribune* All-Star Game."

When I challenged him on that statement, he said it was part of the contract they had with the Chicago *Tribune*. I asked him to produce the contract, which, of course, he would not. At the end of the discussion, I felt reasonably confident about who they believed. Finks had blown it. But would they strike even if they sided with us?

When we left, Finks told the press, "It was heated at times, but not between Ed Garvey and myself. We both respect one another." I made a few innocuous statements saying that I hoped the players would join with us, and then I joined Alan Page and his wife, Diane; Dan Dierdorf; and others while we awaited the outcome. Most of the players doubted that the rookies would have the guts to strike, but the longer they were in there, the more exciting it got. The babysitters were milling around looking concerned. Suddenly, the door opened, and All-Stars David Casper and John Hicks came out to read a statement: "We will not practice until there are good faith negotiations, and there will be no game until a contract is signed."

Diane Page, Alan's wife, let out a cheer, and the All-Stars took off for their rooms with the stunned babysitters in hot pursuit. There was bedlam. Finks, who just a few minutes before had talked about our mutual respect, was now saying, ". . . near to physical violence at times; the players received incredibly bad counsel." One thing was clear: They would never debate with us again.

We were at an all-time high. The All-Stars understood the importance of the collective action and stood with the veterans. Finks had spoken of the moral obligation the rookies owed to their clubs, but David Jaynes, Kansas City's first-round draft choice, stood and said during our debate, "I feel an obligation to my team, but I also have an obligation to my future *teammates* on the picket lines." Finks couldn't handle those arguments.

Diane and Alan Page, Dierdorf, Dobler, and I headed out of the unfriendly terrain of the Orrington Hotel to grab a sandwich.

Neither side wanted to be with us. Many rookies were afraid to be seen with us; yes, they had voted to strike, but why go to the next step and be seen with public enemy number one? The looks of hate from the babysitters were real. Every one of them felt that he had personally lost the battle. After all, they were there to persuade their "property" to avoid the union and to play the game. How would they explain their failure to the general manager? We were happy to get away from the Orrington for a few hours.

It was time to celebrate, but we knew from experience that it was too early to claim victory. The league would really put pressure on the All-Stars to hold another vote. Now the coaches would get into the battle.

In 1970, under the leadership of Steve Tannen, the All-Stars had walked out on strike to support the veterans after a talk by Alex Karras and Dick Butkus, but within twenty-four hours they were back inside the Orrington Hotel, having felt the fear of God through phone calls from Vince Lombardi, Norm Van Brocklin, and other head coaches. Now, as we sat in a little restaurant near the Orrington, we knew how the league would react: Get the coaches on the phone, get Garvey out of Chicago, threaten every one of the rookies.

Soon Jim Searce, Usery's deputy of FMCS, called to suggest an immediate meeting in Washington. That would take care of priority number one of the owners: To get Garvey out of town. Now they would work on the rookies. While we fell for the first ploy and I returned to Washington, we moved quickly to meet the expected threats. We sent out an SOS for Bill Curry, Bobby Bryant, and Charlie West of the Vikings; Doug Swift and Marline Briscoe of the Dolphins; and others to come to Chicago, and they did. The next day I met with the federal mediator while Bill Curry and the other players arrived to mop up.

Various meetings were held, but the rookies stood firm. Within forty-eight hours, the *Chicago Tribune* decided to call off the game. For the first time in fifty years, the Chicago All-Star Game was not played. For the first time in the history of the NFLPA, a union decision was carried out in the best interests of the whole and not in the interests of a few. We believed that the All-Stars would return to their respective teams and help us spread the gospel. We were riding high!

On to Canton

Our All-Star victory convinced the owners to intensify their efforts. The Canton Hall of Fame Game, the first preseason game of the year, would be played at any cost. They prepared with the zeal of army generals. We still did not fully understand that they were out to destroy us, to win the war, to demand nothing less than unconditional surrender with our heads on a stake. We naively believed that it remained a fight among combatants who must ultimately live with one another and that this fact alone dictated aboveboard tactics and recognition that total victory in a labor-management dispute is as bad as total defeat. After all, labor disputes are different from most other disputes. If two businessmen have a falling out and sue each other, they need not ever work together again. But no matter how bitter a labor dispute becomes, when it's over, the parties must work together. If labor is defeated and humiliated, they will go at it even worse the next time around. We understood that the best contract is one that neither side is completely happy with, but the NFL wanted victory—and it had to be total.

Mara and Rozelle were determined to get back at us and to demonstrate once and for all that collective action would never force the NFL to do anything. They would have us believe that only subservience, total respect for authority, and acceptance of their system would allow players to continue to earn the privilege of making a living in the NFL. They were determined to force the players back to the days when, after the owners had agreed to establish a pension program in 1963, Carroll Rosenbloom told NFLPA president Billy Howton, "You go in there and say, 'Thank you, gentlemen' and leave." And he did. They were confident they would uncover another Kemp or Alan Miller; they would be done with militants. They had beaten the Teamsters; they had forced Shulman out; surely they could get rid of Garvey.

The annual Hall of Fame contest between St. Louis and Buffalo was scheduled for July 26 in Canton. The owners concentrated on making sure the rookies on those teams would be "protected from outside influence." No way would they allow a repeat of the Finks-Garvey debate and confrontation.

The Cardinals were training at a college in downstate Illinois. The team's veterans were always among the most pro-union in the league, so we thought we would have a shot at convincing their rookies to boycott the Canton game by sending several vets to camp to talk with them, just as we had with the All-Stars. Dan Dierdorf organized the Cardinals players for the trip. He got damn near everyone. Jim Bakken, Jackie Smith, Jim Hart, Bob Rowe, Roger Wehrli, and fifteen others arrived to picket the camp. By now the owners had perfected the "San Diego technique": Allow the union to have one and only one meeting with the rookies; make sure that the coaches and a management representative sit in on the meeting (and for God's sake don't leave the room); keep the rookies away from the pickets; and treat the rookies like they are in a country club. After all, no one was fooling anyone; these free agents would be cut the minute the veterans came into camp, so why work them too hard? Why risk injuries? Why get them mad?

Cardinals management went to the extreme at league direction because they were determined to play at Canton. Rookies were bused to movies and to a leased swimming pool, so they had no free time to go into town or mingle with the veterans who might "corrupt" them. Management was careful not to work the rookies too hard for fear they would get rebellious.

When the veterans decided to go onto the campus to talk with the rookies, the local prosecutor threatened to have all of them arrested. The Cardinals players said they were willing to be arrested, so we moved toward the confrontation.

I had sent Dan Lindsay, staff attorney on loan from Lindquist and Vennum, to work with Dierdorf. We also hired local counsel, who assured us that any arrest would violate Illinois state law. When I advised the prosecutor of this, he hollered at me over the phone and continued his threats, but when the bluff was called, he backed down. No one was arrested, but the efforts to get through to the rookies still failed because the Cardinals, despite a great effort by the vets and Ken Bowman, just could not break through the barriers established by management. Every time a veteran talked to rookies, a management rep was present.

The Cardinals scabs would go to Canton, but the NFL feared sabotage. The Cardinals would send three equipment trucks to fool us in case we were going to hijack their truck! The Cleveland Browns rookies were waiting to play if either the Cardinals or Bills were stopped. False information was given out about the team hotels near Canton in case we intended to confront them.

We were also working in Canton to shut down the game if at all possible. Ed Podolak, a Kansas City Chiefs running back who was an honorary member of the United Auto Workers (UAW), went to Cleveland to talk with UAW official Bill Castevens. Castevens agreed to do everything he could to help us. He provided UAW picketers for the game, legal help, and a lot of encouragement.

Management countered with an anti-labor judge who issued an injunction to limit the number of pickets at the game. Police on horseback were there to enforce the court order. Four old-timers who had played before 1959, who sided with management, were there to picket the NFLPA, so the press focused on them and *not* on the hundreds of our picketers, including a busload of Buffalo players. The picture circulating nationwide was of two alumni picketing us!

Then there were our friends in television. Howard Cosell called our office and asked us not to picket because he did not want to cross the picket line. We said, "Don't cross the line, but we will picket." Cosell blew a cork. He started shouting on the speakerphone that we were idiots and incompetent and then hurled more personal insults at Kermit Alexander and me. He reminded us that he had walked the picket line for the American Federation of Television and Radio Artists (AFTRA), and, finally, he told us of his obligation to the wonderful people of ABC. It was a Cosell diatribe. At the end, I assured him that the pickets would be there, Cosell or no Cosell.

ABC decided not to televise the game. Was it Cosell's refusal to cross the picket line? Or did ABC refuse to televise a second-rate game played by rookies and scabs but advertised as NFL football? Whatever motivated ABC, CBS Sports—a virtual extension of the NFL establishment—rushed in to take over for them. Brent Musburger and Pat Summerall, NFL cheerleaders, even joked on the air about ABC not covering the game. They weren't bothered by pickets or a second-rate game.

I was alone in Washington when the game began. As I watched the opening remarks, I couldn't believe how far CBS would go to espouse the owners' line. We always knew CBS Sports was pro-owner. As a matter of fact, when CBS sports commentator Heywood Hale Broun wanted to do a special on me, his producer was careful to explain to us that they were CBS *news*—not *sports*—and were, therefore, independent of the league's influence. *60 Minutes* personnel emphasized the same distinction. But on this day, Musburger and Summerall went overboard. They praised the rookies and talked about "the game," *not* the veterans, as the important attraction. The veterans somehow weren't missed. It was as if the vets had disappeared and CBS felt obligated to praise the brave replacements. There was no discussion of police on horseback keeping picketers away, the judge's order, the issues in the strike, or the total absurdity of charging admission and televising a game that could only be described as a sandlot pickup game at the NFL Hall of Fame.

As I watched the game, I couldn't help but feel that the tide had turned and now we were losing. A "football atmosphere" had been created. Praise for the rookies by the CBS shills would scare veterans worried about their positions. The sellout crowd would make us believe that fans would come out to see anything with an NFL logo on it. Never mind that the players on the field were bartenders, teachers, and even a refugee from the Hell's Angels. It was NFL football! If we couldn't shut down this game despite Herculean efforts by the veterans from Buffalo, St. Louis, and other teams from around the league, how could we have any impact the next week when our efforts would be spread to thirteen different locations?

The pickets were supposed to stop other unions from crossing the lines and selling hot dogs, televising the game, turning on the lights. It hadn't worked. The pickets were supposed to convince the rookies not to play the game. They ignored us. The pickets were supposed to get our message across to the public. CBS made certain that didn't happen. And the wire services focused not on our pickets but on some old-timers picketing us.

It was a PR disaster. We again felt the power of the NFL: If ABC doesn't show, get CBS; feed them the lines; get the judge to restrict pickets; get some clown to picket us; get wire services to focus on them. It scared some of us. But no one was giving up.

Canton was a disaster in many ways, but it also provided our first contact with organized labor outside of the International Association of Machinists (IAM). (Our offices were in the IAM's headquarters in Washington, DC, and that union helped us in every conceivable way.) The UAW had also been a tremendous help. They got pickets, helped in court, welcomed all the players to the union hall for beers afterward, and generally educated the players in attendance about unionism.

The veteran players who had been at the game to support us left impressed and excited. After all, we hadn't shut down the game, but we had learned a lot. We could build on that experience and, we hoped, shut down some of the other preseason games. Besides, the veterans were still on strike.

However, I couldn't help but wonder what would have happened if we had shut down the Hall of Fame Game. In retrospect, I'm sure nothing would have happened because the Rozelle game plan called for destruction of the union, but at the time, some of us were still under the impression that we were dealing with a rational opponent who wanted an agreement. Three years later, we would understand that the impression was nonsense.

Negotiations Continue

Meantime, at the Labor Department, Bill Usery was calling for more "negotiations" while a trickle of veterans started to go into camp the week after the Canton game. Our inability to stop that game made it obvious that most other games would be played. Our mistake was to strike preseason rather than regular-season games because preseason games were more like rookie scrimmages than standard NFL football. The owners acted as if it were only a matter of time before we would capitulate. Usery also seemed confident he would get an early agreement because he felt we would be much more "reasonable" on the freedom issues as more and more veterans crossed picket lines.

By July 29, the All-Star Game had been canceled, the Canton game played. Ken Reaves, super rep and iconic player for Atlanta, had been traded off the picket line to New Orleans. News of that trade came during a bargaining session, and we exploded. Reaves had gathered the veterans at the Falcons training camp in Greenville, South Carolina, to picket the campsite. The first day of the picketing, Falcons owner Rankin Smith and Falcons coach Norm Van Brocklin drove to the picket line and asked Reaves to get into their Cadillac; they told him that he could "take his picket sign to New Orleans" because he was now a New Orleans Saint! To say this had a chilling effect on the Falcons vets as well as other reps around the league would be an understatement. Reaves was an original Falcon, and he had played in every game the Falcons had ever played. He was the defensive captain, a player popular with fans, and a highly respected leader of the team.

If owners could pick on a star like Reaves, no one was safe. They had traded and cut reps for years in their efforts to disrupt the NFLPA. Teams like the 49ers with Lou Spaida and Jack White traded one rep after another, including Howard Mudd, Clark Miller, and Kermit Alexander. Atlanta would unload Reaves and then John Zook. Every rep or NFLPA officer on the Eagles was traded or cut: Ron Medved, Tom Dempsey, Nate Ramsey, Ron Porter, Jerry Patton, and finally Kermit Alexander. The Bears got rid of Benny McRae, Wayne Mass, Mac Percival, Bob Grim. The list is long: Pat Matson, Bengals; Pat Richter and Len Hauss, R******s; Bill Curry and Al Clark, Rams; Jon Morris, Patriots. But the blatancy of the Reaves trade infuriated everyone because we knew management was using it to send us a message.

In addition to their intimidation via the Reaves trade, the use of signing bonuses to force rookies to stay in camp and veterans to report reached incredible proportions. Because the WFL had started that year, many veterans signed new contracts with signing bonuses, but management told them they would forfeit the bonus unless they reported to camp. Some of the vets succumbed to this illegal tactic, while others didn't. But all were concerned. (Two years later, Judge Charles Schneider would declare the owners' threats to be a violation of the National Labor Relations Act, but the threats were effective in scaring veteran players.)

The owners also raised pay for all veterans who were under contract prior to July 19, which included about 90 percent of the vets. Each was automatically given a 10 percent pay increase to begin as soon as he crossed the picket line. That meant that veterans on the picket line were without insurance and losing as much as $1,000 per week, while those who crossed the picket lines received a bonus of $3,000 to $10,000. The NFL wanted to win, and neither money nor the law was an obstacle. We knew the plan was illegal, and so did they, but so what? What could we do about it? The owners thought we would collapse.

The federal mediators knew owners were doing everything within their power to break us, and they had to understand that most of the owners' activities were illegal. Nevertheless, they did nothing. Were they not worried about the law? To them, the law is irrelevant. The press is important. Power is important. Progress toward any resolution is important. Getting a deal is important.

Some of our cynics believed that the FMCS was part of the NFL team, that their goals were to keep our leadership in a room at the Department of Labor for hundreds of hours rather than out on the lines keeping the troops together; to mislead the players and public through false press releases about "progress at the table"; and to act as a shield for Kheel and the NFL union busters. I prefer to believe that they were *unwilling* coconspirators. In many ways, they helped us by keeping the owners at the table. Usery never deliberately helped cut us up; it just happened that way. But he could not speak out against the owners' illegal conduct.

And so the scenario was played out in a crummy little space at Fourteenth Street and Constitution Avenue, in the Cyrus Ching Room in DC. The owners next door were not to talk to us, and we were to ignore them. We would pass in the hall, use the men's room together, but there was some mystical force keeping us from discussion. Only the mediator could bring us together, which he did infrequently. It was as if somehow two warring parties had discovered a sorcerer who could cast a magic spell and grant victory to both sides, and everyone would be happy. Unfortunately, Usery wasn't a sorcerer. Mediation was a failure.

We met on July 29, 30, and 31 and August 1 and 2 with no progress. The owners broke off negotiations on August 2 to attend their games—games, by the way, that were poorly attended. The St. Louis Cardinals played the Chicago Bears in Champagne, Illinois, and fewer than five thousand fans turned out in the hundred-thousand-seat stadium. Attendance was down around the NFL. We were hurting them financially, but they seemed to harden with every dollar lost. And with good reason. As each day passed, more veterans crossed the picket lines. The owners sensed that the end was near, that we would give up soon and accept their offer.

We met again on August 6, 7, 8, and 9. No progress. The owners were now haughty. More than three hundred veterans had reported, although at least one hundred hadn't played for years but were convinced by the clubs to try out. The press smelled blood, the players were getting weak, the owners knew we would soon collapse, and so did the mediators.

On the night of August 10, the owners once again walked out of negotiations. They did not want to meet again until Thursday, August 15, on the eve of the third week of preseason games. After they walked out, our committee met and began the long struggle that would ultimately succeed. We decided to forgo short-term gains in favor of long-term victory. The NFL would never be the same again.

Cooling Off

After the owners walked out, we headed for the nearby Palm Restaurant for a late dinner, during which we decided to go with plan B the next morning. I had decided that the only way we could survive the owners' efforts to break us with their refusal to bargain was to go back to work *without* a contract. We were determined to avoid another situation like 1970 where we could be forced to accept a long-term bad contract. If we did that again, I doubted that the union would ever pull itself back together. I knew also that they would force us to abandon the *Mackey* case, testing the Rozelle Rule. They were after total victory; therefore, we had to come up with alternatives, and plan B was the answer.

With plan B, we could go forward with confidence, knowing that they could neither break us nor force us to accept a lousy contract. Some questions went unanswered: Would they start to bargain? If not, when should we turn to plan B? Should we wait until the last minute? Should we take it right up to the first regular-season game? We decided that night, August 10, that our strongest people had sacrificed enough and that the time had arrived. Roger Staubach, Bob Griese, and Terry Bradshaw had crossed the picket line a week before. It was time to make a move.

At the late-night dinner, we were exhausted, but for the first time in months, we felt we could again capture the initiative. Management had been on the ascendancy since the Canton game, and they were now close to a route. Art Modell, Ralph Wilson, Wellington Mara, Ted Kheel, and others saw their plans going even better than they could have expected. There were some doubts after the All-Star setback, but they had recovered, and now all of the illegal plans were working beautifully: Rookies would not come out of camp for fear of losing not only a chance to play but also their signing bonus. Veterans were crossing picket lines because of pressure to keep their jobs and to collect the $10,000 bribe. No unions were honoring our picket lines, so the games appeared on television as if nothing were happening. The sportswriters were describing the union members as "lemmings," the leadership as "militant."

Most sportswriters sensed that we were about to be defeated, and they appeared to want that almost as much as the owners did. They wanted to see the players humbled, and a good many wanted to see me ousted from the union. Some writers were so obviously in the owners' pockets that it was easy to figure out their motivation. The anti-union feeling was almost unanimous. Maybe it was that we had exposed the myths of the reserve system that they had written about for all those years as the truth. Maybe they just wanted to see the characters that entertained them, those "overpaid crybabies," get beat. Maybe they still believed that unions had no place in sports. Maybe it was all of the above plus the lobster Newburg they were served at the Super Bowl.

But the writers were far from our thoughts the night we made the decision. Preserving the union was our only concern. The next day we would implement that decision, but first the Board of Representatives had to be polled on the idea. We could not call off the strike without the support of the reps, many of whom were on the picket lines. But once we decided, it was like a tidal wave of emotions sweeping across the committee. Page, Brown, Keating, Owens, Bowman, Curry, Alexander, Podolak—these guys had spent more than a hundred days fighting the owners at the bargaining table, setting up picket lines, begging, cajoling, urging players to stick with the union and stay out of camp. They knew the total frustration of dealing with an employer bent on destroying the union, and now they could, for the first time in a hundred days, relax and not worry about who might go into camp tomorrow; not worry about whether their own teammates would abandon them; not worry whether the owners would bargain tomorrow.

As the only people left in the Palm that night, we felt the tension lifting. We were again seizing the initiative, and there was nothing they could do about it. They could not force us to accept a contract that would have made a mockery of the players' fight. No, they could not force us to meet with them again; they could not bust the union. We left at 1:30 A.M., looking forward to a few hours of sleep before springing the plan on management *and* the mediators.

The next morning, we gathered to discuss our tactics. While we wanted the vote of the reps, we did not want word to get back to management before we announced the plan to the public. We started phoning reps around noon and would call a major press conference for 4:00 P.M. If the reps voted no, we would call off the press conference. In the meantime, we decided to let the mediators know about our plans but only when there was no time for them to do anything.

Curry and I called Usery and asked if he and Searce could join us for lunch at the Mayflower. They agreed to come by at 1:00 P.M. By that time, the Executive Committee was on the phone to the reps, and, to our surprise, many of the reps strongly resisted. They argued that we could hold out for another two, maybe three weeks. Why not stick with our game plan of letting the strongest link make the determination?

At lunch, we stalled, but we eventually told Usery our plan. He suggested that we return to work under his call, not unilaterally. He would call for a cooling-off period, and we could accept. We agreed to discuss the idea with our committee. The four of us headed back to our office.

Approximately an hour before the press conference, we found a confused and divided committee when we walked into our offices. Ken Bowman thought that the committee had been railroaded into the decision. He started asking why we were in such a hurry and whose idea it was in the first place. Tom Keating joined in Ken's questioning, and suddenly Alan Page called from Minneapolis to change his vote because the Vikings didn't want to go back to work! Suddenly, they now wanted to become militant leaders of the strike? I couldn't believe what I was hearing, but a few questions later I found the answer.

The Vikings and Dolphins were scheduled to play a nationally televised preseason game the next week, and the Vikings knew that most Dolphins had been in training camp all along. They wanted to strike just long enough so that they wouldn't look bad against the team that had beaten them in the Super Bowl the previous January. So much for the militant Vikings. Page decided not to change his vote.

Back at the office, the battle raged on. A clear majority of the reps authorized the action, but many were unenthusiastic. By now, several R******s— Billy Kilmer, Len Hauss, Diron Talbert, Ron McDole, Larry Brown, and Brig Owens—had arrived at the office. They supported the decision to return to work. Time was running out. During a thirty-minute discussion, I urged Bowman and Keating to support the return to work. Usery joined in, saying he would support us, so the committee voted, and again it was unanimous, though there was less enthusiasm this time. We headed for the Mayflower Hotel to meet with the press.

We hadn't even had time to discuss what we were going to say, so I just stood and blurted out the news: "At the request of the director of the FMCS, we have accepted the idea of a two-week cooling-off period, and we are asking our members to return to work no later than Wednesday." The news went out like wildfire. For once, Kheel and Co. were caught with their pants down.

As we left the Mayflower, Dick Basoco, then a reporter with the *Baltimore Sun*, walked back to the office with me. He asked, "Do you have any idea how often a cooling-off period has worked?"

I said, "No, and I don't want to know. You and I both know that this isn't your usual 'cooling-off period.' . . . They probably won't come out again after fourteen days, but now that is management's problem, isn't it?"

We laughed and headed for dinner with the rest of the committee.

The owners were furious when they learned of the unilateral decision to call a cooling-off period.

Carroll Rosenbloom demanded that the players sign a "loyalty oath" that they would not leave again once having come back to the womb.

Joe Thomas, then general manager of the Colts, who the day before was bribing players on the Colts to cross the picket lines and who was telling Bert Jones and Marty Domres that whichever quarterback would report to work would be his starting quarterback, was suddenly upset that players were returning. He announced that they would not be allowed back and said something about not having enough room for them!

Houston coach Sid Gillman banned union meetings on the premises and immediately cut seven players who had been active in the strike, including Paul Guidry, who had driven all night to be on time for camp only to learn that he was no longer wanted. The year before, Guidry had broken his back and was out for the year, but he was determined to help the team and had worked extremely hard to rehabilitate. He walked miles each day in a swimming pool to regain his strength, and miraculously he came back before the end of the 1973 season to help the Oilers. But now it was like saying, "Thanks, Paul. You are cut, even though you walked in the pool, because you also walked the picket line."

The owners officially turned down the cooling-off period. Their decision had little impact because the veterans streamed into camp whether or not they had "accepted" the cooling-off period. What could management do? Turn them back? Not likely. One team briefly threatened to turn back the striking veterans (because they were coming back on their feet and not their knees), but the league prevailed on that team, and the vets went back in.

The teams decided that, to be on the safe side, they should keep all rookies and free agents on the payroll, just in case the union actually tried to pull everyone out again after fourteen days. The results were comical. The Rams played the Raiders, and one of the players said that there were so many people in uniform that they could have circled the field if they had held hands. A conservative estimate is that the average team carried eighty-five players into the last two weeks of the preseason.

The NFL Strikes Back

Kermit Alexander was the first vice president of the union and had been an outspoken advocate of the players' position throughout his brilliant career. Alexander started his career with San Francisco but was traded to Los Angeles one day after being elected to the union's Executive Committee in 1970. He stayed there until Carroll Rosenbloom took over the team. Alexander was cut by the Rams in 1973 and picked up by Philadelphia. He played with the Eagles for the balance of the 1973 season and was looking forward to another year there, but when the cooling-off period began, he went to Philadelphia and was told by Coach Mike McCormack that he suddenly did not fit "into the Eagles' plans." McCormack said Alexander could "work out his own trade."

The absurdity of the situation was obvious. How could Alexander make a trade for himself? "Hello, San Diego? Would you give a second-round draft choice to Philadelphia for me?" Soon thereafter, Alexander was cut. Two years later, the Eagles would be ordered to reinstate and pay him for the entire 1974 season. The judge ruled that they had fired him because of his union activity, but in August 1974, we didn't know what recompense he might receive through the justice system. We knew the punishment was just the beginning.

Bill Curry left for Houston. When he arrived at the Oilers camp, seven friends had already been cut, and it was obvious who was next. Coach Sid Gillman said they were "short on playbooks" so Curry could work out on his own. Curry, the starting center the previous season, would work out "on his own" by running laps while the others scrimmaged.

When the cooling-off period ended, Gillman cut Curry. Curry, too, would win his case against the Oilers. The judge ruled two years later that the Oilers had illegally cut the president of the union because of his union activity. He was ordered reinstatement and back pay.

Tom Keating, AFC vice president, returned to Pittsburgh. Coach Chuck Noll, who had cut Roy Jefferson in 1970 because the team didn't "need militant union types around," would take little time with Keating. Keating, a twelve-year veteran and an All-Pro, was told that he could practice only with the rookies. He remained with the team for a couple of weeks but was not allowed to play a single down in a game.

Just before a road trip, Noll addressed the team and said that some players had their roles confused. Some thought they were coaches, some thought they were owners, and the situation would be rectified. After the meeting, Tom Keating was cut as the team left for the airport. Like the others, Keating would also win his case and receive championship pay for the 1974 season. But it didn't help in 1974.

In Pittsburgh, Preston Pearson had been the alternate rep with Terry Hanratty. Both would be gone from Pittsburgh before the start of the season. Any wonder why we wouldn't get a player rep in Pittsburgh for two years thereafter?

There were many other cases: Ken Bowman, two-time committee member, was told by Packers doctors that he had back problems, a diagnosis made on a long-distance phone call! Apparently, his back wasn't so bad; he was quickly signed by the WFL. Del Williams, outspoken New Orleans rep, was immediately released. Don Goich, Giants rep, was not offered a contract by Wellington Mara; Calvin Hill and Jean Fugett would soon be gone from Dallas; Kenny Houston was traded from the Oilers to the

R******s; the Bears cut Mac Percival; and Cleveland's Paul Brown cut Pat Matson.

By year's end, only three player reps remained in office.

The press didn't seem upset when a person like Kermit Alexander was cut. It didn't strike the writers as odd that the president and the two vice presidents of the union were all cut by their teams: "Curry was coming off an injury . . . Alexander was getting too old . . . Keating beaten out by younger players."

The press was confused. They thought we were on the ropes, but we had jumped out of the ring before the owners could throw the knockout punch. The owners didn't know how to react. How do you handle a union that walks away? As we approached the end of the cooling-off period, a certain amount of tension was building. Would we walk out again? Would there be a new offer?

Usery suggested a Chicago meeting for the end of the cooling-off period, another chance to reach agreement. Both sides said okay, and we prepared for another rep meeting. Our focus would be on survival without a contract since we were convinced that owners would not bargain with us and that players would not walk out again. Militants had been burned, and the others were happy to be off the hook.

We met with owners at the Hyatt Regency at O'Hare Airport for ten minutes. Kheel asked for a caucus, and twelve hours later—that's right, *twelve hours later*—Bill Usery entered our room to suggest that we meet again in the morning, saying, "I am convinced that they will make a substantial offer in the morning."

We returned to our hotel to discuss the future. No one even suggested trying to meet with management. Our people had given up on the idea of collective bargaining. At some point during our marathon sessions at the Labor Department, we heard on the radio an advertisement for the Retail Clerks Union. The voice said, "You have a choice: You can beg, or you can bargain." That became our theme. By that night in Chicago, the reps would reaffirm that we would not beg, and the owners made it clear with their "historic" offer that they were not serious about bargaining.

The reps turned to plans for the 1974 season. We discussed the importance of the *Mackey* case, scheduled to go to trial in February, and we decided to raise the dues to $400 per man to help cover the legal fees we would incur. Believe it or not, everyone was enthused about the future. We had been through a lot, and no one was backing down. As far as the twenty-six reps were concerned, we would live to fight another day. We left on a positive note. Keating went back to Pittsburgh; Curry to be cut in Houston; Page to Minnesota; Bowman to certain termination in Green Bay; Willie Brown to Oakland; and I headed out on the Illinois Tollway to Wisconsin.

Had we lost? Maybe, but they knew they were in a fight. There was no "freedom," and there was plenty of football. T-shirts, clenched fists, picket lines, and thousands of man-hours did not affect the NFL giant, or so it seemed. There had to be other ways to go about it. But we were still around.

Occasionally, Ed found time to relax. (Note the loosened tie.)

Facing page, top:
Informal conversations with congressmen such as Peter Rodino and Emanuel Celler helped advance Ed's goals for the NFLPA.

Facing page, bottom:
Ed's meetings with NFL player representatives sometimes appeared relaxed, but the details were always intense.

Right: *There were times when formal attire was deemed appropriate, as was the case at this NFLPA banquet in Washington, DC.*

Below: *NFLPA executive director and Pro Football Hall of Fame member Gene Upshaw intensely strategizes over details with Ed.*

As he kicks off an NFLPA players meeting, Ed clearly displays his pleasure at being their leader.

Judge Alan Page, an NFLPA Executive Committee member and Pro Football Hall of Fame inductee, shows his trademark intensity.

Brig Owens, NFLPA assistant executive director and Washington R°°°°°°s Ring of Fame member, attentively listens to proposals.

John Mackey, NFLPA's first president and Pro Football Hall of Fame member, awaits his turn to speak.

Dick Berthelsen, NFLPA staff attorney; Kermit Alexander,
NFLPA president; and Leonard Lindquist of the NFLPA law firm Lindquist
and Vennum show a mix of emotions during a discussion.

Ed spoke often of the support of his wife, Betty, shown here enjoying time with Ed at a conference.

John Mackey and Ed in one of their many strategic conversations while meeting with Congress.

John Mackey honors attorney Leonard Lindquist's vital service to the union by presenting him with an official NFLPA ring.

5

The 1974 Season

Can We Survive? Damn Right We Can!

While thinking about the problems facing the union in 1974, I couldn't help but look back to the lonely feeling I experienced in 1970 when the strike was over. Almost minutes after we accepted the long-term contract at the league office, John Mackey headed for training camp, instructing me not to call him, that he would call me. Bowman headed to Green Bay, Richter for Washington, Keating for Oakland, and Alexander for his new "home," Los Angeles. They had to shift gears in a hurry. After fighting management for months, they now had to make their respective teams or else everything they had fought for would not help them personally. They did not want to hear about ongoing problems with the newly negotiated contract. As one of the lawyers, I felt deserted as we gathered to draft the "agreement" that had been reached. What to draft for sections that had never been discussed? Whom should we consult about the players' understanding of the agreement?

As the cooling-off period ended in 1974, the regular season marched into America's living room, and the strike and bitterness were covered up by CBS, NBC, and ABC announcers in order to package their product in the best and most salable wrappings. I had that same feeling of loneliness, but this time I could only blame myself.

In 1970, others were to blame for the defeat: Jack Kemp; Alan Miller; a young and inexperienced negotiating committee; the absence of a staff to contact the players; a severe lack of funds. In 1974, it was my fault. We had a staff; we knew what players wanted; we had the funds; and we had plenty of negotiating experience. Yet we had lost just as badly as we had four years before. This time the mistakes were mine.

Had we demanded too much? Had the clenched fists turned off our membership and fans? Had we overestimated the desire of players to get into camp once they saw rookies trying to take their jobs? Had we underestimated management and its strength? As the regular season started, the answer seemed clear, and it was "Yes!" to all of the above.

It is not difficult to get roasted in the press. When mistakes are made in a highly publicized dispute, the press is merciless in assessing blame. Given the antipathy of the press toward our goals to begin with, our loss of the strike was fuel for their fire. Granted, we had made mistakes, but why couldn't they see that management had tried to break the union? Why wouldn't one of them other than Larry Batson in Minneapolis, Red Smith in New York, and Dick Basoco in Baltimore even ask who should shoulder the blame on the other side of the table? And management would now go to work to seal my fate. If Rozelle had suggested to Mackey that players would have received a million dollars more in the pension fund if it had not been for Dan Shulman's militancy in 1968, what would they say about *my* militancy, which made Shulman look almost like a sweetheart?

The answers soon came filtering back to our offices from the teams and league office, who were hoping to undermine future activism with the same old promises: "If it had not been for the introduction to the demands . . . if you had said 'proposals' instead of 'demands' . . . the picket lines were the last straw; we were willing to compromise, but those picket signs . . . the clenched fist made us determined to fight . . . the freedom demands would destroy the game, and we were not going to sit by and watch Garvey and a few militant Blacks destroy the game we love . . ."

Although management's reaction was predictable, my concern was with the reaction of our own members. The most troubling questions were how management would react to our decision to return to work and how the union would survive when owners started to punish our leadership.

One of the outstanding people to emerge from the strike was tight end Pettis Norman. Here was a real leader, although never an elected player rep, in part because he played most of his career in conservative Dallas. When we walked the first picket lines in San Diego, it was Norman who said, "No cause worth fighting for has been won unless people were willing to go to jail for the cause." And he was ready to go. (Some of our players did go to jail in Green Bay when they were arrested for picketing: Ken Bowman, Norm Thompson, Mac Percival, Joe Moore, Dave Hale, Glen Holloway, Willie Holman, MacArthur Lane, Cal Withrow, Paul Staroba, Larry Krause, Dick Himes, Tom McLeod, Scott Hunter, Clarence Williams, Carlton Oats, Rich McGeorge, Bill Lueck, Bill Hayhoe, and Gale Gillingham.)

Pettis told the rookies, "If they have enslaved us . . . they will enslave you." Norman, like many of us, saw the 1974 strike as a part of the Civil Rights Movement, as a strike for dignity; a strike against discrimination and racism; a strike for due process and fairness. After the strike, Norman failed the physical exam, as we knew he would. After standing on that car in front of Prothro and his staff, there was no way Norman would be welcomed back to the Chargers.

I called Pettis at a particularly low point in September and asked if he would come to Washington to spend the weekend with my family. I told him that I needed help. Two days later, he was in our house. During that weekend, Pettis explained his belief about the players. He said, first of all, that those who had believed in the struggle would understand the overwhelming strength of management and its decision to break us. Black players understood from the outset that this was a struggle for civil rights, and they would support the union. And then Pettis wisely counseled that we continue the same openness and honesty that had saved us throughout the strike by admitting that we had indeed lost the battle, saying, "Players understand winning and they understand losing better than almost any other people in our society because they face it every Sunday. They do not understand, nor do they accept, a tie. So let's face it. We lost, and you should tell them we lost. More than that, you can tell them that this has been one step in the overall battle and that we will eventually win because of the attitudes that were changed during this loss."

That was the best advice that I could have received in 1974 or, for that matter, at any time thereafter.

Before heading out to visit all twenty-six teams, our staff counsel Dick Berthelsen and I made one more visit to John Thompson's office in New York. He was still the negotiator for the NFL. Nothing had changed except that they had recovered from the anger of our cooling-off maneuver and now they were like buzzards waiting to pick the carcass of any remaining meat. They knew the end was in sight. The message was clear. The NFL would not check off NFLPA dues from player paychecks, nor would they cooperate in any way with the union's survival. They would go for the jugular.

Tom Keating always urged me to visit every team, even when I got sick and tired of airports, rent-a-car booths, and lousy meals, not to mention being away from my family. He argued persuasively that it was important for the players to have the opportunity to raise questions and criticize us for everything that had gone wrong. While some of the questioning that year was initially hostile, almost every team visit was a pleasure. (Miami was no bargain, however, as players blamed me for the loss of their All-Star Game check.)

Once I admitted that we had made mistakes and once the initial questioning was over, I could concentrate on the battle ahead: The *Mackey* case. After all, players crossing picket lines was the reason we lost. We spent hours in meetings talking about the power of management and how they used the press to their advantage. We discussed the vulnerability of the NFLPA and our underestimation of management's reaction to questioning of, and possible abolition of, the reserve system.

When I started the three-month trek around the country, I feared it would be a disaster, but I ended with a strong belief in our ultimate success. I was convinced that the players would pay dues, support the lawsuit, and stay loyal to the cause. We would have to bob and weave for a while, or, more appropriately as Muhammad Ali said, "rope-a-dope" them for a year or two and then deliver a punch.

More than a few in the association leadership felt otherwise. Several writers suggested that if I were thrown out, management would bargain with the union, and some players believed those stories. Rozelle and Co. were experts at getting rid of people in the NFLPA: John Gordy, Bernie Parrish, Dan Shulman, John Mackey, and now Kermit Alexander, Tom Keating, and Del Williams. I would be next. This time they knew that they would succeed and return to the sweetheart days. Yes, there would have to be concessions. No, things would never be quite the same after the 1974 war, but as long as the basic power relationships continued, they could afford to throw some bones to those who would get me out. "Garvey" had become a code word used to describe the "militant Blacks" and "crazy whites" who had dominated the NFLPA since 1970.

To start with in 1974, Houston management cut Bill Curry, the president of the NFLPA. Objective types within the union conceded that Curry had not properly recovered from a knee injury of the previous season, and though he expected to get cut, it still shocked him when the axe fell. Suddenly he was without a job and without a career. He returned to Atlanta and waited to hear from other teams. Never one to miss a trick, Carroll Rosenbloom called Curry and asked him to fly to LA for a tryout. When Curry called me with the "good news," I warned him that Rosenbloom would hire him for a price and that the price would be more than a few months on the field. Curry said he understood, and soon he had signed a contract and a few days later was on his way across the country for a secret meeting at Pete Rozelle's home. Curry called from JFK Airport to tell me about the scheduled meeting but cautioned me not to tell anyone else. I said that I couldn't operate that way and that both of us had an obligation to inform the Executive Committee of all such contacts.

Curry met with Rozelle at his home, and the two "just talked." A second meeting was arranged, but this time Rozelle would come to LA and meet alone with Curry at the Rosenbloom estate in Bel Air. By now Kermit Alexander, Tom Keating, Alan Page, Willie Holman, and others had been informed about the meetings, and they were understandably cynical. Seeds of doubt were sown among the committee members because we never received a detailed report of the meetings but broad hints were being dropped by management that "progress was being made by the more reasonable people in our committee and *certain* management people." It didn't take a genius to figure out that I was *not* one of the reasonable people, nor was Kermit Alexander. Curry was.

Despite my positive reading of the players' attitudes, Curry soon started assuring me that there was a revolt brewing among players. The fact that only three hundred players had paid dues at the end of the season seemed to lend credence to his prediction of doom, but I couldn't believe a revolt was underway because my experiences with the team meetings indicated otherwise. I had heard similar warnings before our actions in 1970. Maybe I was crazy. Maybe I was looking through rose-colored glasses or, as writers kept chanting, I was trying to "save my job."

The rest of the committee seemed solid, despite pressure from management. Kermit Alexander had joined the staff after losing his job in Philadelphia. A constant source of strength, he had, after all, made the sacrifice of putting his job as a player on the line for the union and its cause. There weren't a lot of players in the NFL who could look Kermit in the eye and say that he was doing this for a selfish reason.

Tom Keating was now with Coach Hank Stram and the Kansas City Chiefs; the league could get to a lot of people, but not to Tom. After Pittsburgh refused to allow Keating to practice with veterans or to play a single down in the preseason following the cooling-off period, Chuck Noll waived him. Hank Stram of the Chiefs claimed him. Stram talked with Keating, telling him that some people had "warned" him about his union activity but assuring him that he would get fair treatment in Kansas City, and he did.

Alan Page called twice a week to say hello and to keep up morale.

Willie Brown, the great defensive back from Oakland, rarely called, but we always knew we could count on him.

Ken Bowman had been cut by Green Bay and was now with Hawaii of the WFL, so he was out of touch. Few had given as much to the union as Ken. Whatever gains we made, much was largely due to his persistence. We badly needed him in 1974, but he was out of the NFL for good.

Only Curry and Ed Podolak of Kansas City talked of revolt from our constituents against our leadership. Others talked of the courts as our only hope. As the season came to a close, we started last-minute preparations for the *Mackey* case, which was finally to go to trial on February 3, 1975. Despite the fact that our friends at FMCS were no longer interested in our plight, and despite the fact that the NLRB had still done nothing about the owners' illegal conduct that helped them defeat us in 1974, there was a glimmer of light at the end of the tunnel. (We joked in the office that it might well be an onrushing locomotive, but we saw it nevertheless.)

As I prepared for trial, the staff pledged to get a majority of players to pay dues before the critical meeting of the Board of Representatives in mid-February. This would give the staff a month to get the dues paid and put an end to the charge that the players would never support the union without a collective bargaining agreement. Those who wanted us out and who wanted the NFLPA to become more moderate were actually hoping that a majority of players would *not* pay dues, in order to buttress their own arguments about our lack of support. By the time the board meeting took place, we were a majority union, thanks in part to Joe Kapp's court victory, which gave everyone hope that we could also win. Some reps got nearly 100 percent of their teammates to pay. We had survived.

We thought that once we started the *Mackey* case there was little anyone could do to sell out the union. I sat with John Mackey at a restaurant in Minneapolis on the night of February 3, 1975, and said, "John, you got me into this battle, and I told you I would never desert the players as long as the fight was on. I now feel like I have fulfilled that commitment, because we now have them in court and the system will fall."

John agreed that the opening day of court was the beginning of the end for the NFL system, which he characterized best as "an arbitrary abuse of power." But he warned that the battle was far from over.

The first two weeks of trial went so well that when we opened the Executive Committee meeting preceding the board meeting, I was almost exuberant about the prospects for the future. That optimism ended abruptly. The first public indication of a revolt came in a wire service story from New Orleans. Rick Kingrea, the new player rep for the Saints, was quoted as saying that he was coming to the board meeting to find out "how much Garvey earns and whether or not he is worth it." He added that he favored "firing Garvey." I was used to writers going after me, but I was not used to the idea of a player rep calling for my ouster. It was okay with me if outsiders or players who weren't involved went after us, but when a rep started, it stung.

I had never met Kingrea and had never heard of him as a player, and I thought it a bit odd that he would be issuing press statements about firing me, so I called him. Kingrea hemmed and hawed and said he was "misquoted." My first indication that he had indeed been quoted accurately came from Del Williams, who had been the player rep for New Orleans during the strike. Williams called to tell me about a conversation he had just had with Dick Gordon, former astronaut and then general manager of the Saints. Gordon was bragging to Williams that "this time we are going to get Garvey. There are enough votes on the board to oust him." To put it mildly, Gordon was happy, according to Williams, who was concerned enough to fly to the meeting, paying his own way. I thanked him for the information but assured him that "our people" would survive the Rick Kingreas of the world (that is, I hoped we would).

By the start of the meeting, various friends heard that there would be "serious charges" made against me by certain officers of the union and that once the reps heard these charges, my dismissal would be inevitable. When asked about the nature of the charges, all they would get was "Wait till the meeting."

The first day of the rep meeting began with little indication of trouble, except for unmistakable tension in the air. There were caucuses all over the place and unusual attention paid to everything said from the chair. Those who had never paid attention before, and who never would again, feigned great interest in every statement.

After a couple of hours of discussion, including my report on the progress of the *Mackey* lawsuit, Dick Anderson, the newly elected player rep from the Dolphins, raised his hand and was recognized. (Anderson's predecessor, Doug Swift, was one of the most outspoken and militant reps throughout the strike.) Anderson told me the Dolphins had given him a mandate to call for my resignation. I asked if he was putting that in the form of a motion. He said he was. I then asked for a second to the motion, and Joe Beauchamp from San Diego quickly seconded it. This was Anderson's first meeting. Of all of the reps, only Brig Owens, Dan Dierdorf, and Reggie McKenzie had attended a meeting of the board before. With that, I announced that the motion had been made and seconded and that the floor was open for discussion.

I handed the gavel to President Curry, left the stage, and walked down the steps to sit among the player reps. Now we would hear those "serious charges" of impropriety. Now rumors would cease; we would get down to the facts.

The debate, if one could call it that, centered more on tactics of the 1974 strike than anything else. The most serious accusation was that I "cared too much about freedom for the players and had therefore lost perspective." There was also a "charge" that the introduction to the demands had not been cleared with the Executive Committee before it was given to the owners, but five of the seven members of the committee denied that charge since they had reviewed it before sending it to management. Throughout the four-hour discussion, Bill Curry remained silent in the chair. Those who wished to dump me counted Curry among their number, and they waited for Curry to drop the axe.

Finally, one of the anti-Garvey group asked Curry for his comments. To our surprise, he said that he had nothing but respect for the job I had performed and that he felt all players would be indebted to me eventually. He suggested that we operate differently but said he knew I was honest.

Tom Keating, until that point silent, walked to the front of the room and started talking about how he felt after Chuck Noll cut him: "Not one Pittsburgh player called me to say 'sorry' or 'thanks' or even 'goodbye.'" He admonished the reps to remember that no one in this business should expect any thanks from the players but that if the reps were going to fire people every time something went wrong, then when they hire my replacement, they should tell him that he only has a job just as long as "we don't lose anything."

The battle was over. Someone called for the vote, and it was four votes in favor of my resignation, eighteen against, and two abstentions. Dick Gordon was wrong—they didn't have the votes. Now we could concentrate on the *Mackey* case.

I forgot to mention that management had been so convinced that I would be fired that our lone bargaining session in late January before the board meeting was a joke. Kheel and Schramm literally laughed at me and Kermit Alexander. You could see it written all over their faces that soon there would be new negotiators for the union—no need to deal with us. Someone on our side was talking to them. As our meeting ended, I walked up to Tex Schramm with a smile and stuck out my hand. "I'll see you in Minneapolis, Tex." I left no doubt that I knew what they were thinking and that we were not about to go away. A month later, I got my chance to welcome Schramm to Minneapolis, as I sat at the counsel table and helped prepare his cross-examination, one of many little pleasures.

In May, Bill Curry resigned, and Kermit Alexander became union president. This was a heavy blow for Schramm and Co., as they had to put up with us for another year. But they never slept. They still had cards to play.

6

We Finally Get Them into Court

W e were more than a bit apprehensive as we arrived in Minneapolis on February 1, 1975, eleven months after we had first presented our demands for the next contract between the league and the players. The Executive Committee decided to meet on the eve of the trial to discuss strategy and to be present for the historic opening of the *Mackey* trial. It seemed unbelievable that we were finally starting the trial after waiting nearly three years, during which we saw the NFLPA almost go under in the 1974 labor battle. But here we were, and it did not seem possible that the NFL could stop us from proceeding. While we knew from the past that the NFL "never settles," one of our attorneys was convinced that the NFL would make a settlement offer on the eve of the trial. The *Mackey* case was filed on May 22, 1972. Management's public hand-wringing began at once.

"If this suit is successful, the NFL will be destroyed," wailed Tex Schramm, Jim Finks, Ralph Wilson, and others. Yet, if they believed their rhetoric, wouldn't it occur to them to offer to settle the suit before it actually got underway? I expected some half-hearted minimal offer, but it was business as usual for the NFL. No offers. If you wait for them to offer a settlement, you will get old fast.

Hamilton Carothers had accompanied Rozelle in 1961 when they bamboozled Congress into giving the NFL an exemption from antitrust laws for the purpose of pooling all NFL television rights. He had accompanied Rozelle to Congress when they sought and bought a merger exemption in

1966. Rozelle was quick to say, "Clear it with Ham." Rozelle had great confidence in Carothers, possibly because he was so limited in his own judgment on legal matters. On more than a few occasions when I was trying to work out the Kapp situation, he said to me, "Ham has never let me down—he has never lost a case."

And it was true. Carothers had never lost a case for his commissioner, but Rozelle failed to point out that no cases had ever made it to court during Carothers's reign as Rozelle's aide. And the reason should be obvious: The NFL had very deep pockets. They could outspend almost any adversary. Without question, they could outspend any player acting alone. Frankly, no one could afford to take on the NFL and "super lawyer" Carothers. The commissioner knew what all conglomerates know: The courts are, for the most part, friends of those with money.

But on February 3, 1975, Carothers had still not lost a case and had never been forced to try a case for the NFL. We expected some last-minute maneuver to stall the trial. Just a month before, Carothers had argued to Judge Earl Larson that the trial should be delayed because the plaintiffs were not ready for trial, a rather remarkable argument: "Delay the trial because our opponents aren't ready for trial!"

Our counsel, Ed Glennon, exploded. Glennon suggested that Carothers worry about *his* preparations, not ours! And, to our surprise, management actually was not ready for trial. Or maybe it was just Carothers who wasn't ready or who lost his nerve. The bully in the conference room, the tough guy against twenty-three-year-old athletes, the arrogant lawyer on the phone, the man who had sealed the fate of Joe Kapp and countless others, didn't have the nerve to face us in the real combat of the courtroom. A last-minute substitute was brought in: Jim McKay would handle the trial. Architect Carothers would remain on the sidelines.

All day on February 2, plaintiffs arrived in Minneapolis. John Mackey was one of the first. Welcomed by all, Mackey was truly the symbol of the fight we had undertaken for years. Players Dick Gordon, Charlie West, and Alan Page were all there for a quiet dinner together to review the past and speculate about the opening of the trial. And, yes, we hoped the league might contact us about settlement. As the evening ended, it was obvious that the thought of settlement was as foolish as our hopes of compromise in Joe Kapp's case or a legitimate offer in bargaining.

We were second to arrive at the courthouse. Mackey's lawyer, Ed Glennon, and his assistants had already laid claim to the counsel table directly in front of the witness chair. Six of their lawyers had gathered and were examining documents and buzzing about something. There were no greetings, no hellos. Then Alan Page arrived, and we settled down. It was not long before the clerk ordered, "All rise, this Honorable Court is now in session in the case of *John Mackey, et al. v. NFL, et al.*"

We were underway! Fifty-five years after the NFL was founded, player restraints would be tested in a trial for the first time. Ed Glennon stepped forward and outlined our position. We would show that the NFL had been engaged in, and was still engaged in, a conspiracy to violate the federal anti-trust laws. It was short but damned effective.

McKay stepped forward for the NFL. Whatever else he said, one statement he made to Judge Larson would remain with us throughout the trial and epitomize the NFL's arrogance: "Your Honor, this case is brought by some young men who have grown rich and famous beyond their wildest dreams by this great system which they now malign." There was a muffled roar in the gallery as West, Page, and others heard those words. "Beyond their wildest dreams" became our theme for the trial.

John Mackey was the first witness, and he did an excellent job on the stand. It soon became apparent to us that there was nothing the league attorneys could do except cause as much delay as possible. The illegality of the system seemed obvious. Our job was to describe it to the court, and the rest seemed relatively easy. They could make much of the high salaries that some of our plaintiffs and a few of our witnesses made, but so what? No matter how high their salaries, they would be higher without restraints. Their salaries were a small fraction of what the NFL owners made off their backs through monopolistic elimination of any competition for their labor. Though arguing that the NFL would collapse without the Rozelle Rule, management had to admit that players were damaged by the system. The Rozelle Rule obviously reduced salaries. Absent that admission, they couldn't argue that the NFL would "collapse without the draft and the Rozelle Rule." They were on the horns of a dilemma. For the first time in the NFL's fifty-five-year history, they would be forced to be consistent.

That night I had dinner with Mackey. We were both emotional about the day. As we sat there, we couldn't help but recall the problems of getting people to put their names on the line. Mackey was the first volunteer as the president of the NFLPA, and all of the player reps, except John Niland from Dallas and Nick Buoniconti from Miami, were quick to agree to show their support publicly for Mackey.

We also needed non-reps who had played out the option in 1971 and therefore ought to qualify for free agency, in a fairer league. Out of seventy-five to eighty, only ten volunteered as plaintiffs. Some begged off on the grounds that they had too much to risk or that "my lawyer/agent said I shouldn't." We met with the ten in Minneapolis before the suit was filed. All were Black except for Dan Conners of Oakland. They understood the risk of fighting for the freedom for those who would come after. We explained that their careers would be jeopardized if they put their names on the complaint, and each was asked to say something. Charlie West was one of the first, saying quietly, but with great eloquence, "If I have a son, I would like him to play in the NFL as a free man and a man of dignity. If I have to give up my career for that dream, I'm ready."

There was little left to say. Marlin Briscoe, Charlie West, Clint Jones, Ocie Austin, Dan Connors, John Williams, and Gene Washington said okay, and we were off to the courthouse. The NFL had done everything it could to paint us as Black as possible in the strike. Now they moved to eliminate the one white plaintiff from the lawsuit. On the eve of the trial, Dan Conners withdrew, because he wanted to become a coach. So now all of our plaintiffs, who had become "rich and famous beyond their wildest dreams," were Black, and the league loved it. What they didn't understand was that the racial makeup of the plaintiffs might sound important at league meetings and at their country clubs, but it would not count for much in court.

We had anticipated that the NFL would call a large number of witnesses, but we could never have anticipated the length of the *Mackey* trial. We began on February 3 with temperatures well below zero, and we ended on a hot muggy day in July. Fifty-five days of trial, forty-nine witnesses, hundreds of exhibits, and a lot of sweat went into the work. League attorneys called all of the irrelevant witnesses imaginable. They had but one theme throughout: "Without the Rozelle Rule, the NFL, as we know it today, will be destroyed."

They had TV executives; announcers such as Willie Davis and Bart Starr; coaches Don Shula, Hank Stram, and Chuck Noll; former players Gale Sayers, Paul Flatly, Frank Gifford, and Gino Marchetti; owners Art Modell, Tex Schramm, Paul Brown, Gerald Phipps, and Carroll Rosenbloom; and the league office, including Pete Rozelle and Jim Kensil. They brought in two people who had been enemies of players' rights for years, our old "friends," Congressman Jack Kemp and his protégé, Alan Miller. Pumping for the league was nothing new for either of them, but it was particularly obnoxious to many of the players to have Kemp and Miller testifying against us. After all, they once pretended to be on our side.

Bob Woolf, player agent and author, was one of their witnesses. We thought it strange for Woolf, a lawyer, to testify for the defendants when he had once represented one of our plaintiffs who was playing out his option. Nevertheless, Woolf agreed to testify.

NFL counsel began by qualifying Woolf as an expert by asking questions about all the athletes in various sports he had represented—hockey, basketball, football, and baseball. Yes, he had represented some of the biggest names in pro sports. Yes, he was an expert. Once finished with the preliminaries, they began to ask him about players' salaries. He agreed with his questioner that salaries were "out of line" and that something had to be done. He agreed that the leagues needed some restrictions on the athlete. He agreed that without restrictions the league would become unstable, teams would fold, and players would therefore lose job opportunities.

It seemed that Woolf was giving the league its best performance of the trial. He was the "objective" expert and was agreeing with the doomsayers in the NFL that "all will be lost without a reserve system." It seemed perfect, until Glennon asked his first question on cross-examination: "Mr. Woolf, when you testify that players' salaries are so high that they are jeopardizing the stability of the league, are you talking about *football* players?"

A pause. "No." Incredible, but their star witness was saying his testimony didn't relate to football players!

There was a stir at Covington's counsel table. "Who are you referring to, then?"

Woolf responded, "I'm talking about basketball and hockey players."

"Oh, I see. What do you think of salaries in the NFL, then?" Glennon asked.

"They are way too low."

"And, sir, in your expert opinion, tell the court why they are too low."

"Because of the Rozelle Rule," responded Woolf.

Unbelievable! Ten lawyers were working for the league, and their star witness testified that the heart of our attack on the NFL was absolutely correct. We almost laughed out loud.

By now, the stir at Covington's table had become an obvious effort to distract the court from the show on the witness stand. Woolf became *our* best witness.

Gino Marchetti was another surprise witness. I don't think Gino knew why they had called him, but he had agreed and testified that the Colts had a "family atmosphere" when Rosenbloom was there. The Covington lawyer had him explain the importance of good management on a team's performance, and then, almost as an afterthought, he asked: "Mr. Marchetti, you never played out the option in Baltimore, even though there was *no* Rozelle Rule at the time?"

"That's right."

"Why didn't you?"

Marchetti looked surprised by the question and literally blurted out the answer: "Everyone in the league knew that if you played out the option, you were through!"

Here was another witness informing the court that in the minds of the players, anyone who dared play out the option was added to a list shared among NFL teams at the initiative of the owners. The noise at counsel table started again. We asked a few questions on cross-examination, but we couldn't improve on the job that Covington had done.

Although the league's basic argument was grounded on economics, they called no economists, had no expert testimony on the effect of the draft or the Rozelle Rule, and instead relied on conclusions mouthed by witness after witness that "the game as we know it today will be destroyed." Almost unbelievable.

We produced two expert economists: Roger Noll, who had edited the Brookings Report on *Government and the Sports Business,* and George Burman, an eleven-year NFL veteran who had a Ph.D. in labor economics from the University of Chicago. League attorneys tried to discredit Noll because he hadn't played football and Burman because he played so much football that he didn't have time to publish much! Noll and Burman were excellent witnesses, and they destroyed the NFL's argument that there were no alternatives to the Rozelle Rule. Their basic point was that the free market would improve, not destroy, the game. The NFL couldn't shake their testimony.

I was at counsel table for all but two days of the trial. Trying to run the union and yet be in Minneapolis from February through mid-July was no mean feat. But Ed Glennon's work was nothing short of brilliant. To take on management's best every day for fifty-five days was an unbelievable task. Of those fifty-five grueling days, my biased account showed Glennon beating them on fifty-one of them. Whatever we gained, much of it can be traced back to one lawyer who fought the fight in the *Mackey* trial: Ed Glennon.

I was the final witness, and when management had finished cross-examination, we both rested. It was an emotional experience when they said they had no more witnesses. Enemies had been made during those fifty-five days, so there were few handshakes. We were frustrated by a legal system that allowed a monopoly like the NFL to bring up a parade of witnesses for the purpose of delay. The issues were simple and could have been presented by two or three witnesses on each side. But the NFL split its costs twenty-six ways. If it cost the NFL $2.6 million for fifty-five days, that was only a tax-deductible $100,000 per club or a real cost of $50,000. Why hurry? If they could stay long enough, they reasoned, they could ultimately get the players to settle the lawsuit. Players would become eager for peace. Maybe their representation would get expensive. Rozelle and the clubs would stress to the players: "What has Garvey ever done for you? You won't get a decision for years, and when you do, we will appeal it. You had better settle now." Many, including Dick Anderson, the Miami Dolphins' player rep who had called for my resignation, would buy that line of thinking.

Many things would happen before Judge Larson's historic decision. The Patriots would strike, and a few teams would go with them. The players would vote on two offers from management calculated to defeat the lawsuit, and there would be one more attempt to get rid of me. But, ultimately, on December 29, 1975, Judge Larson ruled that the Rozelle Rule was a per se violation of the federal antitrust laws. We were on the way to victory.

Six months later, Judge William Bryant would rule that the common draft was a violation of the antitrust laws. By the fall of 1976, when the Eighth Circuit upheld Judge Larson's ruling, we could finally say that we had beaten the NFL at its own game. They could bribe veterans to cross picket lines, and they could impress the sports media, but they couldn't sway the courts.

7

The Year of the Patriots—1975

The *Mackey* trial ended as training camps opened throughout the league. Because Glennon had done such a remarkable job, we were regaining our confidence in the ultimate success of the union. Team visits this year would be fun compared with our visits of a year before.

As we approached the end of the 1975 preseason, the union leadership was pleased, almost cocky, about the future of the NFLPA. The *Kapp* case had given us a shot of adrenalin in late 1974. We needed it to become a majority union to get through the rep meeting and to continue the *Mackey* case, which was now before the court, with confidence.

At a staff meeting in mid-August, all present expressed confidence that the players would pay dues this year because of the *Kapp* case and because our marathon trial was over. We called a rep meeting for late August primarily to assess our strength. We had asked every team to meet so each rep could come to the board meeting fully informed on player attitudes. Would they authorize a selective strike? Should the Pro Bowl be the target? If there was no contract this year, would they pay dues to keep the fight going in Congress, the courts, and the NLRB?

Three days before the meeting, Alan Page, who had just completed two courses at the University of Texas Law School, called me at home. He had left the Vikings team meeting early in utter disgust because the focus seemed to him the same as a year ago. Fran Tarkenton argued that it was the *union's* fault that there was no collective bargaining agreement. Tarkenton didn't suggest what the union could do to pressure owners into a more reasonable posture; he thought firing me was all that was needed.

At 7:00 A.M. the next day, I received a surprise call from Jim Klobuchar, an on-again, off-again sports-style writer in Minneapolis. I had sometimes admired his writings but strangely had never talked with him before. He asked if I had heard about the Vikings meeting. I said, "Yes, but only a few comments from Alan."

He went on, "Did the player rep, Ed White, call you?"

"No." Now I was considering what in hell could have happened.

He said, "Let me read a press statement the players issued at two A.M.: 'By a near unanimous vote, the Vikings players ask for Ed Garvey's resignation. His interests and those of the players are at odds.' Any comments?" Klobuchar asked.

"No."

"Did Alan Page ask you to resign?"

I responded, "Are you kidding? If Alan Page ever told me to resign, I would. He is one of my best friends."

"Will you resign?"

"No. I work for all twenty-six teams, not just the Vikings, but if a majority of the board wants me to, of course I will resign."

When I left for the office, it occurred to me that management was making one last-ditch effort to get rid of the current leadership and the lawsuit. The bellwether would be Dallas. If Dallas voted the same way, then we could be sure of a conspiracy. Schramm and Rozelle were at work again. Buffalo and Cincinnati would follow suit. If nothing came out of Dallas, then maybe the Vikings vote was a case of isolated frustration.

I called Jean Fugett, who had just resigned as the Cowboys' player rep, but he was unavailable. I spoke with Roger Staubach and asked if he would be in Chicago for the rep meeting. He said Blaine Nye and John Fitzgerald would be there as the new rep and alternate. Then he reluctantly explained that they, too, had voted for my resignation because "you won't compromise on the Rozelle Rule." We had a long conversation about the compromises we had suggested to the league, and Staubach ended up saying, "I feel like a hypocrite voting to fire you on poor information." I laughed and suggested that Dallas and Minnesota don't run the union so he shouldn't worry, but I suggested that next time he check with someone other than Tex Schramm before making judgments.

My primary concern was that the player reps might be pressured to drop their support of the *Mackey* case. Would the board snatch defeat from the jaws of victory? How successful had management been at team meetings in convincing players to give up on the *Mackey* case and to fire their "militant" leadership? To say the least, we were eager, but a little apprehensive, to hear from other player reps.

The day before the rep meeting, Pete Rozelle was interviewed on national TV by Howard Cosell at the Kennedy Celebrity Tennis Tournament. Cosell asked Pete if he agreed with the Vikings' call for my resignation. After a slight hesitation, Rozelle seemed to redden, and then he said that "it might help get an agreement." I thought it incredible that he would show his hand on national TV, an indication that there was a serious effort by the NFL to get rid of me again.

Dick Anderson, who had been the first player to call for my removal at the previous year's meeting, was first to arrive in Chicago. He said that other teams had voted on whether I should be fired and that he thought it would be a tough meeting. (How did he know? Who suggested a vote?) Anderson was a management favorite, and he obviously knew the results of the votes but wasn't saying. Then he said that Wellington Mara had told him that the owners' committee was ready to come to Chicago to present a new bargaining proposal "after Garvey is fired." Anderson's task was to call Mara after I got fired and tell them when to catch a plane!

The rest of the reps arrived, and Kermit Alexander opened the meeting by saying that if anyone had anything to say about the leadership of the union, to say it now. Silence. Then he asked me to bring everyone up to date on the *Mackey* case and the NLRB proceedings. The "crisis" was over. The Vikings were unrepresented, and that made everyone angry, the sentiment being, "Come to the meeting and say it—don't tell the press and then not have the nerve to show up!" Dallas and Buffalo kept quiet. Another management-orchestrated revolt was over. Not even Tarkenton's phone calls to other reps had helped. League management had again overestimated its influence on player opinion.

We talked about strike possibilities, discussed delaying games to screw up the television people, skipping practices, and holding a general strike. About half the teams said they could strike—half, including the Patriots, said they couldn't. Most were depending on the *Mackey* case's outcome.

I then suggested some alternatives: (1) call a selective strike, involving only a few teams; (2) forget about a strike, collect dues, and wait for the court's decision on *Mackey*; and (3) pressure the owners to come up with an offer by setting a deadline of September 1 and then submit that to the players for a vote.

The board rallied to the third option. It would force players to get involved by showing how little was being offered, or it would force owners to come up with a decent offer. In any event, it would take some pressure off the union leadership. If the players turned down any underwhelming offer, it wouldn't be "Ed Garvey's fault" or "Kermit Alexander's fault" or even the "board's fault"—it would be the players speaking out.

This was a risky course of action because we knew the owners would put up some money to "buy" the Rozelle Rule. But we all seemed to feel that if the players wanted a bad contract, so be it.

We then boxed management into a meeting. I called the federal mediator, told him that Mara and the committee planned to fly to Chicago, and asked if he would be willing to fly in. (I "forgot" to tell him that Mara told Anderson that they would fly in "after Garvey was fired." Oh well, a minor condition.) Searce, the FMCS mediator, agreed and then called Mara. Mara couldn't refuse, nor could he condition a session on my firing when discussing it with the mediator.

By 2:00 P.M. we learned that the NFL Management Council was flying to Chicago. We had set the trap. Nearly all the reps wanted to sit in on the meeting because only a few had ever witnessed a bargaining session. Now they would see Ted Kheel, Sarge Karch, and Wellington Mara firsthand. We would educate a new group of reps.

The owners wanted to exclude the player reps, but Oakland's Gene Upshaw said, "Let's all go over, and they can tell *me* we aren't welcome." The vote was almost unanimous for all to go. When the federal mediator learned of the decision, he panicked and threatened to return to Washington. Kermit told him there was a plane leaving every hour. The mediator quickly called to "warn" the owners that we were all coming over. Dick Anderson was so upset he didn't arrive for nearly an hour.

Jack Youngblood, Fred Willis, Al Clark, Bruce Gossett, Tom Banks, Doug Van Horn, Gene Upshaw, and Willie Brown were just some of the players who went to the owners' palatial suite. Schramm, Mara, Kheel, and Karch were there with their PR man. To describe them as nervous would be an understatement. Owners never like to meet with players in a group—none like to expose their true positions in front of players. If the players hear it firsthand, it's that much harder to distort, harder to say, "Did you hear what Garvey did?"

In some ways, this was to be the most humorous session of all. The owners sat at a small table in the center of the room, while the players were arrayed on a huge wall-length couch. To Kheel's consternation, Oakland rep Gene Upshaw put a chair on the opposite site of the table from him. Gene was so imposing a presence that Mara and Kheel had to look around him to address players directly. Kheel actually became afraid of Upshaw, and once, when Kheel started his usual act of outtalking everyone, Upshaw pointed at him and said, "You shut up. We want to hear from Tex." Kheel shut up for a while, but only a while.

When Kheel went into his act, he insisted that the union agree to negotiate on removing the Rozelle Rule; it was time "to remove it [the issue] from the court." I responded that it was illegal and therefore not a mandatory subject of bargaining and that the court case would go on. I pointed out that we had just concluded a fifty-five-day trial and that the matter would be decided by the court. We were, nevertheless, willing to discuss the subject in return for a commitment to negotiate all *other* subjects. We told them that whatever was on the bargaining table on September 1 would be sent to the players for a vote. They seemed to know our position in advance. Had Anderson briefed them? They started getting excited because they believed that it was only the "militant leadership" and not the members who wanted freedom. When they agreed to negotiate everything, we suggested six alternatives to the Rozelle Rule.

- No team that finished in the playoffs could sign a free agent the following off-season.
- We could set a limit on the number of free agents a club could sign in one year.
- We could agree on a maximum budget for player salaries.
- An impartial arbitrator could name a draft-choice compensation for the team losing its free agent from the signing team in advance of the player's signing.
- If the team desirous of the player doesn't have the requested draft choice, the team would have to pay to the team losing the player whatever the team offered the player in terms of salary.
- Salary arbitration plus draft choices could be named in advance.

These arrangements maintained some principle of the Rozelle Rule for the league, with signing teams compensating the team losing the free agent or with other protections holding free agency in check, while preserving some degree of free agency for players by making those protections predictable and outside the commissioner's arbitrary discretion. The owners said they were pleased to receive these ideas and would "consider them" overnight. When we then insisted on negotiations on impartial arbitration, minimum salary, squad size, and pension, they suddenly became quite "tired." Kheel urged a break until Wednesday; he knew all reps would be gone by then, so we protested. Finally, Kheel said that their full committee was waiting to be called to Chicago and that they would meet with us at 2:00 P.M. on Tuesday, to give us a better idea of their "package offer."

We left at 1:30 A.M., and I knew we wouldn't see them again. They had accomplished their goal—or at least they thought they had. This was the first on-the-record discussion of the Rozelle Rule, and they were almost giddy with the prospect of running into court to say that we had "negotiated on the rule." More than that, they thought they could convince the players to accept a restrictive system. The players' vote was their hope.

At 7:00 A.M. the following day, Minneapolis sportswriter Dick Gordon called and said he had been told we were "dismissing the *Mackey* case and negotiating the Rozelle Rule." I assured him that that was *not* true; that we could not settle the *Mackey* case; that we strongly believed the rule was illegal and had proven it in court.

Our fears were confirmed. Within the hour, Searce, the mediator, called to say that Kheel had returned to New York City and that therefore the Management Council saw no reason for a bargaining session, a position he agreed with. I insisted strongly that we have a meeting. They had promised to stay and negotiate all issues, and our people had stayed over for it. He called back and said they would come over at 12:30 P.M. for an "informal" session.

Kermit Alexander and I drafted a letter to make our position clear: Any change in the Rozelle Rule would have to be approved by the antitrust counsel before it could be submitted to the players. We would give the letter to them at 12:30 P.M.

Blowup

Tex Schramm, Jim Finks, George Halas, Wellington Mara, and attorney Sargent Karch came over at 12:30 P.M. They were in a great mood, laughing and talking. "Smug" would best describe their attitude.

We sat down and talked for a while about inane subjects. Schramm was upset about rookies who get paid when they get hurt. He wondered aloud if we could somehow agree not to pay them. I laughed, and Schramm got angry. "This isn't funny, goddammit! No wonder you can't make a deal. You don't even know how to talk."

I explained that the humor rested in the fact that after two years of negotiations, we were no longer discussing freedom; we were, instead, listening to a desire to screw rookies out of $10,000. He wasn't amused. We then discussed the mechanics of getting the new offer out to the players with our ballot.

When it appeared the meeting was almost over, I handed them the letter. It was like someone taking the cap off a geyser. To put it mildly, they went bananas.

Karch started asking questions, but by now Tex Schramm had seen enough. He was on his feet pacing and shaking the letter. Finally, he spurted, "Ed, what the hell is this—what the hell is this?"

I explained that some might have misunderstood our position on the Rozelle Rule and that this just cleared it up. Schramm said, "I thought you were going to submit our proposal to the players without a recommendation!"

"We are, Tex, but if any part of it is illegal, then we have a duty to advise the players of the illegality. If it's illegal, it wouldn't do any good if the players voted in favor. We would be back where we started." This was the fundamental difference. The NFL said that even if it's illegal, they could sprinkle holy water on it, put it in an agreement, and make it legal. We disagreed.

Schramm exploded. "I guarantee you that we will not make a proposal on option compensation that your lawyers will consider to be legal!"

I almost laughed as Kermit looked at Schramm, who was hovering over us, and said, "I wouldn't have said that, Tex."

Mara then started shouting that we were back to March 16, 1974: "Nothing has changed." Schramm was so nervous he was having trouble opening his briefcase.

We suggested a break and headed for the door. Alexander and Ray May, the Broncos' player rep, were the last ones out of the room. Mara rose and threw his yellow pad on the table. Alexander smiled and shut the door.

The mediator was ashen. He had not seen anything like it and asked if we would withdraw the letter. We said no and then returned to the room. Little was said, but Schramm was shaking so badly he couldn't hold the letter in his hands. Dick Anderson tried in vain to explain that all we were saying was that we would have to check everything out with our lawyers, just as they would. Then Anderson suggested that if "we like it and our lawyers say it is illegal, we will get different lawyers." An intriguing possibility!

Karch responded by suggesting that the committee didn't understand what I was "pulling" here. As if he were exposing a complete fraud, Karch said, "Dick, he is even quoting from a Supreme Court decision! Don't you see what he is trying to do?" It was interesting that they all talked to Dick Anderson—not to me and not to the president of the union, Kermit Alexander.

They thought they could buy the Rozelle Rule by going directly to the players, as if the law were whatever the NFL collectively decided. The letter let them know that we would still consider it illegal—even if accepted by the players—because it would have been *bought, not negotiated.*

They were unhappy as they departed Chicago.

––––––––––

On Thursday, August 28, I held a press conference announcing that a vote of the players would be taken on the NFL's offer. Immediately, the NFL Management Council said there would be no offer "because of the roadblock created by Garvey's legal letter of the 16th." Once again, they blamed it all on me.

We had been concerned about the logistics of getting the proposal to the players, but with no new offer forthcoming, our task was easier. We took the pending proposal given on July 23 and summarized all major points. We sent a comparison of the economics of the NFL's proposal with the amount needed if a cost-of-living increase had been granted. Their offer would not come close to a cost-of-living increase. On Labor Day, we gathered at the office to copy, stuff, and mail the "offer" to the players.

We had begun hearings on the owners' illegal conduct during the 1974 strike at the New York regional office of the NLRB in early August, two weeks after the *Mackey* trial ended. The hearings dragged on as management tried to stall the proceedings to avoid judgment day. It had been incredible. Fifty-five days in the *Mackey* trial, a short break, the NLRB hearings, then the rep meeting in Chicago. We had a three-day summer.

We nervously awaited the results of the players' vote. "If it's close, we are in trouble," Alexander said. He was right.

Throughout the week of September 8, votes piled in. I called a press conference for Wednesday the tenth to announce a near unanimous, 910–11, rejection of the offer. This time, the *players* rejected the offer, *not* the leaders. Maybe the owners would get the message.

A few days later, I left for Atlanta, where I was to speak to a lawyers' group on antitrust law and pro sports. Before leaving, I talked with player rep Randy Vataha, who said the New England Patriots wanted to strike. I didn't take it too seriously because it was clear that we couldn't get a two-thirds authorization from the full NFLPA, and I never imaged a team striking alone. Nevertheless, we did send a message to the reps asking them to poll their players on whether to strike. We assumed a negative response.

I left feeling that everything was going relatively well. We were regaining momentum. The *Mackey* case would soon be decided. The players had clearly rejected the owners' offer. And the fear of the unknown was now on the owners. They would still have to worry about a strike.

Just before I spoke in Atlanta, a messenger told me to call my office immediately. I always fear the worst on those occasions. When I called, staff member Gary Ballman told me that player rep Tom Banks had just phoned to say that the St. Louis Cardinals were considering a strike of their Sunday preseason game against Denver. I told Gary to tell Tom to hang on, that I would call as soon as possible, and I went back and gave a speech about the illegality of the NFL system.

After the speech, we learned that the Cardinals would vote on Saturday and that the Patriots would decide the same day whether to strike their game with the Jets. I grabbed the jammed Eastern Airlines flight through a thunderstorm back to DC. When we arrived at the office at 5:00 P.M., everyone was excited. It could happen! Only the Patriots-Jets and the Broncos-Cardinals games remained to be played on the Sunday before the opening game. It was to be a CBS doubleheader.

Randy Vataha from the Patriots was on the phone again: "If we strike, could we get protection? Would it be legal? What about liability?"

I had told Dick Berthelsen from Atlanta to get the answers from Lindquist and Vennum. If players were fined or fired, we might not have been able to protect them, but Leonard Lindquist advised, "If they stick together, they will be okay."

The Patriots were scheduled to play the Jets at the Yale Bowl. The Cardinals and Broncos were scheduled for Denver.

At midnight, I made my last call to Vataha: "Call before you leave for practice in the morning. Let's think about it tonight."

No one on the staff really thought the Pats would do it, but what if they did? It was fun again.

6:30 A.M.: Saturday, September 13, I was up making notes: "If they do . . . if they don't . . ."

7:00 A.M.: I got Leonard Lindquist out of bed: "Tell them to go ahead if they know they could be discriminated against. Whatever they do . . . stick together."

7:30 A.M.: I called Kermit Alexander, union president, at 4:30 A.M. his time and said, "We will back them. Pay for any fines, et cetera. Good luck."

9:00 A.M.: I called Vataha. "We will protect you every way possible. We will pay any fines. Our lawyers will be at your disposal. But it's up to you guys. Frankly, Randy, I'd have to recommend against it. The risks are too great—the owners too vicious. We can still wait for the *Mackey* decision."

"I agree," said Vataha. "But I don't know what my team will do. I'm going to recommend against it to see if they really understand."

"Hey, if you do it, we will do everything for you. Good luck. If you do strike, set a meeting for tomorrow to keep everyone together."

10:30 A.M.: Tom Banks of the Cardinals called. "I think our guys will do it. I'll call you back after the vote."

12 Noon: No word.

12:30 P.M.: No word.

1:30 P.M.: The bus was scheduled to leave the Patriots training site for the Yale Bowl, where the game was scheduled for the next day.

2:00 P.M.: Vataha, on speakerphone, asked me, "If we strike and the other teams don't go out with us, would you give a no-strike pledge to get us off the hook?" I understood that Vataha was seeking protection for himself and his teammates, so I quickly responded, "Yes. If other players around the league won't support you, why not?"

Another player's voice: "If others won't support us, we will withdraw from the union."

"I understand. I wouldn't blame you. I would resign, as would Kermit and the others. Tom Keating said it all just now on the phone: 'It's either the beginning or the end.'"

Vataha concluded the discussion: "I'll get back to you after we meet with the players."

3:00 P.M.: Vataha called. "They went home. The buses are gone. We are on strike! I've got to meet with management, and I'll call you back."

All hell broke loose in our office. Nobody in the country knew what the hell was going on, but within minutes the phones were going crazy. AP, United Press International (UPI), WBZ, CBS, with more than a "news" interest, wanted all the details—for their own understanding or for Pete Rozelle's? We had earlier told Tom Seppy of AP to stay in touch with us in case a story broke.

Now what would we say? We couldn't reach the Jets. What would they do? Camera crews started arriving at the office. We wanted to keep the focus on New England, not us.

We arrived at the Sheraton Park at 7:30 P.M. for a dinner honoring R******s quarterback Sonny Jurgensen. There was more excitement on the faces of R******s players Billy Kilmer, Ron McDole, Len Hauss, Brig Owens, Bill Brundige, and Diron Talbert than I had seen since our convention in March 1974.

"By God, they have done it!" shouted Kilmer.

Others said, "This is great. We're with them. What can we do?"

I said, "Come to the office tomorrow and convince other teams to support them."

They said they would be there at 2:30 P.M. the next day to call other players for support.

The dinner went on.

The NFL was now awake and moving quickly. Our PR man, Joe Blair, came to me when dinner began and indicated that Jim Searce, the federal mediator, had just called and dictated a message he planned on releasing to the press. Searce knew from management that within the hour the Patriots team would be meeting at a local restaurant, the Red Snapper, in Foxborough, and I assumed there was contact between the federal mediator and Sargent Karch, who was undoubtedly going crazy trying to frustrate strike activity.

The message from Searce said in part, "I urge the Patriots to forgo strike activity as any strike at this time will impede negotiations." But there were no negotiations! How in the hell would the strike "impede negotiations" when the owners had refused to meet with us or even make a new offer?

I immediately called Searce. "Jim, this is Ed. What in the hell do you think you're doing? Who asked you to say anything? Impede negotiations, my ass! There aren't any negotiations, and you know it!" He agreed to say nothing. I relaxed, but I shouldn't have.

An hour later, I received an "important" message to call Searce. When I called, he said, "This is the message I have sent to both parties but not to the press." His message urged the Patriots to forgo a strike and called on both sides to commence negotiations. I said, "I told you to stay out of it, goddammit!" but it was too late. The damage was done. Searce had done what the NFL wanted.

Before we could reach Vataha to measure Searce's damage, we reached Richard Neal, the Jets' player rep, at midnight. He said there was "no problem"; the Jets would strike. Jets general manager Al Ward had met with Jets players and warned that if they did not show up at the Yale Bowl on Sunday, they would be locked out the next week, even though the Patriots would not be there, and that they should not issue any public statement in support of the Patriots. Too late! Richard had already publicly stated that the Jets had voted 28–6 in support of the Patriots. He had indicated to me that they would not go to the game, but he was concerned that the Patriots might change their minds at the last minute. I assured him that I would call him as soon as I reached Vataha.

When we finally got through to the Red Snapper, we were told that Vataha and all the players had just left, that various management people had been there, but that they had left earlier. The questions were obvious:

Did management convince them to go to New Haven? Had Searce been the decisive factor? Were the players now on their way to the buses? Had they been intimidated? Or were they still on strike?

At about 1:15 A.M., the Patriots players voted again to stay on strike. This time the vote was unanimous. At the start of the Red Snapper meeting, Patriots coach Chuck Fairbanks, owner Billy Sullivan, club president Robert Marr, and others had marched into the meeting without an invitation. Marr walked to the front of the room and said, "Randy Vataha may be a pretty fair football player, but he is a lousy labor leader." Then he played a tape of mediator Searce's statement urging the players to avoid striking. (Searce forgot to tell me that they had taped his statement.) Marr pointed out that even the mediator opposed the strike, so the players should not listen to Garvey and Vataha.

That ended management's ability to control the situation. Every player in that room knew he had put his career on the line by voting to strike. It was not Randy Vataha's decision, and they weren't going to let him take the blame.

Marr's statement had insulted every player present, but this is the kind of unthinking response to problems that we expected from management of the NFL. It was another example of the "devil theory": Behind every problem they saw a Garvey, a Vataha, or an Upshaw. They could not accept the idea that players had their own thoughts and convictions that they were willing to fight for. Management assumed that somebody had given the players a better speech or lied to them in some way. "We can straighten them out" went management's thinking. Denigrate the leader, and they will believe us again.

Owner Billy Sullivan's plea was the most interesting. It went along the lines that he could "understand it if it were Pittsburgh," since they "had won the championship," but he couldn't understand how the New England Patriots could strike, since "You guys have never won anything." The logic escaped most.

In any event, after five management people and agent Bob Woolf pleaded with them to go and play the game, the players voted unanimously to stay on strike. Two players who had abstained the first time were so angry with management's approach that they now voted to strike.

I contacted the Jets' player rep Richard Neal at 2:00 A.M. and told him that the game was off. We left for home, feeling tired, exhilarated, excited, but apprehensive. Would the Cardinals do it? Did we have a union? Tom Keating's statement of earlier that day, "It is either the beginning or the end," seemed to haunt us all. In any event, it was a hell of a lot of fun to feel the pulse of the NFLPA beating again. It had been a long time since the cooling-off period of August 27, 1974, when we had last had that kind of excitement.

Sunday

I arrived at the office at about 9:00 A.M. Phones were ringing off the hook. The main question was whether there was a chance that the Patriots would still play the game. We figured by now there was absolutely no chance, and we said so to the press. Brent Musburger called me and invited me to be on the pregame show by telephone. I suggested to Brent that he was already worried about the reply for a fairness doctrine complaint, or he wouldn't ask me to be on. He laughed and said that was true. He suggested that I watch the program, since Karch would be on TV, and he would ask me to respond to him on the phone.

A couple of calls to Tom Banks in Denver indicated that he thought the Cardinals would definitely strike now that the Patriots had walked out. They scheduled their meeting for 9:00 A.M. Denver time. He would call as soon as it was over. If the Cardinals did strike, then maybe Denver could say they would honor the wishes of the visiting team, but we knew that the Broncos would not strike on their own.

Banks called at 11:45 A.M. "We did it! The vote was 30–10 to strike. I'm going to my room to draft a statement for the press."

He said he would call back in twenty minutes, and all of us in the office shook hands and announced that a union had been born. I joked with Gary Ballman: "If a union has been born, then Randy Vataha was the midwife."

There was great excitement because the players had canceled both games and no one could tell what kind of momentum that would generate with other teams in the league.

Just then, Len Shapiro and Ken Denlinger of the *Washington Post* arrived, and Joe Blair told them the results of the Cardinals' vote. It was understood that they wouldn't say anything and would not call the wire service. They moved into the other room to start watching *The NFL Today* on CBS.

Vataha had wisely observed that if the Patriots had gone to New Haven, they would be pressured into playing. He felt that if they were going to strike, they would have to agree not to go because, once there, they would find it difficult not to go to the stadium.

Within minutes, Ray May, the Broncos' player rep, called and asked if I knew whether the Cardinals had voted, and I told him the results. He seemed to be talking in front of other people, and it was a strange conversation. He almost shouted, "We voted to play the game by a 17–15 vote, but all of us, even those who voted to strike, are going to the stadium as a team!" Would they take the field if the St. Louis Cardinals were not there? Incredibly, he suggested that management probably would not let them. I said that we needed a commitment that they would *not* take the field because if they did, it would be terribly embarrassing to the Cardinals and would pressure them into playing.

Just then, we got a call through to the hotel in Denver where the Cardinals were staying, and I spoke with Cardinals player Ernie McMillan. I told him the results of the Denver vote, and he said that would blow everything apart. He was afraid that the Cardinals would then change their minds. I urged him to do everything he could. At the same time, I kept Ray May on hold. Then I received word that Brent Musburger was waiting for me on one of the other lines.

I grabbed the phone and took Musbuger's questions on live national TV. We indicated support for the Patriots, complete surprise that they actually voted to strike, and uncertainty about the Cardinals game. We said it would be up to the players and that as soon as we heard, we would be happy to inform CBS. Denlinger and Shapiro from the *Washington Post* were in the next room, and they had learned just a few minutes earlier that the vote was 30–10, so I am sure they wondered what was going on as they watched *CBS Today* and heard me saying that we weren't certain about the Cardinals game!

Twenty minutes later, Tom Banks called to say in a disheartened voice that the Cardinals had voted 30–16 to strike, which, he added, was not the required 75 percent, so they would play. *But who required 75 percent?* Some management people had told the players they needed 75 percent and had forced six non-dues-paying players into the room for a second vote. They had upset the balance, so Tom was on his way to the game. I urged him not to give up; this was the turning point. If he said anything negative, it would be extremely detrimental, and I urged him to issue a statement saying that most players wanted to strike, that they supported the Patriots, and that they would vote on Monday whether or not to play the opening game. Tom put his best face forward and said that he would. We quickly announced that the game would be played, despite the fact that most of the players wished to strike.

We indicated the Cardinals' complete support for the Patriots. We all looked at one another. The union began to die a little. We did our best under the difficult circumstances. It was important to keep spirits up at that point, but it wasn't easy. Momentum was back on the other side.

I knew Vataha would be troubled and quickly called him to explain what had happened. Though he was upset, he took it in stride, and no one seemed to panic.

The CBS program continued on and on in place of the struck game, with superficial analysis from the self-appointed philosopher of the sports world, Jack Whitaker, making an absolutely ludicrous analogy between the madman who slashed Rembrandt's *Night Watch* in Holland and those who were striking. CBS's programming had been upset. They would work hand in glove with management to end the strike and get the season underway. CBS took the lead in discrediting the union leadership and the Patriots and their leader, Randy Vataha.

About 3:00 P.M., a number of players who lived locally arrived at our DC office to be in on the action. Ron McDole, Billy Kilmer, Diron Talbert, and Lenny Hauss talked to player reps, encouraged them to strike, indicated that the R°°°°°°s would go out on strike in support of the Patriots, and did one hell of a job rallying the troops. It was also good for the morale of the people in the office.

R°°°°°°s team president and part owner Edward Bennett Williams called the office and asked if I could meet with him downtown for half an hour. I agreed to meet at 4:30 P.M. I then informed the R°°°°°°s in the office that I was going over to see "Panic Button," as they referred to him.

When I arrived at his office, Williams told me that if I would put together a memo on the main issues, he would go to New York the next day for the owners' meeting and argue for the players. I reviewed the issues, and Williams said he agreed with our position. I said I would put the memo together and give it to him sometime the next day. We left his office together, and he dropped me off at my office, where I reported Williams's attitude to the R°°°°°°s players.

The next development should have been anticipated. Player reps Reggie McKenzie of Buffalo, Blaine Nye of Dallas, and Bob Johnson of the Bengals were quoted by CBS as saying that they "opposed the Patriots' strike" and would not go along with it under any circumstances. CBS was doing its job. Brent Musburger kept repeating that message. He was isolating the Patriots. Finally, Billy Kilmer went on the air live to say that the R°°°°°°s favored the Patriots' action, that they admired their courage, and that the R°°°°°°s would undoubtedly go on strike to support them.

After Kilmer's call, the NFL and CBS did the best they could to confuse the situation by quickly indicating that "CBS learned" that the R°°°°°°s "had not voted yet." Obviously, the Bengals, Bills, and Cowboys hadn't voted either, but that didn't count; they were on the NFL and CBS's side—

against the strike. Further, they said, "Brig Owens, the player rep, disagrees with Kilmer!" Owens called the office and said he had never talked to CBS, and so the usual NFL-CBS tie-in continued to broadcast the negative news for the union's solidarity while suppressing the positive.

In any event, the Kilmer call was an inspiration to a lot of reps around the country, and they started calling to say they were delighted that he had spoken out. It was nice to have a quarterback say something since a lot of the quarterbacks had led the walk across the picket lines in 1974 that had helped break the back of the union.

Finally, at about 8:30 P.M., the whole group headed for dinner. I stayed behind, taking some calls and responding to others. Out of the blue, Edward Bennett Williams called and, in a strange discussion, said that he was going to resign as president of the R°°°°°°s the next day and that as far as he was concerned, he didn't have to "take this crap anymore." He said that Billy Kilmer calling in on national television saying he supports the strike was the last straw, since that "no-talent quarterback" had been paid over $100,000 by Williams. Then he made a strange proposition: He asked me to call a press conference and propose that he, Edward Bennett Williams, be named as the "impartial arbitrator of the entire dispute." He said that if I did, it would be the greatest PR coup in history if the owners turned it down. If they agreed, I should feel comfortable because I already knew his position on the key issues. I couldn't believe what I was hearing.

I said that I would have to think it over and call him back. I went to dinner with Joe Blair, Leonard Lindquist, Gary Ballman, and my wife, Betty, and we discussed Williams's suggestion. We decided it would be a good idea to get together with him first thing in the morning. I called him and asked if he would meet at my house so no one would see us, but he preferred the Metropolitan Club. He said he would be there at 8:00 A.M. after having breakfast with R°°°°°°s coach George Allen. He stressed the importance of the meeting, and I said that Leonard Lindquist and I would both be there. I got home at about 2:00 A.M. and set the alarm for 6:00 A.M. so I would be sure to be at the Metropolitan Club on time.

I could hardly open my eyes when the 6:00 A.M. alarm went off. On the way to the Metropolitan Club, I had the strange thought that maybe something would finally get settled. Uncertainty was now a major factor in the dispute, and possibly Williams was a key to settling the whole thing. We would never suggest him as the arbitrator, but, in any event, I knew that he was going to play a role for the first time.

I met Lindquist inside the Metropolitan Club, which was reminiscent of an eighteenth-century British dining club, and after waiting for about half an hour, we told the person at the door that we would like a cup of coffee. He told us not to go to the dining room, but we did. It was now almost 9:00 A.M., and Lindquist was supposed to be on the shuttle heading for New York to meet with Pete Rozelle to see if there was some way the two of them could find the key to this marathon dispute. Lindquist suggested I call Williams to make sure he hadn't forgotten about the breakfast meeting.

I called and was shocked to learn that he had forgotten, or pretended to have forgotten. He was at his office a block away but never offered to come over. He acted as though he knew nothing about the meeting. He simply said that he had "blown it." He asked if I could meet with him after 11:30 A.M. since he had a morning meeting. I agreed and wondered to myself whether he had forgotten about his resignation from the R°°°°°°s as well.

We were furious as we left the Metropolitan Club. Leonard had delayed his trip to New York, and I was exhausted, but most of all we were upset by the insult from Williams.

Williams then called me at about 11:30 A.M. and indicated that he still wanted to get together but that he had to meet with George Allen. He asked if I could see him just before dinner. I said sure but knew immediately that he must be headed for R°°°°°°s Park, where the team would be deciding whether to strike in support of the Patriots. I acted on my intuition and got the word through to the R°°°°°°s locker room that Williams was going there to give a big speech

Sure enough, before long I heard that Williams and George Allen had the players in a meeting at R°°°°°°s Park. Our PR expert, Joe Blair, was like a frog on dry ice as we waited to hear word from the R°°°°°°s locker room. The phone rang, and it was Diron Talbert and Lenny Hauss saying that Williams had pleaded with the players not to strike and, in any event, not to make any announcement for twenty-four hours. He told them he was meeting with me and "working closely" with me to get this matter settled. He urged them to give him some time. The players told him to go to hell and voted unanimously to go out on strike if the Patriots were locked out. I never heard from Ed Williams again—that's how closely he was working with me.

By then, I had heard from Lindquist, who was encouraged by his meeting with Rozelle at Rozelle's estate in Long Island. He said that Pete had suggested that the Rozelle Rule be left to the courts, and this was, of course, acceptable to us.

I called Bill Usery, who had been part of the labor movement as an International Association of Machinists organizer before his position at the FMCS, and suggested a meeting. When he arrived at our office, I told him that this time we had some clout, that we had some leverage because the

Patriots were out; the R°°°°°°s, Lions, and Giants would follow; and the regular season was in jeopardy. If a mediator had ever walked into a better situation, we were unaware of it. Now, we would watch Usery in action. Time was short. The pressure was on. Usery smelled a settlement.

When the afternoon call from Usery indicated a late-night meeting with management, I had hopes of a compromise as we headed for the Department of Labor. Mara, Karch, and Kheel were there when we arrived. By then, one team had been locked out, the Jets had gone on strike earlier in the day, and surely the R°°°°°°s, Falcons, Lions, and Giants would follow on Tuesday.

The Giants were playing the Dolphins in the Orange Bowl the night the Patriots voted to strike. Doug Van Horn of the Giants had heard about the Patriots' vote. He immediately phoned my office to learn the details and then called the Giants together and told them about the Patriots' decision. He asked the Giants players if they wanted to do anything, and to his surprise they decided to delay the game in order to screw up the television people who were sending the game back to the New York area.

After their warm-ups, the players remained in the locker room. Mara stormed in and demanded that the players take the field on time or they would all be suspended. Doug Van Horn informed him that it had been a team vote and that he would have to suspend all of them, because they would not be out on the field on time for the 8:00 P.M. start.

Mara raced out, and a few minutes later Dolphins coach Don Shula entered the Giants' locker room with his quarterback, Bob Griese, at his side. Mara, unsuccessful in his threats, had appealed to the opposition for help. Imagine the thoughts running through the players' minds as the opposing coach and quarterback were now in the "enemy" locker room urging them to come out onto the field!

Shula started by telling them that the Giants players were insulting "my fans who are here to see this game." Griese then urged them to play the game. Finally, Giants quarterback Craig Morton had heard enough. He told them to get the hell out of the locker room; that they had no right to come in the first place; and that they were insulting the intelligence of the players. One of the other players started to taunt Griese by telling him, "It's fine for you with your two-hundred-thousand-dollar contract to tell us not to strike, but what about those of us who are making eighteen thousand dollars and who are depending on the pension?"

Shula and Griese departed. They had been no more successful than Mara.

Enter Bill Arnsparger, the Giants' head coach. All the players liked "Arns," and there was a hush in the room when he spoke. He told them that his job was on the line if they didn't get out onto the field. While some of the players were prepared to test that threat, most of them felt that they had made their point, and the team decided to go out and play the game. It didn't start exactly on time, but it was close. Nevertheless, Mara had been embarrassed. He could no longer control his own team. Don Shula may have learned a few things as well—the players of 1975 were a little different from the players of the late 1960s and early 1970s.

The Giants players learned something as well: If they stuck together, they could put management in an impossible situation. Two days later, they would strike in the face of even more threats.

Ever the optimist, I again thought the stage was set for a quick settlement, or at least some honest bargaining, in a DC meeting at FMCS. After all, this was the first time that the regular season had ever been threatened, and the pressure on the owners from the television people alone would be incredible.

It didn't take long for Kheel to destroy my optimism: "We are not here to negotiate; we are here to discuss the Patriots problem."

During the 1974 fiasco, Usery had said on several occasions that the problem was that the pressure wasn't really on the owners, because regular-season games weren't threatened. Now that they were, Wellington Mara announced to the group, "We will not negotiate with a gun to our heads." All I could think was that if they wouldn't negotiate when there was no pressure and they wouldn't negotiate when there was some, we were in a lot of trouble.

Rather than bargaining, they started another grand plan to destroy the union. They would sacrifice the opening game if they could use it as a device to get rid of the leadership or bust the union. After all, the *Mackey* decision had not yet come down. Reason was missing on their side. I suggested that the dispute had gone far enough and that it was time for compromise and good faith on both sides. While admitting that we had made some mistakes, I stated that now was the time to put bitterness aside and reach agreement.

Instead of having the desired effect, it sparked something in Mara: "We will make an offer to the players if you, Ed Garvey, will let them vote on it! I guarantee you"—he was now almost shouting—"that the players will accept our offer if you let them vote on it!"

There it was. Once again Mara believed that it was my diabolical plotting to keep the players from voting that stood in the way of a settlement. I told him that we were not prepared to stay there to listen to insults and that we were convinced that union busting was still their goal. I suggested that they no longer cared about anything else. The well-being of the league was secondary to their goal of "getting the union." Usery called for a caucus.

Thirty minutes later, Usery came into our meeting room and said, "They are adamant; I don't think there is any way to get through to them. We might as well forget it."

I had a thought: "Listen, Bill, what if *you* suggest something so reasonable that they would look crazy turning it down?"

"Like what?"

"Suppose that you suggest that we put the 1970 agreement into effect for two weeks, both sides preserve all of their legal arguments in the *Mackey* case, and the players go back to work."

Usery liked it. "Let's get a list of the issues and give it a try."

We proposed four basic points:

1. The Patriots will go back to work and there will be no reprisals against them.
2. There will be no strike or lockout for two weeks.
3. The 1970 agreement goes into effect for the two-week period.
4. We will continue to negotiate during the two-week period.

When we had finished, it was close to 2:00 A.M., and Usery left to try it out on the owners, but he was back in a few minutes. The only thing they would agree to as proposed was number one. In other words, the Patriots' strike would have been wasted completely. I told Usery there was no way the Patriots would return to work unless they saw some concession, some movement, some good faith on the part of the Management Council.

Suddenly Karch, executive director of the Management Council, asked to meet with me alone. He seemed panicked, and, in fact, I thought he might pass out. It was probably just an act. He urged me to get the Patriots back to work and then try to work something out. I told him, "Give me something so the Patriots won't feel the effort was in vain."

"No," said Karch. "We can't give you anything. But it is *vital* that they return to work."

In effect, he was saying, "Do as I say, or else."

I suggested that both sides submit a proposed settlement and that we let Usery decide on one or the other. Each side would argue their respective positions, and then whatever he recommended would bind both sides. "No," said Karch. "We won't let the mediator impose a settlement."

I decided to smoke him out completely and offered, "Well, I will go this far, Sarge. I will agree to sell to our players whatever Rozelle recommends." He hesitated, then refused and said, "No, they must go back to work."

My response was "Stick it!" They would try to break us again.

Kheel, ever the maneuverer, had a thought. He proposed a six-point package—by dividing our first point into six points!

1. No lockout.
2. No strike.
3. No reprisals.
4. A new offer next week.
5. Set the date for negotiations.
6. Patriots go back immediately.

We suggested they jump in a lake, and we left at 6:00 A.M. for the office.

Why had they bothered coming to Washington? Was it to tire us out? To keep us from the phones? They had never been serious about a settlement.

The Machine Cranks Up

When we walked into the NFLPA office, we tiptoed past AP's Tom Seppy, in vain, it turned out. We had told the paper by phone at 4:00 A.M. that it looked bad, and now we summed up the session.

Seppy was about as friendly as a bear awakened from a midwinter's nap: "Oh, for Christ's sake, what do you mean you can't tell me what happened?" I reminded him of Usery's ground rules: That he alone makes the statements. We were still playing by the rules.

As I left the building, Seppy received a call from his headquarters, New York AP, with a tape-recorded statement from the Management Council's PR man, Terry Bledsoe, saying, "Management offered a six-point proposal, but the union turned it down." So much for Usery's ground rules. Bledsoe had taped it outside Usery's office and called it into the AP! When I heard about the Bledsoe message, I quickly dictated a memo of what had happened and asked the secretaries to read it to all reps. I called Randy Vataha, explained the lack of progress, and urged him to go off strike to test the lockout.

For a moment, we were on the defensive. "Why did *you* turn down the six-point proposal?" came the question from the press. We quickly prepared a press release based on my hastily dictated memo and got it out to the wire services. We made it clear that the *owners* had rejected Usery's proposal—the *owners* had rejected the extension of the 1970 agreement.

The NFL had released the so-called six points from Usery's office and was now screaming that we had no right to release the fact that it was Usery's offer or that they had even refused to let Rozelle make recommendations. How dare we tell what really happened!

The owners were desperate. They released a fax saying we were lying—that Usery had not made a recommendation. Our response was simple and direct: Call Usery and ask him. Player rep Richard Neal of the Jets did, and he got the truth; then he called Jets general manager Al Ward and said, "Gee, Al, I guess the Management Council is not telling you the truth." (A year later Neal would be traded.)

Randy Vataha called, and Usery told him the truth. Once again, the NFL was exposed. The battle became more intense. Management went for the jugular, never for a settlement.

Foxborough

Vataha was to call with the latest word immediately after reporting to practice that Tuesday morning. We concluded that if the owners were smart, they would welcome the Patriots back with open arms. This would bring the Jets back quickly, avoid a R°°°°°°s strike, and immediately defuse the situation. On the other hand, they would fear a repeat performance if there were no reprisals, which might encourage another strike.

The NFL took the hard line. Their goal was to punish these "kids" because they got out of line by striking. It was the totalitarian personality—fine them, suspend them, fire them, trade them, or lock them out. To forgive or even accept the Patriots players' action would be to "give in to the radicals."

When the Patriots arrived, Head Coach Chuck Fairbanks had a no-strike pledge ready for the players. He also said that they must accept Kheel's six-point proposal, which I had rejected at 6:00 A.M. Randy said they would accept neither: "We are not on strike. We are ready to practice and play." The response: "Sorry, the facilities are locked."

At about the same time, George Allen was pleading with R°°°°°°s reps to work out at R°°°°°°s Park without supervision from the coaches. This would show their solidarity with New England but at the same time would not hurt their game plan for New Orleans. While they were discussing the Allen idea, Billy Kilmer knocked on the coach's door to say, "I only came to tell you that the guys are gone. We are on strike."

In the meantime, the NFL was busy spreading the word to the other teams that the R°°°°°°s *would* practice at R°°°°°°s Park *without* supervision. The Jets, Giants, and Lions were all told this lie in order to hold off more strike action. If management could convince players that our strongest team, Washington, had not gone on strike, then weaker teams might not strike. Their goal—hold off until Wednesday, then apply maximum pressure on New England. Management saw this as a possible way to deal the final crushing blow to the union. If no team followed the Patriots, then the Patriots would have to return with tails tucked between their legs. Leadership would be blamed for the selective strike and the inability to get others to stand up and fight for them. The kept press would do the rest.

More calls for my resignation would follow as day follows night.

We were desperately trying to counter the constant flow of lies from management, but the task was enormous. Camera crews were all over the place, AP and UPI camped on our steps, our phone lines were all tied up, player reps were out of touch, and the NFL's ever-present fax machine was spewing out lies like a geyser out of control:

"We heard that Garvey is going around Vataha."

"It was a secret plan agreed upon in Chicago and not even shared with the reps."

"The Jets are back practicing."

"The Giants are on the field."

"Detroit decided not to strike."

The Giants

Doug Van Horn of the Giants called me at 11:00 A.M. "I hear the Jets are practicing."

"Not true," I said.

"I hear the S***s decided not to strike."

"They have already left R******s Park," I told him.

"Okay, I'll call you right after the meeting. I think we are okay, but you never know."

More waiting. Richard Neal of the Jets called. "I hear the Giants are practicing."

"No, they are in a meeting. Doug says they will walk."

"Okay, call you later."

Van Horn called me again at 1:00 P.M. and said, "We're on our way down to the Management Council to tell them that the Giants are on strike!"

"Sounds good."

"Can you get ahold of the Jets and have them meet us there?"

"We will try."

We got on the phone with AP and UPI to let them know that both New York teams were on the way down to confront their owners and the entire committee!

I said to my staff, "Get the news to Detroit Lions rep Jim Yarbrough and to Vataha!"

Randy was excited and wanted to know about Detroit and Los Angeles.

Yarborough called me. "No problem, I'm sure we will strike, but we want to announce it tomorrow." Each Lions player had given him a secret ballot, and he would reveal the results Wednesday.

I said, "It would be nice to announce it today to keep the ball rolling, but if you can't, that's okay."

The phones were going crazy. The Rams would vote Wednesday, same for the 49ers. Our message was that no one should play unless the Patriots were allowed to play. New Orleans, Houston, and Buffalo would have no opponents. (The Saints were to play Washington; Houston, the Giants; and Buffalo, the Jets. A three-team strike was suddenly a six-team strike.) The season was in jeopardy. Six to ten teams would be screwed up even if the others didn't strike. It just might work! A crazy plan by a few guys in New England. A union? Maybe.

But now the owners would give it one more push that almost worked.

Usery called again. "Can you and Leonard [Lindquist, our general counsel] join me on the five P.M. shuttle to New York?"

"No problem. See you there."

I called Randy to let him know we were heading to New York City to bargain and told the office to let the reps know.

We arrived at the Management Council's office at 7:00 P.M., three days before the regular season was to open. Usery entered with Mara, Kheel, Bledsoe, and Karch and opened with an appeal to both sides to get the dispute settled: "It's long overdue. Both sides are suffering, and the fans are getting turned off. That should concern both of you."

While Usery was talking in a quiet yet dramatic fashion, the Management Council secretary came in and gave Wellington Mara a note. Mara read it, smiled broadly, and left the room. Soon after, we learned that the note informed him that the Rams had voted *not* to strike. Now the owners were close to the jugular.

The Rams were the first team to formally split with the Patriots. We subsequently learned that Carroll Rosenbloom had walked into the players' meeting and told them if "you vote against the strike, I guarantee you that all economic benefits will be increased by forty percent." Rams players believed him and voted against a strike. Guess what? Economic benefits were not increased, but the NFL would say whatever it took to defeat the union.

At around 9:00 P.M., Usery asked Kheel to speak. Kheel urged a solution. He said they were present in good faith, but he again made it clear they were not going to bargain. Usery called on me, but I decided to yield to Lindquist. I thought, "If I speak, it will be used against us, no matter what I say. Leonard is not such an easy target." I guess I let them intimidate me into a silent role—stupid in retrospect because they would say whatever they thought would help their cause no matter who spoke for the union.

Lindquist made an emotional appeal for reason: "Let's get this dispute settled. We should all reexamine our positions, seek harmony, not discord." Eloquent, but not well received.

Usery called a caucus. During the break, I phoned Richard Neal, who was waiting at a restaurant to hear from me. Neal reported that the Jets had voted to return to work!

Just then, Usery came in to tell us about the owners' mood: "They are in no mood to negotiate. They got word of the Rams' vote, and they now think you have no power. The other teams will play Sunday." (They must have known about the Jets as well.) "It's all over as far as the strike. They know they have you. I've never seen them in a more intransigent mood." Was Usery trying to soften us, or was it a warning?

Lindquist said, "What in hell is the matter with those bastards? They don't even know what 'good faith' is all about!"

Usery said he was working on a proposal and would get back to us. By then it was after 11:00 P.M., and I called the office to learn that we couldn't reach Randy Vataha. I said not to worry, that Randy had never let us down before and he wouldn't now. Then I gave him the bad news about the Rams.

At midnight, we broke for dinner. I told Richard Neal we would meet him and the other Jets downstairs. A reporter was there and asked, "Do these players know what the hell they are doing? Who do they think they are?"

I responded that they know what they are doing but declined to debate since her position was obvious.

"Well, they aren't going to get any sympathy," she said.

"If not, that's okay. They believe strongly that a player should have rights, just like other workers."

"Who are you, by the way?" she asked.

"Doesn't matter."

"Who are you? I'm with NBC."

"I'm Ed Garvey."

"Oh, could I interview you?"

"No, but I'm sure you will report this dispute with complete objectivity!"

At dinner, several Giants—Doug Van Horn, John Hicks, and Dick Enderle—joined us to discuss strategy. We huddled around one small table. Richard said the Jets were going back to work on Thursday. Most other teams probably would not go on strike. Someone suggested that we call a national meeting. It could get us past the first game. The response was immediate: Let's try.

I called the office and told Dick to get union president Kermit Alexander's reaction to the idea of a national meeting.

We headed back to the Management Council. When we walked up to the office, the AP reporter asked, "How do you feel about Buffalo Bills player rep Reggie McKenzie's call for your resignation?"

"Bug off!" I said.

When we entered, Wellington was smiling and having a good time with Kheel, but when he saw Hicks, Enderle, Hill, Neal, and Van Horn, he stopped smiling. He was upset. "Who invited them?" They hated to see players. They wanted only me present for the final coup. Then it would be their word against mine. The players would screw that up.

Usery cooperated by asking for only the negotiating committee members to meet with the Management Council. I turned to the players and said, "To hell with it; I won't go in there without you." Winston Hill of the Jets urged me to go in, but, instead, I insisted the owners and their representatives come into *our* room and speak in front of all the players.

Finally, at about 2:00 A.M., they agreed to come in and said, "We have no offer. Accept the six-point proposal we gave you two days ago. That is our final position." The players heard it themselves this time.

After they left, John Hicks called Rams player rep Jack Youngblood. "How in the hell could you do that?" Youngblood told us about Carroll Rosenbloom's promise of a 40 percent across-the-board economic increase. If they didn't deliver, "Carroll said he would publicly blast the Management Council. He would destroy them." That promise was good enough for the Rams because "Carroll had a lot of influence. The NFLPA won't dare give the Rams more nonsense."

Total nonsense on his part, but it worked.

Around 3:30 to 4:00 A.M., an idea came to me. A little while later, I told Usery in a meeting that included Van Horn, Neal, the Jets' Winston Hill, and Enderle that if on Monday he assured our committee that the Management Council would make an offer that was a substantial improvement over the present position, and that they would bargain with us in good faith for three days, then I could buy the six-point proposal. But I *insisted* that he make a public statement to this effect.

Usery paced back and forth. "I won't give that assurance lightly! Let me get back to you."

I turned to the guys who were with me. "Okay?" I asked.

"Okay," they said.

Why not put Usery's feet to the fire?

At 6:00 A.M. Usery returned. "I am satisfied they will bargain in good faith for three days. They will make an offer on Monday, and it will be a substantial improvement. I'll say so publicly."

Were we giving up, making progress, or trying to get our best people off the hook? With the Jets going back, with no new teams joining the strike, and with the Rams' vote, I was confident that we had to get our people off strike or face the prospect of a broken union.

I then insisted to Usery that he fly to Boston with me to explain the offer to the Patriots, saying, "We had discussed the problem ourselves. We can't afford to lose our most militant members. We had better convince them."

Usery hesitated, but said, "I'll go with you, but I want someone from management." He seemed excited. He had achieved his goal, namely, a strike settlement. The opening game would be played; he considered it a success.

I quickly called Kermit Alexander, and he said, "Okay, go ahead. We don't have a lot of options, thanks to the Rams."

We reached Vataha, who said, "I'll talk to you when you get here. I've got a lot to tell you."

Len Hauss and Brig Owens said, "Okay," and Jim Yarbrough said, "Okay, but call me from Boston."

Usery returned to read the statement. We signed and made a brief press announcement, and then Lindquist and I headed for the airport. On the way, I said to him, "I hope it's the right decision."

Lindquist made a terrific response: "Even if it isn't, mistakes are for this world, perfection for the next."

I got off the shuttle flight first because the others were toward the rear. I was shocked as I looked up and saw TV cameras, photographers, and a number of writers waiting for us to deplane.

I made a quick statement: "I am hopeful this will be acceptable to the Patriots . . . hope this will lead to a settlement."

We headed for Foxborough. All the Patriots players were there. Randy Vataha introduced me, and I told them we got nothing except a pledge to make a substantial offer on Monday followed by three days of good faith negotiations. The only reason I recommended it was because the best we could get was Usery stating publicly that they would follow through.

I said, "We put his reputation on the line—maybe that will work. We don't want to sacrifice you guys; I think you have made your point by forcing them to make a new offer, forcing them to bargain." Clearly, it was selling. Tough questions followed:

"What assurance do you have?"

"Why couldn't they make one concession?"

Then someone suggested getting Usery and Karch down there in person.

The association office called me before Usery's arrival. The Detroit players were angry. Management had threatened the team with fines unless they went to practice immediately. Yarborough was holding them out until the Patriots made a decision. When Sargent Karch and Usery arrived, I told them Yarborough's position, and Usery responded immediately, "Goddammit, Sarge, we don't need this." Karch called our office and said there would be no fines against the Lions.

The Patriots players reassembled. Usery started in by congratulating them, saying they really got things moving, adding, "Now, don't overplay your hand. Have confidence in your leadership." Players listened, but it sounded all too familiar.

Karch got up. "I want to congratulate you. You have forced us to come up with a good proposal, and we will. I also want to tell you that you will get paid for last week's game." (Murmurs, as the players were insulted. They didn't give a damn about the money.) "I also want to tell you that Ed Garvey has done everything in his power to properly represent you. He has acted most responsibly." (Praise from Karch was like a kiss of death!)

Then the players' questions and comments started:

"Why are you sending the offer to the players directly?"

"You are still trying to bust the union by going around our leadership, and we resent it!"

"Absolutely not," said Karch. "We have never tried to break the union."

At that point, I had to contradict him. "Of course they have tried to bust us, and maybe they are still trying. There is no legitimate reason for sending the offer to the players. They have cut our leaders and refused to bargain. Nevertheless, I believe we should test them to see if they still will not bargain."

Players asked Karch, "Why does league management continue lying to us? Why don't you give in on one point just to show good faith?"

Now Karch was beginning to panic. He had never faced more than five players before; he didn't know how militant they were. Nor did I!

When a player asked, "Why won't you allow a neutral arbitrator to settle this?" Karch started shouting: "Bill Usery will tell you that if you allow neutrals to come into it, you destroy the bargaining process! Isn't that right, Bill?"

Silence.

"Well, Mr. Usery, I'm waiting!"

The scene was almost comical as Usery looked straight ahead, puffing on his pipe.

Again, Karch said, "Well, Mr. Usery!"

Usery slowly rose and said, "Well, Sarge, sometimes what you say is true, but there are many ways to settle a dispute, and neutrals can be very helpful."

Karch was finished. No one in that room would ever believe him again; he now looked the complete fool. Suddenly, he turned to the players and screamed, "Collective bargaining won't work because Ed Garvey is here telling you that our offer on Monday will be nothing but a pile of crap!"

Real shouts from the players—some now out of their seats, others moving forward. Karch was afraid. Even I was concerned.

I jumped up and asked for order. "Let's settle this quickly. Anyone here who heard me say, 'Their offer won't be good,' raise your hand."

No hands went up. Players started shouting, "Get your hand up, Karch. Get it up! Get it up! Get it up!"

Theater of the absurd. Karch put his hand up, and everyone started laughing as he headed for the door.

Vataha said to me that there was "no way" back now. Quite frankly, I started wondering how I would feel if they said no. Maybe that's the answer. My God, I had no idea how strong these guys were. What would I think with a full night's sleep? We took a short break. I told Usery to stick around. When we were ready to start, Ron Bolton and Randy Vataha reported that their quick poll indicated that a majority would reject the settlement.

Despite our misgivings, we started again. I told them to forget Karch. I said, "We've all been up two out of three nights; he's tired, and so forget his last statement. We have to decide what is in *our* best interests without worrying about management jerks." But soon the master plan started coming out.

Even I was shocked as the picture of management's plot of the previous night unfolded. Randy Vataha was out of touch; Patriots president Bob Marr asked Ron Bolton and Vataha to come to his office. Once there, he asked if they would agree to sell a package to the team. They said not unless it was worthwhile.

Marr said, "We have an offer you can't refuse, but before you see it, you have to promise to call a team meeting and you have to agree to sell it. Finally, you cannot talk to Garvey or the union office."

Vataha and Bolton said they couldn't possibly agree to those terms. After some discussion, they agreed to get the players to the stadium and not to call me. There they would receive an offer "they couldn't refuse." Rozelle called to "assure" Vataha that the NFL would help if possible.

When the Patriots got to the stadium, Head Coach Chuck Fairbanks told them that once they accepted the offer, they would turn on the lights and have a midnight practice to "show everyone that the Patriots were back together."

Finally, they gave the Patriots the "improved" offer. It was almost exactly what I was then trying to sell them! But the team voted it down unanimously at midnight. Had they accepted at midnight, I would have been sitting in New York refusing the very thing the Patriots had accepted. We could then be written off as crazy militants who did not represent the players. No player would be with me. It would all be laid at my doorstep. A brilliant scheme, but it didn't work, thanks to the Patriots players and the participation of Giants and Jets players at our all-night sessions.

The debate then turned on whether guys would strike again the next week if the offer were no good. The vote was unanimous to go back on strike. One speaker said we needed 70 percent of Patriots players to agree to go back to work.

I intervened. "You need a big majority to go out, but you can't allow thirty percent to keep you out. Make it a majority."

Randy took a vote. "Those in favor of fifty-one percent, raise your hand . . . those for seventy percent." Fifty-one percent carried.

More debate. Many players were upset because they had rejected the same proposal the night before; now here they were again voting on the same thing, with nothing changed except that Usery had agreed to pressure the owners. Because of the Searce tape urging them not to strike, few of the players had any confidence in Usery or Searce. They viewed them as part of management's team.

I invited all the Patriots to Chicago for the bargaining session.

The vote came: 28–15 to go back to work. I headed for Usery, who was waiting with Karch. I told him, "Okay, they will play."

Karch looked shaky, put his hand out, and said, "Thanks."

I responded, "Your offer had better be good."

Usery was clearly relieved, and, frankly, so was I. The crisis was over for now. We faced the cameras and headed for the airport. It occurred to me on the way that we hadn't eaten since midnight, but who cared? We could now get ready for negotiations.

The next day we decided to have not just the NFLPA Executive Committee but all reps, alternates, and all other players interested to go to Chicago to receive the owners' offer. For sure, we wanted most of the Patriots. We would not be isolated again.

Brent Musburger of CBS called and asked me to appear on the pre-game program before the first regular-season game, a game made possible by our no-strike pledge and the Patriots' vote. I readily agreed for several reasons, the main one being that I could bring pressure on management to come up with a decent offer and live up to their agreement. After all, I would have twenty million fans watching while I told them that the NFL had promised to negotiate in good faith and that Usery had given his word that the new offer would be substantial. I reasoned that if management refused, if they acted as they had in the past, the public would really condemn them. The CBS program would give me the forum to put the pressure on management.

But then came Musburger's infamous introduction of "alleged bomb-thrower, Ed Garvey."

Musburger planted in the minds of millions of fans that I was some kind of kook, a screwball. He was finishing his task, which had begun one week before, to assassinate the character of the union "militants." Rozelle could pontificate, but the "bomb-thrower" could hardly put pressure on anyone to come up with anything. Only later would I realize that a new management plot was in the works and that CBS had done its part, or had been used by the NFL to do its part.

That afternoon, before leaving for Chicago, we went to a friend's house to meet a little-known former governor from Georgia named Jimmy Carter, who was running for president. He would talk of honesty and integrity, words foreign to the NFL.

That night, we headed for Chicago again. One month earlier, the players had met in Chicago and started, almost inadvertently, the chain reaction that led to the strike. Would it finally end there?

On Monday, September 22, we met the reps for breakfast. We set a 10:00 A.M. meeting, and the committee left to receive the offer at the Palmer House in Chicago.

I sensed disaster as we approached the Palmer House. Reporters and cameras were all over the place. One reporter told me that the "offer" was going to be released to the press at 10:00 A.M.! How could that be? The press would receive it at the same time we would see it!

We met Usery, and he directed us to the meeting room. He said he had made one more fruitless appeal to the Management Council and Rozelle: "Don't send the offer out to the players and the press—it's a mistake." But the plot had already been hatched; they would now triumph over the union by getting players to vote for the Rozelle Rule in order to get more pension benefits. We quickly learned that all head coaches had told players after Sunday's games to come to the stadium at 10:00 A.M. to get the offer. The coaches would sell it while the reps were tied up in Chicago. They would get the weakest teams to vote first to set the trend—Minnesota, Buffalo, Pittsburgh, Cincinnati, Dallas. The offer must have been in the mail when Karch was promising the Patriots that the offer would now be substantial and would be negotiated in good faith!

When Kheel, Mara, Ralph Wilson, and Tex Schramm came in, I knew it was all over. The cockiness, the friendliness, the condescending attitude. Just another performance. There was no pressure. Shit! Why had I signed that damned no-strike agreement? Why had I convinced the Patriots?

The reps decided to ask questions and force bargaining, if possible. After all, they had promised, in writing, to bargain for three days. Usery had given public assurance. The Patriots, R******s, Giants, and Lions had called off their strikes. The few reps who thought they were on the inside with management felt betrayed. Dick Anderson kept saying, "They'll do better than this." Sadly, he probably believed it.

Our main goal was to keep the owners in Chicago as long as possible and let the players see Kheel, Karch, and Mara in action, in living color, and possibly force them to bargain.

On Monday afternoon we put hundreds of questions to Kheel so the reps would thoroughly understand how bad the offer was in order to explain it fully to their players. The offer called for the *Mackey* case to be settled; for Rozelle to be arbitrator of all important issues; for an end to the injury grievance procedure; for a five-year contract. The session exposed Kheel and Karch. They seemed to have lost the ability to distinguish truth from falsehood. Everyone was angry as we left for dinner.

The rep meeting began that night without reps from San Diego, Philadelphia, and Cincinnati, and the two Pittsburgh reps left early. A Patriots player said, "I'll guarantee you that the Steelers will vote to accept. Those two didn't want to hear the negative aspects and took off." (Pittsburgh did vote to accept.)

The offer was an insult, the refusal to bargain was a violation of their promise, and the outcome of the vote was obvious by the midpoint of the meeting. So we talked of another strike, of waiting for the *Mackey* decision. It was an excellent union meeting. Every player rep spoke, and everyone had something positive to say about the future of the union. The vote among those assembled was unanimous to reject the offer, but we decided not to announce the vote. The meeting ended at 2:00 A.M.; then it would be a few hours of sleep and back to the Palmer House at 10:00 A.M. to confront the owners again.

———

Day two began with more questions. Kheel became quite agitated. He shouted at Usery, "We are not going to bargain; we are not going to be told what to do by you or anyone else!" They wanted to leave. Usery called for a caucus. He told us to come up with six or seven things we "must" have. He left, and immediately everyone had an idea, and after a few arguments and a few laughs, we narrowed it down to six points:

1. Impartial arbitration
2. Rozelle Rule left to the court
3. No limit on our right to negotiate changes in working conditions
4. The old preseason-pay formula
5. Retention of equal representation on the Retirement Board
6. An increase in squad size

What about union security? I argued for it, but Jack Youngblood said, "Everyone will pay dues. If it's a big problem for them, let's drop it."

Usery heard the six points, and knowing that the only concession he could get from them was in the form of union security, he said, "I wouldn't give that up. Try for it." It was added as a seventh item.

The management team returned. I began by saying that the seeds of our problems were sown on August 2, 1970, when we were forced to accept a bad contract. We took it but started to build for a fight. If we were now forced to accept another bad agreement, everyone would be in trouble. If, on the other hand, the board could recommend a contract, there would be real peace. I said, "In that light, here are the seven items we must have. Please consider them."

Usery later told me it was our best effort. Even Tex Schramm seemed to recognize the importance of what we were trying to say.

They stayed in caucus for over two hours. Kermit Alexander and I talked: "Are they smart enough to agree to everything *except* the Rozelle Rule?" If so, it would be the moment of truth. Our backs would be against the wall. The suspense was building. Kermit and I agreed that we would both resign if the players gave up the *Mackey* case.

The owners returned. Karch began. Impartial arbitration: "No."

Preseason pay: "No."

Squad size increase: "No."

Rozelle Rule left to court: "No."

"But, on union security, we agree to an agency shop next year for rookies. This is our *final, final, final offer!*"

Players started whispering obscenities. Screwed again. Mara got up. "Let me speak to the players. If we were to accept your seven points, we would lose the battle that has been going on for five years. We may be stupid and we may be stubborn, but we aren't crazy."

One of the players said aloud, "Two out of three ain't bad, Wellington!"

By now everyone was angry enough to blast them in the press and to convince their players to vote no.

Before they left, I made one more plea: "If we can't reach agreement, can we at least agree on a method of settling? Would you agree to impartial arbitration of the dispute?"

The answer came quickly: "No."

The session ended. Everyone prepared to leave Chicago—angrier but wiser.

The Patriots' efforts had ended with a whimper, not a bang. But the lesson would not soon be forgotten. Forty guys in New England taught us how to strike. Taught us a lot about trust, guts, and character.

8

In Good Faith

Despite the careful work of the owners to bypass the leadership, the players voted overwhelmingly to reject the offer. Even Dallas and Buffalo voted against it. After that, we somehow finished the 1975 season without any major casualties. There were no negotiating sessions for the rest of the year. Both sides waited anxiously for the *Mackey* decision because the owners knew that if we lost *Mackey*, we were finished. Almost miraculously, a majority of the players paid dues by personal check, briefs were submitted to the court in the *Mackey* case, and a calm seemed to be present as we awaited the outcome.

When the *Mackey* decision came in late December, we were ready for the celebration. I got the call from Tom Seppy of the AP. He began by casually saying, "Congratulations."

He assumed that I knew the outcome, but I had to ask, "Why the congratulations?"

He read part of Judge Larson's decision:

The Rozelle Rule constitutes a *per se* violation of the antitrust laws . . . The Rozelle Rule is so clearly contrary to public policy that it is *per se* illegal under the Sherman Act . . . The Court finds that the existence of the Rozelle Rule has not had any material effect on competitive balance in the NFL.

And, finally,

> There is no labor exemption available for defendants. . . *the Rozelle Rule is a non-mandatory, illegal subject of bargaining.*

I let out a "Whoop!" and started to celebrate. We had survived! It was a total victory. Surely, they would now talk settlement! Ah, but had I forgotten already that the NFL never settles? I had indeed.

The NFL's response? "We will appeal." And appeal they did. And they still held out hope that the players would fire me and drop the *Mackey* suit. Our celebration was a short one, but we had finally defeated the NFL in a full trial.

Kermit Alexander's term as president was up in January 1976, and we had to think about elections. Randy Vataha had demonstrated great leadership under fire during the Patriots' strike, and he was the natural favorite of the "radicals." Dolphins defensive back Dick Anderson was clearly the candidate of the owners and the "We need a contract at any price" faction. After all, aside from the *Mackey* decision, and even with strikes ended, we still had no collective bargaining agreement.

Given our court victory, we guessed that most reps would be satisfied to continue our strategy. Without the Rozelle Rule, the NFL would be forced to bargain. Since Anderson, the Dolphins' player rep, had only five or six dues-paying members supporting him, we assumed that he would be defeated for not doing his job. Anderson had also come to the office during the Patriots' strike and used the toll-free line to call reps and urge them not to strike in sympathy with the Patriots.

Rozelle saw another Jack Kemp in Anderson and did what he could to get him elected. Word circulated that we needed "some class" in our leadership. We needed a "businessman who understands management" to get a deal. We, of course, wanted a proven leader. We needed strong leadership while we awaited the appellate court decision, and Randy Vataha had proven himself under fire. The choice seemed obvious.

However, there were those who wanted a deal "at any price," and there were a lot more who thought we should try to have a conservative figurehead deal with the NFL for a while to see if it would help. Dick Anderson was elected over Randy Vataha. It was also clear that management had pushed some players to become reps. Several of the strong reps told me not to worry as they would watch him and that I would, in any event, offset his pro-management sentiments.

Anderson opposed unions. In running for the presidency of the NFLPA, a certified union, he had difficulty rationalizing his philosophy. He didn't believe in strikes, so what would he do to exert pressure on the NFL to get them to bargain? Because he thought the election too close to call, he had to make some concessions in order to pick up support. His concession was that he would support our plan to file a class action lawsuit against the league, seeking damages for all players who had played during the past four years under the recently declared illegal Rozelle Rule, a position he had previously vehemently opposed.

We voted before the election, and the vote to file the class action suit was almost unanimous. (One rep humorously suggested that he favored putting all the player reps' names on the suit, but he insisted they be listed alphabetically. His name? John Zook of Atlanta.) The night of Anderson's election, some of us laughed about champagne corks popping in every club office in the NFL at that news and then management trying to push the corks back into the bottles when they heard about the class action decision.

By a quirk, three Anderson supporters were elected to the Executive Committee: Skip Butler and Fred Willis of the Oilers and Jack Youngblood of the Rams. Anderson's vote gave them a majority on the Executive Committee. The "Anderson Four" were pro-agreement-at-any-price. With their election went any hope that the NFL would work out a compromise settlement.

Once again, NFL management rode high, believing we would roll over. Their arrogance returned. They *knew* they had us now. It was only a question of time before they would act to sell a new agreement to Anderson. Only the filing of the class action baffled them. Even if Anderson and his crew wanted to sell out, how could they dismiss the class action suit controlled by Glennon, Garvey, and three members of the Executive Committee? Absent the class action, they would have moved quickly to buy the agreement. On the eve of filing, Fred Willis called me and seemed almost frantic in his plea not to file. But file we did.

The NFL decided to wait. Presumably, Anderson and Rozelle wanted to hold off on offering their new contract until the players were back in training camp, so a quick vote could help ratify the agreement they knew Anderson would accept. By the spring of 1976, Anderson was positive he would get a deal. He told us he was talking with his coach Don Shula and sometimes the team's principal owner, Joe Robbie. As the summer wore on, we had had a few bargaining sessions but made little progress. We won our NLRB case against the NFL on June 30. In that decision, nearly every charge against the NFL was upheld by Judge Charles Schneider, and the NFL was held guilty of massive unfair labor practices. Another shot in the arm for us.

However, it seemed clear that as long as I was in the room during negotiations, nothing would happen. The NFL negotiators knew that I would ask tough questions, but more important, they felt it was imperative that I receive absolutely no credit for making a deal. After all, if I helped negotiate the deal, my hand would be strengthened and they would have to contend with me in the future. They wanted none of that. The deal had to be made with Anderson alone. They would give him the credit, then he would fire me or I would resign, and they would have another era of "peace and goodwill." Anderson could move in as executive director, or they might even bring back Alan Miller or, as one rumor had it, Nick Buoniconti.

Another fact was becoming too obvious to ignore: We would be out of money soon. The association's credit was not very good, so when we tried to borrow money to make payroll and pay the phone bills, we would get it only if I personally guaranteed the loan. My wife and I signed the note, and we received enough money to keep the office doors open. Because of the funding shortage, I started visiting teams in mid-August on the West Coast and planned to work my way back to the East Coast. It meant more time away from home, but it would save a lot of money.

I started in San Francisco and then went to Seattle. In Seattle, I got a call from Anderson, who wanted an Executive Committee meeting in New York. He said that the owners were coming up with a new offer and that they would negotiate with us. He said that it was imperative we meet immediately. I reminded him of our financial crunch, but he demanded a meeting.

I called Gene Upshaw; he smelled a rat. He told me to return east but said he would stay in Oakland's training camp. In the meantime, he would call Dan Rooney to confirm whether there really was a new offer coming and whether they would bargain with us in New York. He surprised Rooney, who told him that there were no plans to bargain, but he urged Upshaw to attend the New York meeting! Apparently, Rooney knew more about "our" meeting than Gene Upshaw. Upshaw stayed in Oakland.

Lenny Hauss and Doug Van Horn smelled the same rat, so we decided they should attend the New York meeting. When we arrived at Anderson's hotel, it was obvious that Willis, Butler, and Anderson had been in discussion prior to our arrival. Even though Youngblood arrived later, it was soon apparent that he was on the inside track as well. Anderson began the meeting by telling us that he had had discussions with Dan Rooney and that management would soon give us a new offer. He started outlining some of the features but ducked when we asked for the location of these sessions and for details of the deal. He argued that when the deal came it should immediately go to the players without a rep meeting.

They were just too obvious. We noted that our constitution forbade that type of action and asked again what was in the new offer. Anderson started reading from notes, but the so-called offer wasn't in writing. I suggested that when we got it, we should meet again and decide whether or not to call a meeting of the player reps to discuss it. Anderson argued that it was going to be the best deal we would ever get, and Youngblood, supposedly without any prior knowledge, agreed with him.

From March 16, 1974, until August 1976, we had not received a good faith offer. The 1974 strike, the Patriots' strike in 1975, the *Mackey* decision—nothing had forced a new offer. Yet here we were in New York City, hearing that magically we were about to receive "the best deal we would ever get." It stretched credulity a bit far.

Len Hauss asked what the hurry was all about, and he was quickly accused of "not wanting an agreement." Hauss laughed, and he, Van Horn, and I headed for the door. We told Anderson to get it to us as soon as possible. The rat was starting to stink. (Three years later we would learn that Rooney and Rozelle were waiting to meet with Anderson and his supporters in Rozelle's office. After we left, they had a meeting, and Rozelle's lawyers worked out the details of their deal.)

One week later, my wife and I were scheduled to leave for a European vacation. It was a reunion with old friends. Hauss, Van Horn, and Upshaw told me to go ahead and not to worry about Anderson. They were the only ones who knew I was leaving the country, and they wouldn't let any meeting take place while I was gone.

Two days later, my wife and I arrived in Holland. I called the office to find out if anything had transpired. Sure enough, Anderson had called for an emergency meeting of the player reps. We hadn't received the offer, which meant the Executive Committee had nothing to review, but we were expected to have a meeting.

Rozelle's orchestration had begun. The press received leaks saying that a deal had been made. The image of Anderson and Rooney, sleeves rolled, going at it for hours, was soon created: Anderson, the hard but reasonable bargainer, looking out for the players' interests; Rooney, the tough but generous owner, looking out for the interests of his fellow owners. Most important, both were looking out for the best interests of *the game*. It was almost funny to watch the league work with its sportswriters.

In the meantime, I was making reservations to return to the battle, leaving my wife with friends in Holland. I told the staff to get John Mackey,

Kermit Alexander, and Alan Page to the meeting and took off for Chicago. By the time I arrived, the AP was carrying a story explaining that the Executive Committee had already approved a deal worked out privately with Rooney and would recommend it to the reps.

When the committee gathered in the O'Hare Hilton, there was so much tension that there were no handshakes, no greetings. All pretenses were dropped. Anderson began by saying that we should recommend the agreement. Upshaw asked if it would be too much of an imposition to see it before voting on it. Finally, Anderson dispatched his fellow "Anderson Four" committee member Skip Butler to get the box of agreements.

On the box, I noted the label from the Chicago Bears: "Deliver only to Dick Anderson." After distributing the agreements, but before anyone could look at the lengthy document, Anderson and Butler began asking for a vote.

Upshaw hit the roof. He asked about the press story saying that we had already voted to accept; he asked about the secret meetings; and he asked how it could be that a meeting like this had been called over his objection. The Chargers' Fred Willis told him to be quiet and suggested that he was only saying what "Garvey wants you to say."

Upshaw was on his feet in a flash. "Let's settle this real fast, Fred. Come on out in the hall."

Willis said he would but he had a bad shoulder, and then he added, "I'm sick of this. I quit."

With that, Len Hauss gave him the umpire's thumb and motioned for the door. Willis refused to leave. The scene was extraordinarily tense. Clearly, there would be no vote, because there wouldn't be a quorum. Anderson looked panicked. The plan was falling apart. He hadn't expected me there. Somehow he had learned that I was in Holland. He wasn't prepared to handle an angry Upshaw and Hauss. He quickly tried to defend the agreement to the group, but he didn't have answers to any of their questions. I asked where Rooney was, and he told me he was at the Regency in New York. That was all we needed.

The group left my room at 2:00 A.M. I read the agreement and listed my questions. At 6:00 A.M. I awakened Dan Rooney. I told him we had a few questions, but Rooney made it clear that it was a take-it-or-leave-it deal. There would be no changes. I then invited him to fly to Chicago to meet with the reps. He refused. I asked if Karch could go, and he said, "No, we are through with meeting."

As the player rep meeting began, people were extremely uptight. In order to make sure everyone went to the meeting, management faxed all teams telling them a deal had been made and to make certain their player rep was at the meeting to vote on it. The stage was set, and Anderson walked to the microphone to start the meeting. He began by saying that he had been elected to "get a deal" and that now he had one. This was the "best contract you are ever going to get from management. You had better accept it."

Then he started in on me: "We have listened to Garvey's legal advice for too long. What has it gotten us? I say it's time that the players decide what they want." He then said *he* would run the meeting, not "Garvey," and asked if I had anything to say.

I went to the microphone and told the reps that in 1974 Lonnie Warwick had asked me in the Atlanta team meeting if management had ever offered me a bribe. I answered, "No, but never stop asking the question." I suggested to the reps that they ask that question today.

I sat down, and the meeting started. Anderson was shocked to see John Mackey, Alan Page, and Kermit Alexander walk in. He stared at me and said, "Who invited them?"

Anderson also took a shot at Lindquist and Vennum by stating that their advice had not helped to get an agreement, so he had sought outside counsel to get an objective view of our struggle with the NFL. (All that Lindquist and Glennon had done was to win every case brought against the NFL! The *Mackey* case had not been paid for; we hadn't paid them in months because of our financial crisis, yet they were at the meeting to lend assistance.) Anderson knew that his only chance at the meeting was to silence me and to discredit Lindquist. A major part of the offer he hammered out with Rooney was dismissal of the class action suit "with prejudice" (meaning that no one could bring a similar suit in the future) and termination of the *Mackey* case, which was scheduled for a fall decision by the Eighth Circuit Court of Appeals.

Anderson went on to say that Dean Burch, former Barry Goldwater aide and former Republican Party chairman, had been his "unpaid legal consultant." Anderson told the reps that Burch favored dismissal of the lawsuits and agreed with Anderson's assessment of the legal situation. How did Dick Anderson get in contact with Dean Burch? You don't suppose that Jack Kemp arranged the meeting, or how about a helpful Pete Rozelle?

But, once again, Anderson underestimated his fellow players, just as management had. He thought that to get the players to go along with him he only had to inform them that Lindquist and Glennon were wrong, that Garvey hadn't gotten an agreement, that Burch knew more about the NFL and antitrust laws than we did. I knew better. Too many people sensed victory nearing, too many had sacrificed their careers to win the battles, too many realized that the legal representation had been excellent. More than that, who was Dean Burch? There weren't many Republican player reps, and few players were impressed with Burch's credentials. If he was so good, why wasn't he here to explain and defend his position?

For most of our rep meetings, players would buy their own tickets and then the NFLPA would reimburse them. For this meeting, in the middle of training camp, teams had prepaid the tickets for the reps and the teams were ordered to aid the players in their efforts to attend the meeting. Some club officials were so happy about the Anderson-Rooney deal that they couldn't refrain from commenting to the reps. R******'s executive Tim Timerario was typical. He approached Lenny Hauss and told him how happy he was that "We finally have a deal." He did this soon after our abortive New York Executive Committee session. Hauss asked, "What deal?" and Timerario responded that it had already been agreed to and "Ed Garvey can't stop it this time."

As the meeting progressed, Anderson started fielding questions. Every time he faced opposition about a section of the agreement, he would say, "No problem. Dan told me they would be willing to change that." Or, "I'm sure they wouldn't object to that change." He was really selling—overselling. I told the players Rooney had assured me that it was a take-it-or-leave-it offer and that there would be no negotiations on any subject. Anderson then said that he had talked with Rooney after I did, that he knew how to deal with management, and that I did not.

Then John Mackey was asked what he thought, and his only response was to ask why we were in such a hurry. Anderson had Andy Russell attend for Pittsburgh and Fred Cox and Ed White for Minnesota in order to bolster his forces. But Alan Page quickly challenged White's credentials. It turned out that he had never been elected as the player rep. Russell had not paid dues. They were no match for Alexander, Mackey, and Page. Throughout the day, Hauss, Van Horn, and Upshaw talked with the reps and filled them in on the maneuvers that had led to a secret deal.

At 5:00 P.M., with the press begging for news that the reps had accepted, we were about to vote. Anderson, sensing defeat, was now desperate. He shouted that this was "the best deal you are ever going to get! There is no sense in returning to the bargaining table. There is no more for them to give."

 The vote was 22–4 to table the agreement. Once again, management had lost. Maybe now they would understand that they would have to deal with the union—above the table.

Two weeks later, Dick Anderson called Lenny Hauss and asked if he would hold a team meeting with the R°°°°°°s so Anderson could tell players the details of the Anderson-Rooney agreement. (Some of the reps started to refer to it as the "Anderson-Looney" or "Looney-Rooney" agreement.) Anderson also wanted a private dinner meeting with Hauss and Dan Rooney. Hauss agreed to both but added me to the invitation list.

At the R°°°°°°s team meeting, Hauss asked Anderson if he wanted to start the meeting, but Anderson deferred to me. Lenny then gave me a very complimentary introduction, and I proceeded to tell the team about the Anderson-Rooney near fiasco and reaffirmed our commitment to openness within the union.

R°°°°°°s player Bill Brundige then asked Anderson to defend himself. As Anderson was about to speak, his former Dolphins teammate Jake Scott, now playing for Washington, requested permission to speak. I expected a vote of confidence for Anderson, but Scott said, "All I want to say, Dick, is that anyone who would sell out the players' right to impartial arbitration and name Rozelle as the arbitrator is a goddamned idiot."

Anderson was stunned! "Thanks, Jake" was his only response. Then he started in on how good the pension would be under his agreement. He was speaking to older veterans, and apparently he thought that if he could sell them on the agreement, then the other teammates would fall in line.

Within minutes, R°°°°°°s player Ron McDole took the floor to tell Anderson that the older vets were too smart to fall for the pension crap. He said, "We have been around too long and have been screwed too many times to listen to talk about a pension." Players Jean Fugett and Calvin Hill then discussed the importance of freedom and players' rights, and it was all over.

Anderson had failed to convince anyone. The meeting ended shortly thereafter, and Anderson, Hauss, and I headed for dinner with Dan Rooney. Prior to the dinner meeting, we had heard from one general manager that there was a signed agreement between Anderson and Rooney. We were determined to find out if that was true.

Rooney was a friendly person, and Lenny and I liked him. While he had pulled a fast one with the agreement, we couldn't blame him for trying to take advantage of a sweetheart on our side. After all, he was only first violinist; Rozelle was the conductor.

After some banter about training camp, I asked Rooney to clear up the rumor about a signed agreement between himself and Dick Anderson. Rooney responded, "That is an inappropriate question." I suggested that I would rephrase it, but he said he wouldn't respond. I then turned to Anderson and asked him. He also declined to answer.

By now, Lenny Hauss was a little hot. He said, "Let me get this straight. Neither of you will tell me, a vice president of the union, and Ed, the executive director of the union, whether or not you signed a deal?" They said that was correct, and there was a long pause while we ordered dinner.

There was little left to say. If they would hide a signed agreement from us, what good would conversation be? We had some heated exchanges but ended dinner on a friendly note. After all, it was just another meeting between the union and management.

Anderson and the NFL still had an ace in the pile: The *Mackey* appeal. If we were to lose the appeal, then Anderson be proven correct in saying that our legal advice was bad and that we might never reach agreement. If we were to win the appeal, the NFL would be out of places to turn. The chances of the U.S. Supreme Court overturning the Eighth Circuit were remote.

The court ruled in October, and, once again, we won. The decision was unanimous. The district court decision was affirmed with an important modification. The appeals court said that the Rozelle Rule was "unreasonably restrictive" but *not* "illegal, *per se*." The court went on to say that a restriction on player movement would be legal if the union, after good faith, arm's-length collective bargaining, accepted a substitute restriction.

The decision assured the union of some ultimate success but also placed a tremendous burden on us. Now that we had won the appeal, there would be nothing standing in the way of winning damages in the class action suit. While damages were virtually assured, the fact that we could legalize their otherwise illegal conduct by agreeing with that conduct gave many of us considerable pause while Dick Anderson was still president. He would argue that now we could agree with the system that he and Rooney had worked out! Never mind that it was worked out when the union had little strength or that it was worked out by two people who did not believe in the free movement of players.

Thus, the Eighth Circuit appeal was a success, but it was also a heavy burden.

In November, a month after the appellate court ruling, Sarge Karch called and asked to meet with me to discuss a possible settlement. I was immediately suspicious. Rooney and Rozelle had had their secret meeting with

Anderson—that didn't work, so they figured, "Let's try Garvey." I called the Executive Committee, and they told me to meet with Karch. These would not be "secret" meetings.

I arrived at his suite at the Madison Hotel in Washington at 10:00 A.M. The discussion lasted several hours. I found a "new" Karch. He was relaxed, friendly, and actually humorous. He asked what it would take to settle the contract. I was still suspicious as I thought they might well accept a few items, add in some money, and, with Anderson's help, once again try to sell a deal to the players over the heads of the player reps.

Nevertheless, I told him we needed several things. First, I said, Rozelle must go as the arbitrator: "We will never agree on a contract with Rozelle as arbitrator, and that is final." Then I listed injury protection for the veterans, more jobs, union security, higher squad size, and a system that would allow lower-paid athletes freedom of movement. Karch began a discussion of these points while trying to determine exactly how far they would have to go to meet our needs. I had been down the primrose path before, so I took it with a grain of salt, but I reported to the Executive Committee that he appeared to be serious.

A few weeks later, I met Karch again in New York at the Waldorf. He wanted to know how much money it would take to settle the lawsuits, and I told him $20 million. He urged me to be more realistic, but I stuck to the figure. Little else was discussed, but Karch wanted assurances that there would be no more lawsuits or strikes for the life of the agreement. I agreed, but if we settled the suits and had an impartial arbitrator, we wouldn't need to go to court. We agreed to meet at Super Bowl time and left on a positive note.

Our Super Bowl meetings in Los Angeles added little. Carroll Rosenbloom set up a private meeting with Rozelle, Anderson, and me. Now that we were making progress, we thought Rozelle might get involved in order to get some publicity, but at his hotel suite, it was immediately apparent that he had decided to make the meeting meaningless. After some chitchat about the upcoming Super Bowl, I suggested that we leave. It had been a complete waste of time.

The Pro Bowl was scheduled for a week later in Seattle, but the practices were held in San Diego. Gene Upshaw was a perennial All-Pro, so we decided to meet with the management committee there. We began with a luncheon meeting with Rozelle. The only memorable thing from that luncheon was Rozelle's offhand comment to Upshaw that "This is your last Pro Bowl." Upshaw and I looked quizzically at each other. But Rozelle was almost right—it was Gene's second-to-last Pro Bowl! (A cynic might have wondered then about Pro Bowl selections.)

Upshaw and I next spent about two hours with management's committee, and, unbelievably, they accepted an increase in squad size and came close to our demand on minimum salary. We left impressed with the idea that they did, indeed, want to bargain. The lawsuits were putting them under pressure.

Characterizing the Karch-Garvey meeting and the San Diego meetings as the first collective bargaining sessions in NFL history would be 100 percent accurate. For the first time in fifty-seven years, NFL negotiators were actually giving something to the union that the union wanted. No longer were they telling us simply what they wanted, what they would give up, and that we had to take it or shove it.

Our full committees met in New Orleans ten days later. Three days of intensive bargaining convinced even the doubters that they wanted an agreement. They needed the draft and feared lawsuits if they held it with no agreement, and they needed compensation for free agents now that the Rozelle Rule had been struck down by the appeals court. They also needed to settle their lawsuits with us or face enormous damages. Apparently, however, from what I subsequently learned, even then, Rozelle and Ham Carothers opposed a settlement. They wanted to litigate until the end and were never happy with the efforts to get an agreement. They wanted one more chance to get rid of me. An agreement would only strengthen the "radicals," in their assessment. But by the end of the New Orleans session, it was obvious that we were on the way to settlement.

Two weeks later, in some tense sessions in New York, the final pages of the agreement were written. There was a lot of give-and-take, and several times we were about to break off negotiations, but for once *they* wanted to stay and bargain.

Anderson arrived late to the sessions, and when he was convinced that there would be no further progress, he returned to Miami. Four hours later, we reached across the table and shook hands with the management team. The "militants"—Kermit Alexander, Doug Van Horn, and I—had settled the contract. Seven years of fighting with the NFL had finally ended. We gained a lot:

- $15,675,000 for the settled lawsuits
- Impartial arbitration
- Fifty-six more jobs
- Injury protection for veterans
- Freedom for the lower-paid athletes
- A graduated minimum salary level

- Union security
- And more

We gave them a lot as well:

- Draft of rookies (with some protection for the rookies)
- Control over the movement of higher-paid players
- Stability
- And this five-year agreement five months before the announcement of their new television contract, which would more than double their profits

We joined Mara, Rooney, and Karch for a beer and then headed back to our hotel, where Van Horn, Alexander, and I had another beer to discuss the contract. Had we done the right thing? I remembered Leonard Lindquist's comment after we signed the no-strike pledge: "Don't worry, mistakes are for this world, perfection is for the next." We believed the contract would help most of the players, and that had been the goal. Among other things, it marked an end to Rozelle's absolute control. All in all, not a bad deal.

The reps unanimously approved the agreement, and the court accepted the settlement. Ninety percent of the players who voted favored the agreement. We were finished fighting. Ah, but not for long. Within months, the NFL fired Karch, his assistant Terry Bledsoe resigned, and they removed Mara and Rooney from their committee. Then they dropped the bomb.

They claimed to have a "perpetual option" on all players—meaning that, once a free agent's contract with his team was up, that team would still hold his rights and could match the terms of and demand draft-pick compensation from another team interested in acquiring that player, albeit compensation based on a preapproved structure rather than the whims of the commissioner. Even though it was not written into the agreement, that was their "good faith" interpretation of the contract, an interpretation agreed upon in a secret meeting of owner-monopolists in Seattle. If all monopolists agree on an interpretation, what could anyone do to fight it? Dan Rooney explained to me that the owners had agreed to that interpretation a month before we had reached agreement! When I asked Rooney whether he felt any obligation to tell us that at the bargaining table, he said "maybe" they should have.

On May 16, 1978, one year and three months after reaching agreement, we were back in court arguing that the owners had perpetrated a fraud on the court. We asked that Judge Larson take the case again to knock out the "new reserve clause," but Judge Larson refused. He told us to work it out under the new agreement. Ah yes, "in good faith." The owners didn't yet understand the meaning of the words, but next time it would all be spelled out.

We learned yet another lesson from teacher Rozelle: Interpretation of an agreement by a monopoly is as important as the language itself. But the clock was running on the old tactics employed by the NFL.

Despite it all, I honestly believed that professional sports would never return to the old days, because of the gallant efforts of players who cared more about dignity, freedom, and their fellow players than about their own careers. We didn't win as much as we thought we had, but gradually the loopholes were closing. Gradually, we were establishing player rights. Gradually, we were establishing a union.

goal

9

The Future

The decision of the NFL owners to interpret the collective bargaining agreement as a perpetually renewable option (like the baseball reserve clause of the 1800s) meant that our long fight for freedom through true free agency had been a waste of time for all but a few throughout the life of our five-year contract. The old illegal Rozelle Rule was adopted in 1963 at a secret meeting of owner-monopolists. Wishing to avoid court challenges of the rule, club owners tried to avoid having a large number of option "play outs" because the chilling effect of the rule would be too obvious if a significant number of players could not move. In particular, clubs made certain that no star athlete would play out the option and become a free agent. Had John Unitas, Bart Starr, or Jim Brown become free agents in the 1960s or early 1970s and not received offers, the restrictive nature of the Rozelle Rule would have been publicly exposed. A court challenge would surely have followed.

The result of the Rozelle Rule was that very few players annually became free agents and a few stars did quite well financially. Between 1963 and the *Mackey* trial in 1975, a year with as many as twelve to fifteen free agents would be unusual. The one exception was 1971, when President Richard Nixon froze wages. An extraordinary number of players became free agents the next year because the teams could not offer more than a 5.5 percent increase. Over seventy players were declared free on May 1, 1972, and ten of those became plaintiffs in the *Mackey* case to test the legality of the Rozelle

Rule. Absent the wage freeze, we would have had difficulty finding representative plaintiffs.

When the court of appeals ruled that restrictions accepted by the union were legal, everything changed. Owners no longer attempted to mask their conspiracy, which was their wage scale. Rather, they would flaunt their collusion because it was "legal." In 1977, 37 players played out their deals and became free agents; by 1979, there were 139; and by 1980, there were 137. In other words, there were four to five times the number of free agents between 1978 and 1981 than in the previous twelve years.

As hundreds of players became free agents, we witnessed a complete boycott of all but two or three free agents. Only one player, Norm Thompson of St. Louis, moved to another team under our elaborate new compensation system. The other three hundred signed new contracts with their old clubs, retired, or went to Canada. Even stars were allowed or challenged to play out the option by confident general managers who knew that no offers would be forthcoming from other teams.

Jim Finks, general manager of the Bears, challenged All-Pro Wally Chambers to "go ahead and play out the option." Joe Sullivan did the same with Terry Metcalf, even tearing up the last year of his contract. They understood that the NFL had cleverly returned to the 1950s and 1960s, but this time they would do it within the law—or at least they were confident they wouldn't be challenged. Price fixing, agreement on wages, and a boycott of free agents would still be illegal, but now they had an excuse—draft choices as compensation would be held up as the reason no offers were made.

―――――――

From 1963 through the *Mackey* trial, club owners and general managers defended the refusal to make offers to free agents on two grounds: (1) they feared the unknown compensation that Rozelle would name; and (2) veteran players might—and probably would—be named as compensation.

They argued that if clubs knew in advance exactly what it would cost to sign a free agent, then they would make offers, particularly if an established veteran could never be the price of signing another proven veteran. Most clubs privately agreed that after the first couple of rounds, the draft was a crapshoot. You might get a blue-chip performer in the third, fifth, or tenth rounds, but statistically your chances weren't good. Coaches generally preferred a veteran who had demonstrated that he could perform in the NFL to the future draft choice of a rookie who may be overrated.

Our concept in the 1977 agreement was designed to address the precise reason why veteran free agents had not received offers under the Rozelle

Rule. Compensation would be fixed in advance, and only draft choices could be used as compensation. Perfect! Now we could test the free market in the NFL.

Pete Rozelle once said that Chiefs owner Lamar Hunt would use the "Pro Bowl program like a Sears catalogue" if free agency came to the NFL. We would give him a chance. Ego, we thought, would bring some owners into the bidding in order to win. And then there was always George Allen, who worked exclusively with veterans.

———————

owners

Our high hopes had been dashed by the secret interpretation of the option as being renewable if a veteran free agent failed to receive an offer, but still we had confidence that offers would be made. Confident, that is, until news stories began appearing quoting Schramm, Rooney, and Finks that a team "must build strength through the draft." Dallas and Pittsburgh were successful "because of the draft." Suddenly, draft choices became their most important asset. "Fear of the unknown" quickly gave way to "fear of the known." Tested veterans were no less valuable in the new market than third-round crapshoots. George Allen, with his preference for veterans, was fired and blackballed. Walter Payton, Vince Ferragamo, James Scott, Jim Hart, and Dan Dierdorf became free agents but were "not worth" draft choices in the future. Nonsense!

What should have been obvious to us had not been: Free agency would never work in the NFL because owners agreed not to bid for free agents.

Think of the history of organized team sports. One theme that dominates all others is the reserve clause, designed to hold down wages. First it was the option, then the draft, then the perpetually renewable option, then the Rozelle Rule, all with the purpose of holding down wages. ✳ ✳

Owners adopted the Rozelle Rule in 1963 to eliminate bidding for players and escalating salaries. In 1977, they met in Seattle and agreed to interpret any future agreement with the union as a renewable option—just like the old days. In 1981, Rozelle and twenty-seven owners would call themselves "partners" in the *LA Coliseum/Al Davis* trial. They would insist that they were not competitors off the field—they were part of a "single business entity," a "unitary partnership."

Would partners within a single economic entity bid against one another? It did not seem possible to me. The NFL's attorney explained the NFL's business practice in the *Davis* trial. He said the key is "close, exciting games in which the outcome is unclear; in which there is an element of uncertainty. The NFL has from 1920 forward consistently met change, fine-tuned its rules to assure that the kind of competitors that the Raiders were trying to sell here will never determine who the prevalent team on the playing field will be. . . . The league is a special kind a business animal . . . it is a single business." In other words, balance in the league is what counts; making certain the richer teams cannot dominate—by bidding for free agents—is what counts. They were telling us that to expect the Chicago Bears to compete with their partner in Minneapolis makes as much sense as two Sears stores trying to drive each other out of business or as a gas war within Exxon.

In case the message was too subtle for us, Tampa Bay owner Hugh Culverhouse explained it clearly to me and Gene Upshaw in New York, three years before the *Davis* trial. Culverhouse asked what the union would seek in 1982, and I responded that we would seek a percentage of gross revenues and a wage scale.

He seemed genuinely surprised and asked why.

I said, "Because you bastards will never bid for free agents even if all compensation is eliminated."

Culverhouse agreed with that assertion. As he put it, "If I bid for one of Bud Adams's boys [Houston Oilers], he will get mad and bid for two of my boys. The end result will be that I lose two boys and overpay one. It's better if we leave each other's boys alone." Spoken like a partner of Bud Adams and a coconspirator of all other owners. Obviously, he had been carefully schooled on the value of not bidding on free agents by teacher Rozelle, but apparently the teacher had forgotten to warn him to keep their little secret quiet.

Balance within the league, close games, that was the goal. As Bill Ray, NFL treasurer, explained the role of the Competition Committee of the NFL: "They address themselves to control of players because there is a very strict monitoring of the number of players that any club can control because if you have more . . . you have a competitive advantage, and they want to equalize the competitive aspect."

Exactly. Listen carefully: The Competition Committee made rules to insure against domination by one team. Keep them equal and the league will succeed.

Revenue Sharing

A decision to share revenues equally helped the NFL "partners" maintain their plan to equalize teams. Some owners would break stride and try to win by paying more money to, and for, players. But the NFL solved that problem by sharing revenue equally among winners and losers, starless teams and star-filled teams. Economic reward for success was eliminated early. Here's how:

Gate receipts—During the preseason, the two teams split revenues fifty-fifty after agreed-upon expenses. During the regular season, the home team kept 60 percent of revenue and the visiting team got 40 percent after deducting 15 percent for rental and other expenses.

A losing team got 40 percent on the road even if no one wanted to see them play the home team. With nearly all seats sold in advance of the NFL's relatively short season, the loser was guaranteed as much from gate receipts as the winner. In 1980, 92.4 percent of all seats were filled in NFL stadiums, including 72 percent by season ticket sales long before anyone put on a helmet.

The result: Winners and losers received roughly the same at home as on the road, the only difference being stadium size and ticket prices. There was no reward from gate receipts for excellence.

Television receipts—Each team received the same amount from the networks. In 1976 that was $2.4 million; in 1981 it was $5.8 million; and in 1982 it was expected to be $12.5–$14 million per team, regardless of a team's record or its TV ratings. Also in 1982, the NFL reached agreement on a $2 billion, five-year agreement guaranteeing over $14 million per team per year. All teams shared equally.

NFL Films—Bill Ray testified that the subsidiary monopoly NFL Films made a profit and that each team received 1/28 of it.

NFL Properties—Ray said, "It is split if you are a popular club or an unpopular club. You get the same."

Luxury boxes—The eleven teams with loges, or so-called luxury boxes, would keep the money now but not for long. Ray testified: "We are looking into the matter of [sharing] income that comes from loge boxes."

Playoffs—A basic tenet of team sports holds that players who get into the championship contests must be rewarded for excellence. The unstated reason is to convince the fans that athletes have an incentive to perform well all season long even though they are paid a high salary. But NFL owner-monopolists-partners apparently eschewed the "What's good for the goose is good for the gander" saying. In the NFL, "postseason revenues are pooled and belong equally to each of the 28 clubs," according to Bill Ray's *Davis* testimony:

> The clubs themselves don't make a great deal, if any, money from the postseason games, the ones that compete. They don't make any more than the ones who don't compete.

The message was clear: The NFL did not want to reward owners whose teams made the playoffs. Success is not incentivized financially, so competition for the best players is not truly incentivized either. John Mecom's 1–15 Saints made as much from the 1981 Super Bowl as did Al Davis, whose Raiders team won. Raiders players received a $32,000 bonus for their excellence. Would they have tried as hard without the money? Who knows?

Let's return to the free agent seeking offers from the twenty-eight NFL partners. Would any "partner" bid for him? Why would they? If he went to a new team and that team did better, that team would not make any more money, even if the team made the playoffs and he were the sole reason (highly unlikely).

Faced with these realities, the NFLPA searched for a new approach. In 1968, 1970, and 1974–1977, the union attempted to help athletes negotiate more effectively. In 1968, we won the right to have a lawyer accompany the players in their negotiations with their teams; in 1970, the right to have a lawyer or an agent; in 1977, modified free agency, higher minimum wages, and a "good faith bargaining" requirement with resort to an outside arbitrator. But none of these improvements helped much because of the owners' revenue-sharing plan and their secret agreements with one another.

We thought about reforming the system next time around, but the more we studied the NFL, the more obvious it became that individual negotiations in the NFL simply would not work no matter what we did. We began to review our bargaining efforts from 1968 through 1977, and we realized we were tilting against windmills. Our efforts had been to make individual negotiations work—to give leverage to the individual. But that effort was based on the premise that owners would compete for talent if we removed artificial restraints such as the Rozelle Rule.

We concluded that individual negotiations could not possibly help the athlete gain a fair percentage of the revenues he generates in the NFL. In 1977, we finally achieved the right to review all individual contracts. Upon a review of all contracts in the NFL, certain patterns became obvious, patterns that in retrospect should have been predictable.

Draft choices throughout the NFL received nearly identical salaries depending on the round in which they were selected. Third-round choices in Miami received the same salary as the Chicago third-round choice; 100 percent of fourth-round choices in 1970 had first-year salaries between $30,000 and $35,000. If the teams were truly "negotiating" with agents and players, there would be a much greater range. Eighth-year tackles were within a few thousand dollars of each other whether they played for Minnesota or Los Angeles.

When it hit us, I couldn't believe how naive we had been. Why hadn't we seen it before? There was a wage scale in the NFL, agreed to by twenty-eight "partners" in a single business.

As we approached collective bargaining in 1982, for the fourth time in NFL history, almost everything had changed. No longer would the union try to make individual bargaining work. Instead, players would, for the first time in sports history, demand a fixed percentage of gross revenues for wages and fringe benefits. No longer would we believe owner-partners and their commissioner who said that "owners will do anything to win." (Anything, that is, except negotiate fair contracts, sign free agents, and spend money.)

We learned a lesson or two from teachers Rozelle, Schramm, and Carothers. I was reminded of a demand made by the NFL of the union in 1970:

> NFLPA Continuity: Since the emergence of the Players Association as an active unit, there has been a continued lack of continuity in its personnel and direction. It is certainly urged by the members of the NFL that the NFLPA establish an organization which provides a major degree of permanency. It is only in this way that a proper working relationship and confidence can be developed between the Member Clubs and the NFLPA.

The NFL wrote those statements as they edged Dan Shulman out and just two years after they convinced players to reject the "continuity" provided by the Teamsters. Then they benched and fired John Mackey, Bill Curry, Tom Keating, and Kermit Alexander. Continuity, my foot! The demand should have read: "We demand continuity in the NFLPA, and we will provide it if you let us name your officers and staff."

While calling for continuity in the NFLPA, the owners and Rozelle loved the *lack* of continuity. New negotiators could be fooled into believing that the battle should always center on free agency, on making the draft less restrictive. We should fight to loosen the cuffs, not to have them removed. We should worry about per diem, minimum wages, and squad size. We should not seek a piece of the action. Partnership among owners is acceptable, but partnership with the performer-athlete is not what they had in mind.

But after twelve years of experience, we realized that we needed to focus on the real issue: A fair share of the revenue.

How Much Is Fair?

Many sportswriters were shocked at first when we announced that we wanted 55 percent of gross revenue in 1982, but after listening to our concept, many thought it made sense. The first question asked was "After the success of free agency in baseball, why wouldn't you go for it in the NFL?"

I explained that owners in baseball rewarded winning clubs with money, providing an incentive to win. Also, baseball's television revenues were generated locally, and the local baseball team got to keep 100 percent of that money. Winning baseball teams had better TV ratings and, therefore, made more money. Not so in football. Winners and losers got the same. Also, the baseball schedule was much longer than the NFL schedule, generating more games and more revenue from those streams. In addition, free agent baseball stars like Pete Rose, Catfish Hunter, Reggie Jackson, and others helped draw crowds over the long schedule, so there was an economic incentive for owners to sign big-name free agents.

In the NFL, a free agent Pete Rose would go wanting. For example, the R******s would not have made an additional dime had they signed free agent Walter Payton. All their season tickets were sold in advance, with thousands of people on the waiting list. TV monies were shared equally, and had Payton taken the R******s to the playoffs, the organization's share would have been the same as other teams'! The result was that Payton did not receive an offer from the R******s or anyone else because *no other team would earn an additional dime by signing one of the greatest backs in NFL history.*

Edward Bennett Williams, trial lawyer, R******s president, and owner of the baseball Orioles, told the *Washington Post* and the *Wall Street Journal* in separate interviews in the spring of 1981 that baseball needed the "quasi-socialism" of the NFL to solve its free agent "problem." Williams's message was quite simple: Eliminate economic rewards for star players and for winning. Once you do that, free agents become a drag on the market. Then owners could get on with the important business of making money.

Because of NFL "socialism," our only hope of obtaining a fair share was to seek a percentage. The second question became "What is a fair percentage?"

We researched the percentage of gross going to National Hockey League (NHL) players and learned that they received 48 percent in 1979. Baseball players got about 50 percent. National Basketball Association (NBA) players got over 70 percent. During the WFL-NFL competition (albeit only two years), players in the NFL received 45 percent of gross. In 1966, the last year of direct competition with the AFL, players on the NFL teams received an estimated 52–60 percent of all revenues. The U.S. Census Bureau told us that players in the AFL and NFL in 1967 received an incredible 67 percent of gross.

Originally, we settled on 55 percent per player as being fair to both players and owners. Players are the game—they provide the entertainment, and they take all the risks; therefore, 55 percent seemed a moderate demand, a reasonable share.

In 1981, NFL players received less than 30 percent of the gross, and with television revenues slated to double in 1982, that percentage would drop substantially if we allowed individual negotiations to continue. There would be several side benefits for management under our proposal, although, admittedly, they would make less money. But why not? They were really promoters more than owners. They really own very little.

Let's compare them with a concert promoter: The promoter of a Barry Manilow concert hires Manilow, rents a hall, prints tickets, and advertises the event. What does Dan Rooney, owner of the Steelers, do? He hires the performers, rents the hall (field), prints the tickets, and advertises the performance (game). Owner? Promoter? Whatever you call him, he has no risk. The performers in football take on tremendous risk on every play, yet Barry Manilow keeps 90 percent of the gross while the promoter takes 10 percent, which makes sense. But in football, Rooney keeps 70 percent, which doesn't make sense.

Our question was simple: "Isn't it time to reward the performer as well as the promoter in team sports?" To us, the answer was obvious.

How Much Money Is Involved?

The amount of money involved was staggering. The *LA Coliseum/Davis* trial provided some extremely valuable information. For the first time, we saw the gate receipts of every NFL team, the average ticket price, and the actual home-and-away split. It helped us tremendously. No longer were we speculating about team revenues. Now we knew.

Total ticket sales in 1980 were $184 million league-wide, or an impressive $6.6 million per team (including preseason, regular season, and postseason). Television and radio revenues were $6.3 million per team, or $176,400,000 league-wide. Total revenues were over $400 million. The myth that TV brings in the lion's share of the money was exploded. Gate actually accounted for nearly 45 percent of revenues.

The average team in 1980 had gross revenues of $14.3 million. Teams paid players an average salary of $78,500, only 28 percent of gross revenues. With gate receipts expected to increase by 30 percent in 1982 (prices go up by 15 percent a year on average), and TV revenues to double to over $12 million per team, players would receive an ever-declining piece of the pie if we allowed individual negotiations to continue. Average team revenues in 1982 were estimated at $22.5 million. If players received an average of $100,000, they would be receiving only 20–22 percent of the gross—a decline of 6–8 percent. And there was absolutely no assurance that the average salary would climb to $100,000.

Some owners called our concept radical, while others were more understanding. The question asked most often was why athletes deserved a piece of the pie. We responded by explaining that NFL owners were really "promoters." They don't own anything except player contracts and monopoly rights bestowed by fellow "partners" and their commissioner. Why should the promoters get 70 percent of the gross to spend any way they want?

In the *LA Coliseum* case against the NFL, Don Shula was called as an NFL witness. The NFL attorney asked what was needed to play football. Shula responded, "Ball, players, equipment, and a field." Had he been pressed, he might have added coaches, but one doubts he thought owners or commissioners were necessary. Good answer, Shula.

Under our proposal, players would receive a *fair share* of revenues, which *they*, not the owner-promoters, generate. No longer would fans read about players walking out of camp over a contract dispute. And contracts would be real. Players would be paid even if cut in midseason. "Renegotiate" would be a word of the past. "Agent" would likewise be placed in the archives. Who needed an agent to take $50,000 or $100,000 from the players in meaningless individual negotiations?

This system would be fair to all players who walked onto a football field. For too long the owner-promoter had paid a star or two while exploiting hundreds of players. Now there would be a sensible way to reward those who risked their involvement in the NFL—the players. A player performed for eight years in high school and college, ran thousands of miles, lifted tons of weights, suffered through several operations. He risked that investment on every play. That risk should be rewarded. The only way the non-stars could be rewarded was through our proposal—the sharing of revenues. For the most part, football players lacked individual statistics to prove their worth, so they became "interchangeable parts." John Mackey commented, "There are parts factories all over the country called colleges turning out hundreds of new ones every year."

1982

Predictably, most owners reacted negatively to our proposals, and some, like Chuck Sullivan of New England, threw down the gauntlet. Yet a few agreed with Art Modell of Cleveland, who told *Los Angeles Times* reporter Bob Oates that the idea had merit. Modell left the door open by saying that the NFL adjusted when it had to.

The main line used by the NFL and their apologists in the trade press was "The owners will never agree; therefore, forget it." The answer was not "Your plan is unfair or unworkable"; it was just "No!"

I am reminded of that great line, "'Shut up!' he explained."

It would be an interesting fight. Our hope was that fans and writers would understand this time.

The NFLPA reached out for help before the battle could start. The players, eleven years after turning down the Teamsters, were welcomed into the fourteen-million-member AFL-CIO. The NFLPA also organized athletes in the North American Soccer League (NASL) into a union. We also organized the Major Indoor Soccer League players and, in so doing, entered into the first agreement in sports completely eliminating the reserve system. As NFL players went into battle with owner-promoters, they enjoyed the support of the soccer players and 120 affiliates of the AFL-CIO.

While we reached out for help, owners were already changing the landscape. In this case, a player could have said, "*Same* circus, *same* clowns." Cross-ownership in sports had become the rule. Joe Robbie owned the Miami Dolphins; his wife owned the Fort Lauderdale Strikers in the NASL. Lamar Hunt owned all or part of the Kansas City Chiefs in the NFL, the Dallas Tornado in the NASL, the Chicago Bulls in the NBA, and World Championship Tennis. Jerry Buss owned the Forum, the NBA Lakers, and the NHL Kings. Madison Square Garden, a subsidiary of Gulf and Western, owned the NBA Knicks and NHL Rangers. Ted Turner owned the NASL Chiefs, baseball's Braves, and the NBA Hawks. Ed Williams owned part of the Washington R******s and all of the baseball Orioles. Lee Stern owned the NASL Chicago Sting and part of the baseball White Sox.

To state the obvious, owners in all sports were working on a common strategy on all fronts: Increase profits from pay-TV, control labor relations, and maintain a reserve system. They used the same attorneys; they met together to plan strategy. What happened in football affected baseball and hockey, and they shared their information.

Baseball commissioner Bowie Kuhn gave a testimony before a congressional committee about cable television "on behalf of Major League Baseball, the NFL, NASL, NHL, and NBA."

How did that happen? They were working as if they were part of a larger unregulated monopoly of the sports business. We faced an interlocking directorate of all sports.

So they admitted that they now had a common position and spokesperson on cable television. What about dealing with players' unions? We were amazed to read of a meeting of the negotiators of major sports in the April 28, 1981, edition of the *Washington Post*. The headline of the piece written by *Post* staff sportswriter Thomas Boswell read "Sports Management to Confer," and the article noted that "Representatives of management from all of America's major professional sports have planned a meeting in New York City Thursday to discuss methods of dealing with labor-management problems common to the various sports." Various issues were targeted for discussion by management in a meeting that Boswell characterized as "a sort of sports mogul war council."

Why not? After all, if the sports monopolies were coordinating their television policies, why should we be surprised if they were meeting to overwhelm sports unions?

So, the battle is joined. Management, with weapons from all other sports leagues, against the union, with help from the AFL-CIO. Looming on the horizon are billions of dollars to be generated by paid cable television. When the fight comes, NFL players will understand that the performers deserve most of these revenues, and they will understand that, if we are successful, the reserve system and all of its dehumanizing aspects will have died in the NFL. It will be a battle worth watching, worth participating in.

TABLE 1 SALES PRICE OF TEAMS AND ADJUSTED 2014 VALUES				
Team	Sale Year	Sales Price ($)	Adjusted for Inflation ($)	Current Value ($)
Arizona Cardinals	1932	50,000	847,000,000	961,000,000
Atlanta Falcons	2002	545,000,000	708,712,614	933,000,000
Baltimore Ravens	2004	600,000,000	742,574,257	1,227,000,000
Buffalo Bills	1959	25,000	201,613	870,000,000
Carolina Panthers	1993	206,000,000	333,333,333	1,057,000,000
Chicago Bears	1920	100	1,163	1,252,000,000
Cincinnati Bengals	1967	8,000,000	55,944,056	924,000,000
Cleveland Browns	2012	1,000,000,000	1,018,329,939	1,002,000,000
Dallas Cowboys	1989	150,000,000	283,018,868	2,300,000,000
Denver Broncos	1984	78,000,000	175,000,000	1,161,000,000
Detroit Lions	1964	4,000,000	30,075,188	900,000,000
Green Bay Packers	1919	50	676	1,183,000,000
Houston Texans	1999	700,000,000	981,767,181	1,450,000,000
Indianapolis Colts	1972	15,000,000	83,798,883	1,200,000,000
Jacksonville Jaguars	2012	770,000,000	784,114,053	840,000,000
Kansas City Chiefs	1960	25,000	196,850	1,009,000,000
Miami Dolphins	2008	1,100,000,000	1,194,353,963	1,074,000,000
Minnesota Vikings	2005	600,000,000	718,562,874	1,007,000,000
New England Patriots	1994	172,000,000	271,293,375	1,800,000,000
New Orleans Saints	1985	70,000,000	152,173,913	1,004,000,000
New York Jets	2000	635,000,000	861,601,085	1,380,000,000
Oakland Raiders	1966	25,000	179,856	825,000,000
Philadelphia Eagles	1994	185,0000,000	291,0798,107	1,314,000,000
Pittsburgh Steelers	1933	2,500	44,643	1,118,000,000
San Diego Chargers	1984	70,000,000	156,657,658	949,000,000
San Francisco 49ers	1977	13,000,000	50,193,050	1,224,000,000
Seattle Seahawks	1997	194,000,000	282,798,934	1,081,000,000
St. Louis Rams	2010	750,000,000	803,858,520	875,000,000
Tampa Bay Buccaneers	1995	192,000,000	294,478,528	1,067,000,000
Tennessee Titans	1959	25,000	201,613	1,055,000,000
Washington R°°°°°°s	1999	750,000,000	1,051,893,408	1,700,000,000

Conclusion

I end this book with a deep sense of gratitude to hundreds of NFL players who have sacrificed in order to build a union and to a staff that has fought all the battles, usually with low pay and little credit. Many players were special teams players; many made it for just a year or two; most believed that things worth winning come hard. None could have known how tough this battle would be.

One thing is certain: It was a different union confronting management in 1982 than the one that was cuffed around by Rozelle in 1970, 1974, and 1975. It's different because of John Mackey, Alan Page, Gene Upshaw, Len Hauss, Bobby Moore, Dick Berthelsen, Frank Woschitz, Ken Bowman, Pat Richter, Tom Keating, Kermit Alexander, Jeff Van Note, Mac Percival, Al Clark, Pettis Norman, Elvin Bethea, Doug Van Horn, Calvin Hill, Jean Fugett, Richard Neal, Tony Chursky, Winston Hill, Doug Swift, John Zook, Kenny Reaves, Dan Dierdorf, Ken Houston, Jim Bakken, Mike Stratton, Tom Banks, Ernie McMillan, Willie Lanier, Len Rhode, Bob Grim, Charlie West, Dave Wilcox, Bobby Bryant, Tom Condon, Gene Washington, Denny Vaninger, Henry Sheppard, Victor Hicks, Doug France, Ike Hill, Jim Hart, Conrad Dobler, Brig Owens, Don Hasselbeck, Billy Kilmer, Bobby Douglas, Clarence Williams, Bill Lenkaitis, Randy Vataha, Doug Dieken, Rodrigo Barnes, Leon Gray, and Ron Bolton. And because of dedicated staff members Kathy Hansen, Pat Eubank, Jay Benoit, Janet Velie, John Kerr, John Buck, Gary Ballman, Pat Takach, Kal Weinstein, Betty Sievert, Cheryl Davis, and Buck Briggs.

and advisers kept us going. Leonard Lindquist was, and
Gene Keating, Ed Glennon, Denny Mathison, Dan Shul-
ium, Chip Yablonski, Joe Rauh, and Dan Lindsay have all
ortant part in our success. As for the failures, I will willingly
ie. I must add, however, since none of my friends would believe
it ou.   , that I'll also take my share of the successes.

Finally, I must lift a glass to a great man who inspired all of us: Nate
Feinsinger. We couldn't have made it without his vision, determination, and
plain ol' guts. Thanks, Nate.

Index

Ed Garvey (1940–2017) was a lifelong activist for civil and labor rights. He was an associate at the labor law firm of Lindquist & Vennum in Minneapolis, where he helped organize the National Football League Players Association (NFLPA) to lead the persistent fight for players' rights. He became the NFLPA's first executive director in 1971, a position he held until 1983, after which he was Deputy Attorney General for Wisconsin. As a private practice lawyer, he engaged in a range of political reform initiatives.

Chuck Cascio is an award-winning freelance writer, author, and educator whose work has appeared in numerous publications. He received a Virginia Press Association Award for sportswriting and a Distinguished Teacher Award in the Presidential Scholars Program. He is the author of the novel *The Fire Escape Belongs in Brooklyn*, a finalist for the National Indie Excellence Award. He lives in the Washington, DC, area with his wife, Faye. Visit him online at www.chuckcascioauthor.com/.